THE LITURGY OF FUNERARY OFFERINGS

THE EGYPTIAN TEXTS WITH ENGLISH TRANSLATIONS

E. A. WALLIS BUDGE

DOVER PUBLICATIONS, INC.
NEW YORK

Bibliographical Note

This Dover edition, first published in 1994, is an unabridged and unaltered republication of the work originally published by Kegan Paul, Trench, Trübner & Co. Ltd., London, in 1909.

Library of Congress Cataloging-in-Publication Data

Liturgy of funeral offerings.
The liturgy of funerary offerings : the Egyptian texts with English translations / E.A. Wallis Budge.
p. cm.
Originally published: London : Kegan Paul, Trench, Trübner, 1909.
ISBN 0-486-28335-6
1. Funeral rites and ceremonies—Egypt. I. Budge, E. A. Wallis (Ernest Alfred Wallis), Sir, 1857–1934. II. Title.
PJ1559.L6 1994
299′.31—dc20 94-17824
CIP

Manufactured in the United States of America
Dover Publications, Inc., 31 East 2nd Street, Mineola, N.Y. 11501

TO

THE EARL PERCY

I DEDICATE THESE LITTLE VOLUMES

ON THE

LITURGY OF FUNERARY OFFERINGS

AND THE

BOOK OF OPENING THE MOUTH.

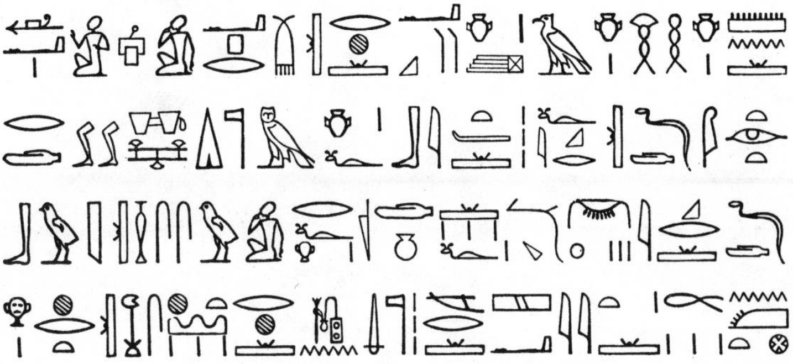

PREFACE

THE present volume contains the Egyptian text and English translations of two copies of one of the most important documents connected with the dead which have come down to us, namely, a detailed list of the offerings which were made to the dead, and also of the consecrating formulae which were recited by the chief officiating priest, as he presented them to a mummified body, or to a statue of the deceased. The ancient title of the composition, if it ever had one in early days, is unknown to us, but it has been called the "Liturgy of Funerary Offerings," because the document deals exclusively with the presentation of offerings to the dead, and because this title is convenient for reference.

This Liturgy is associated in the funerary texts in the tombs and papyri with another work entitled the "Book of Opening the Mouth," and this fact suggests that it is a portion of or a supplement to it, and that it is a development of the canonical List of Offerings which we have reason to believe was in existence under the IIIrd or IVth Dynasty. We know that funerary chapels were attached to the pyramids and maṣṭaba tombs of this period, and that offerings of meat and drink were made in them to the dead daily by properly qualified priests. It follows as a matter of course that the proceedings of the priests were regulated by some system, and that some kind of written service must have been recited regularly, and we are justified in believing that the Liturgy of Funerary Offerings was that which was commonly said for kings and other royal personages, and for men of high civil and ecclesiastical rank.

In the case of the "Book of Opening the Mouth," the object of the recital was, in the earliest times at least, to bring about the reconstitution and resurrection of the dead man, and even in later times, when the work was recited before a statue, on which the accompanying ceremonies were performed, the idea of the Egyptians on this matter remained unchanged. It must be remembered also that the Egyptians intended by means of ceremonies and formulae to bring back the Ka, or double, either to the dead man, from whom it had been temporarily separated, or to a statue which represented him; and when this had been done they believed it to be their bounden duty to provide meat and drink for its maintenance. It was the Ka and the heart-soul (Ba), not the spirit-soul (Khu), which fed upon the offerings, and if meat and drink of a suitable character, and in sufficient quantity, were not provided for them, these suffered from hunger and thirst, and if the supply of offerings failed, they perished by starvation. The texts make it quite clear that the Egyptians believed in a dual-soul; one member could not die, but the other only lived as long as it was fed with offerings by the living, and provided with an abode, i.e., a statue. Offerings were brought to the funerary chapels and tombs daily, and additional gifts were presented on the days of all great festivals.

In very primitive times offerings of meat and drink were brought to the graves, and laid there for the souls of the dead to partake of at pleasure, just as is the case at the present day in many places in the Sûdân. When the ceremonies connected with the Book of Opening the Mouth were evolved, it became customary for the offerings to be brought forward at a certain place in the service, and afterwards, little by little, the canonical List of Offerings, and its later development, the Liturgy of Funerary Offerings, came into being.

As in the Book of Opening the Mouth the words spoken by the Kher-ḥeb, or chief officiating priest, were believed to change the meat, and bread, and wine into divine substances, so in the Liturgy also the formula which was said over each element was supposed to change it into a divine and spiritual food, which was partaken of by the souls of the gods and of the dead. The material elements of the offerings were eaten by the priests and the relatives of the dead, and the act of eating brought them into communion with the blessed dead, and with the gods. The age of the belief in the transmutation of offerings cannot be stated, but it is certain that it was well known to the Egyptians under the Vth Dynasty, and there is reason to think that it was not unknown to their ancestors in the latter part of the Neolithic Period, and that it is coeval with the indigenous African belief in the immortality of the soul, and in a life beyond the grave.

The life of the Liturgy of Funerary Offerings was long. It is found in a more or less complete form in many maṣṭaba tombs of the Ancient Empire, in a very complete form in the pyramids of Unȧs and Pepi II., in incomplete forms on sarcophagi and in tombs of the XIIth Dynasty, and in the tomb of Seti I. of the XIXth Dynasty, and in complete forms in the tomb of Peṭā-Ȧmen-ȧp of the XXVIth Dynasty and in papyri written in the first or second century of the Christian Era. The changes textually in the complete copies of the different periods are very few, and we may say that this work was used by generation after generation, in a practically unaltered form, for about four thousand years.

A description of the labours of my predecessors on this important text will be found in the introductory matter to the present volume.

E. A. WALLIS BUDGE.

BRITISH MUSEUM,
August 5th, 1909.

CONTENTS

CHAP.		PAGE
	PREFACE	vii
I.—THE DOCTRINE OF OFFERINGS		1
II.—THE LITURGY OF FUNERARY OFFERINGS DESCRIBED		33
	First Ceremony	42
	Second Ceremony	46
	Third Ceremony	50
	Fourth Ceremony	56
	Fifth Ceremony	59
	Sixth Ceremony	62
III.—DESCRIPTION OF THE OFFERINGS—		
	Seventh Ceremony	64
	Eighth Ceremony	65
	Ninth Ceremony	67
	Tenth Ceremony	68
	Eleventh Ceremony	69
	Twelfth Ceremony	70
	Thirteenth Ceremony	71
	Fourteenth Ceremony	72
	Fifteenth Ceremony	74
	Sixteenth Ceremony	74
	Seventeenth Ceremony	76
	Eighteenth Ceremony	76
	Nineteenth Ceremony	79
	Twentieth Ceremony	79
	Twenty-first Ceremony	81
	Twenty-second Ceremony	81
	Twenty-third Ceremony	83
	Twenty-fourth Ceremony	84
	Twenty-fifth Ceremony	85

CHAP. PAGE

Twenty-sixth Ceremony 85
Twenty-seventh Ceremony 86
Twenty-eighth—Thirty-fourth Ceremonies . 88
Thirty-fifth Ceremony 91
Thirty-sixth Ceremony 92
Thirty-seventh Ceremony 95
Thirty-eighth Ceremony 96

IV.—THE LITURGY DESCRIBED 98
Thirty-ninth Ceremony 100
Fortieth Ceremony 102
Forty-first Ceremony 103
Forty-second Ceremony 104
Forty-third Ceremony 104
Forty-fourth Ceremony 105
Forty-fifth Ceremony 106
Forty-sixth Ceremony 106
Forty-seventh Ceremony 107
Forty-eighth Ceremony 108
Forty-ninth Ceremony 109
Fiftieth Ceremony 110
Fifty-first Ceremony 111
Fifty-second Ceremony 111
Fifty-third Ceremony 112
Fifty-fourth Ceremony 112
Fifty-fifth Ceremony 113
Fifty-sixth Ceremony 113
Fifty-seventh Ceremony 114
Fifty-eighth Ceremony 114
Fifty-ninth Ceremony 115
Sixtieth Ceremony 115
Sixty-first Ceremony 116
Sixty-second Ceremony 116
Sixty-third Ceremony 117
Sixty-fourth Ceremony 117
Sixty-fifth Ceremony 118
Sixty-sixth Ceremony 118

	PAGE
Sixty-seventh Ceremony	119
Sixty-eighth Ceremony	119
Sixty-ninth Ceremony	120
Seventieth Ceremony	120
Seventy-first Ceremony	121
Seventy-second Ceremony	122
Seventy-third Ceremony	122
Seventy-fourth Ceremony	123
Seventy-fifth Ceremony	123
Seventy-sixth Ceremony	124
Seventy-seventh Ceremony	124
Seventy-eighth Ceremony	125
Seventy-ninth Ceremony	125
Eightieth Ceremony	126
Eighty-first Ceremony	126
Eighty-second Ceremony	127
Eighty-third Ceremony	127
Eighty-fourth Ceremony	128
Eighty-fifth Ceremony	128
Eighty-sixth Ceremony	129
Eighty-seventh Ceremony	129
Eighty-eighth Ceremony	130
Eighty-ninth Ceremony	130
Ninetieth Ceremony	131
Ninety-first Ceremony	131
Ninety-second Ceremony	132
Ninety-third Ceremony	132
Ninety-fourth Ceremony	133
Ninety-fifth Ceremony	133
Ninety-sixth Ceremony	134
Ninety-seventh Ceremony	134
Ninety-eighth Ceremony	135
Ninety-ninth Ceremony	137
One hundred and first Ceremony	138
One hundred and second Ceremony	138
One hundred and third Ceremony	139

PAGE

One hundred and fourth Ceremony 139
One hundred and fifth Ceremony 140
One hundred and sixth Ceremony 140
One hundred and seventh Ceremony 141
One hundred and eighth Ceremony 141
One hundred and ninth Ceremony 142
One hundred and tenth Ceremony 143
One hundred and eleventh Ceremony . . . 143
One hundred and twelfth Ceremony 144
One hundred and thirteenth Ceremony . . 144
One hundred and fourteenth Ceremony . . 145
Section from text of Pepi II. 145

THE LITURGY ACCORDING TO THE TEXT OF UNȦS . . 151

THE LITURGY ACCORDING TO THE TEXT OF PEṬĀ-ȦMEN-ȦP 204

INDEX 257

LIST OF ILLUSTRATIONS

PAGE

1. The Sem priest pouring water from a libation vase . 42
2. The Sem priest carrying the censer 48
3–5. The Sem priest pouring water from a libation vase 51, 57, 60
6. The Sem priest presenting a ball of incense . . 62
7. The Sem priest holding the Kef-pesesh . . . 64
8. The Sem priest presenting the Neterti . . . 66
9. The Sem priest presenting cheese 67
10. The Sem priest presenting shȧku 68
11. The Sem priest presenting milk and whey . . 69
12. The Sem priest pouring water from a libation vase . 70
13. The Sem priest presenting two vessels of wine . 71
14. The Sem priest presenting the Ḥem cake . . 73
15. The Sem priest presenting a ball of incense . . 74
16. The Sem priest presenting the Uṭen cake . . 75
17, 18. The Sem priest presenting a white vessel of wine . 77, 78
19. The Sem priest presenting a vessel of Ḥent beer . 79
20. The Sem priest presenting a table of offerings . 80
21. The Sem priest presenting the Ṭept cake . . 81
22. The Sem priest presenting the Aḥ meal . . 82
23. The Sem priest presenting the breast . . . 83
24. The Sem priest presenting a vessel of wine . . 84
25. The Sem priest presenting a vessel of beer . . 85
26. The Sem priest presenting an iron vessel of beer . 86
27. The Sem priest presenting a stone vessel of beer . 87
28. The Sem priest presenting the Seven Oils . . 89
29. The Sem priest presenting eye-paints . . . 91
30. The Sem priest presenting two bandlets . . 93

PAGE
31. The Sem priest presenting burning incense . . 96
32. The Sem priest pouring water from a libation vase . 97
33. The altar on which the offerings are placed . . 100
34. The Sem priest presenting the two royal-offering cakes 102
35. The Sem priest presenting two vessels of beer . 103
36. A ministrant kneeling by the side of the offering . 104
37. The Sem priest presenting the Ṭua and Shens cakes. 105
38. The Sem priest presenting a Rethḥu cake . . 106
39. The Sem priest presenting a vessel of drink . . 107
40. The Sem priest presenting a vessel of beer . . 107
41. The Sem priest presenting bread and beer . . 108
42. The Sem priest presenting the Ṭua and Shens cakes 109
43. The Sem priest presenting the Sut joint . . 110
44. The Sem priest presenting two vessels of water . 111
45. The Sem priest presenting two vessels of incense . 111
46. The Sem priest presenting the Ṭua and Shens cakes 112
47. The Sem priest presenting two Tut cakes . . 112
48. The Sem priest presenting a Rethḥu cake . . 113
49. The Sem priest presenting Ḥeth cake . . . 113
50. The Sem priest presenting two Neḥrȧ cakes . . 114
51. The Sem priest presenting a Ṭept cake . . . 114
52. The Sem priest presenting a Pasen cake . . 115
53. The Sem priest presenting a Shens cake . . 115
54. The Sem priest presenting an Ȧmta cake . . 116
55. The Sem priest presenting Khenfu cakes . . 116
56. The Sem priest presenting Ḥebennet cakes . . 117
57. The Sem priest presenting cakes of Qemḥ . . 117
58. The Sem priest presenting Ȧtent cakes . . . 118
59. The Sem priest presenting the Pat cake . . 118
60. The Sem priest presenting Ashert cakes . . 119
61. The Sem priest presenting onions 119
62. The Sem priest presenting a haunch of beef . . 120
63. The Sem priest presenting a loin of beef . . 120
64. The Sem priest presenting a breast . . . 121
65. The Sem priest presenting a Sut joint . . . 122

PAGE
66. The Sem priest presenting ribs of beef . . . 122
67. The Sem priest presenting roast meat . . . 123
68. The Sem priest presenting a liver 123
69. The Sem priest presenting a spleen . . . 124
70. The Sem priest presenting a fore-quarter of beef . 124
71. The Sem priest presenting a fore-part of a bull . 125
72. The Sem priest presenting a Re goose . . . 125
73. The Sem priest presenting a Therp goose . . 126
74. The Sem priest presenting a Set goose . . . 126
75. The Sem priest presenting a Sert goose . . . 127
76. The Sem priest presenting a dove 127
77. The Sem priest presenting a Såf cake . . . 128
78. The Sem priest presenting two Shāt cakes . . 128
79. The Sem priest presenting Nepåt grain . . . 129
80. The Sem priest presenting Mest grain . . . 129
81. The Sem priest presenting Tchesert drink . . 130
82. The Sem priest presenting Tchesert drink . . 130
83. The Sem priest presenting Khenemes drink . . 131
84. The Sem priest presenting beer 131
85. The Sem priest presenting Sekhpet grain . . 132
86. The Sem priest presenting Pekh grain . . . 132
87. The Sem priest presenting Nubian beer . . . 133
88. The Sem priest presenting figs 133
89. The Sem priest presenting wine of the North . . 134
90. The Sem priest presenting white wine . . . 134
91. The Sem priest presenting Åmt wine . . . 135
92. The Sem priest presenting Qem wine . . . 136
93. The Sem priest presenting Senu wine . . . 137
94. The Sem priest presenting Ḥebnent wine . . 138
95. The Sem priest presenting Khenfu cakes . . 138
96. The Sem priest presenting Åsheṭ fruit . . . 139
97. The Sem priest presenting Seshet grain . . . 139
98. The Sem priest presenting Seshet grain . . . 140
99. The Sem priest presenting Set grain . . . 140
100. The Sem priest presenting Set grain . . . 141
101. The Sem priest presenting Babat fruit . . . 141

PAGE
102. The Sem priest presenting mulberries 142
103. The Sem priest presenting mulberry cakes . . 143
104. The Sem priest presenting Ḥuā grain 143
105. The Sem priest presenting offerings of all kinds . 144
106. The Sem priest presenting spring products . . 144
107. The Sem priest presenting gifts of every kind. . 145

THE LITURGY
OF
FUNERARY OFFERINGS

CHAPTER I.

The Doctrine of Offerings.

The tombs, temples, and religious literature of all periods of the history of Egypt proclaim with no uncertain voice that the ancient Egyptians believed in the resurrection of the dead, and that they possessed an innate conviction that the souls of the blessed renewed their existence in the world beyond the grave under circumstances and conditions which gave them happiness and prevented them from dying a second time. The consistent, persistent, ineradicable and unalterable belief in immortality is the chief fundamental of the Egyptian Religion, and the attainment of everlasting life was the end to which every religious ceremony was performed, and every funerary text written.

Now, although in the Dynastic Period the Egyptians

believed that the dead rose again because Osiris rose from the dead, and that it was indeed he "who made mortals to be born again,"[1] and who bestowed upon the "re-born" new life, with new powers, spiritual, mental, and material, they spared no pains in performing the works which they thought would help themselves and their dead to put on immortality and to arrive in the dominions of him who was the "king of eternity and the lord of everlastingness." Every tradition which existed concerning the ceremonies that were performed on behalf of the dead Osiris by Horus and his "sons" and "followers" at some period, which even so far back as the time of the IVth Dynasty, or about B.C. 3800, was extremely remote, was carefully preserved and faithfully imitated under succeeding dynasties, and for long after Christianity was established in the northern part of the Nile Valley, and Egypt was filled with Christian monks.

The formulae which were declared to have been recited during the performance of such ceremonies were written down and copied for scores of generations, and every pious, well-to-do Egyptian made arrangements that what had been done and said on behalf of Osiris should be done and said for him outside or inside his tomb after his death. No ceremony, however trivial, was considered unimportant, and no

[1] , *Book of the Dead*, Chapter CLXXXII., line 16.

form of words was thought useless. New ceremonies and words might be added, for it was held possible that they might become a means of salvation, but nothing might be omitted intentionally. The natural result of this religious conservatism was that as centuries rolled on the significance of several funerary ceremonies was forgotten, and the meanings of many liturgical phrases were understood with less and less exactness, until at length they became mere collections of words, which conveyed little to the minds of those who heard them.

Now the oldest religious ceremonies and formulae known to us were invented in connection with the presentation of offerings to the dead. In the Predynastic Period men buried offerings of food, unguents, &c., with their dead, believing that, in some mysterious way, such material gifts would assist their relatives and friends to maintain their existence in the Other World. When this custom first arose cannot be said, but it was certainly general in the late Neolithic Period, and it continued to flourish for several thousands of years. Indeed it is probable that modified forms of it exist at the present day among the pagan, Christian, and Muḥammadan inhabitants of the Nile Valley. We cannot tell now what ideas existed in the minds of those who gave offerings to the dead as to the way in which such gifts benefited the dead. There is little doubt that at first they believed that the life which was led by the departed in the Other World closely resembled life in this world, and it may be reasonably assumed that they thought that the food which they placed in graves with the dead was actually consumed. They must have known that their funerary offerings would last in the ordinary way but a short time, and it seems as if it was only intended to supply the needs of the departed on their journey to the place of departed spirits.

On the other hand, the fact that personal ornaments were buried with the food, and flint weapons of war and the chase, suggests that the living intended them to be used by the dead for an indefinitely long period. The primitive Egyptians appear to have thought that inanimate things possessed spirits like human beings, and if this be so it is probable that they also believed that the spirits of human beings in the Other World fed upon the spirits of the offerings made to them in this world by the living. This being so it would be necessary to renew the supply of offerings of food at regular intervals, so that the spirits of the dead might be prevented from suffering from hunger and thirst, and from dying a second time through exhaustion. There was also another side to the question of an important character. The souls of the dead who lacked food would, it was thought, be driven by hunger to the villages wherein they dwelt during their life, and would eat up such food as they found there, or, in the event of finding nothing suitable for their wants, would cause sickness, disease, and trouble. To avoid such a calamity it was necessary to make offerings at their tombs, and to propitiate them with suitable gifts at regular intervals. Thus the giving of sepulchral offerings profited both the dead and the living.

Among the Egyptians of the Dynastic Period the presentation of offerings to the dead was regarded as one of the chief duties in life of the religious man, and it will here be well to illustrate their views on the subject by references to texts of several periods. In the second section of the great text in the Pyramid of Unȧs[1] the "Chiefs" are called upon to give to king Unȧs in heaven the loaves of bread, cakes, and drink-offerings which he had offered to them upon earth, and Rā himself orders those beings who preside over the roducts of the year to give Unȧs wheat, barley, bread, nd beer from the supplies which they had collected "For, for Unȧs to be hungry and not to eat, and to be "thirsty and not to drink, is an abomination to him" (l. 195). In the text of king Tetȧ[2] the writer addresses hunger and adjures it not to approach Tetȧ, but to depart to the god Nu, for Tetȧ suffers not hunger like the god Shu, nor thirst like the goddess Tefnut, because the hunger which is in the belly of Tetȧ, and the thirst which is on his lips, are destroyed by the four children of Horus, Ḥāp, Ṭuamutef, Qebḥsennuf, and Ȧmset. In a paragraph immediately following allusion is made to the fate which befell the souls of the departed who were not provided with sepulchral offerings, and it is quite clear that the Egyptians thought they were

[1] Maspero, *Pyramides de Saqqarah*, p. 20.

[2] Maspero, *op. cit.*, p. 97.

driven by hunger and thirst to wander about the desert and eat filth and drink polluted water. Small wonder, then, is it that hunger and thirst were held in abomination by departed spirits.

In the text of Pepi I. the king is told that he shall receive each day a thousand loaves of bread, a thousand vessels of beer, a thousand oxen, a thousand geese, a thousand sweet things of all kinds, and a thousand changes of linen,[1] but probably we are not intended to interpret this statement too literally, for such a series of large gifts suggests that these offerings were derived from the supply of the gods who were Pepi's brethren in heaven. In another passage some god is entreated to give bread and beer to Pepi of the bread and beer which are everlasting.[2]

All the above extracts are taken from texts which are cut on the walls of the chambers of the pyramids of kings Unås, Tetå, and Pepi, under the Vth and

[1] Maspero, *op. cit.*, line 46. 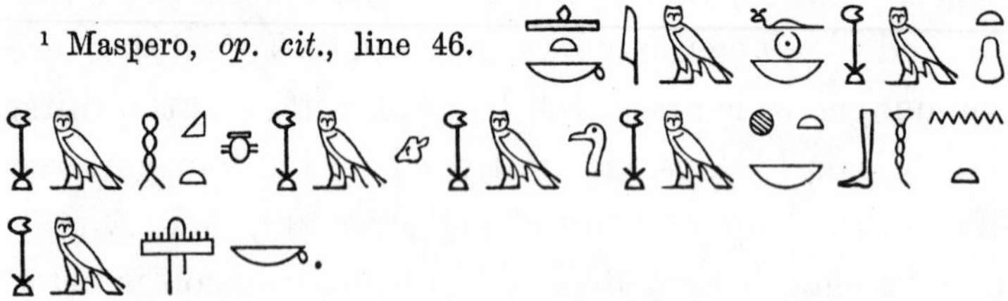

[2] *Ibid.*, line 390. 

VIth Dynasties, but if we look at the inscriptions on the maṣṭaba tombs of earlier dynasties we shall find the same ideas expressed everywhere. Thus on the walls of the tomb of Seker-khā-baiū, which can hardly have been built later than the IVth Dynasty, and may well belong to the IInd or IIIrd Dynasty, lists of offerings are found, e.g., wine of various kinds, sweet beer, cakes of various kinds, fruit, such as raisins, mulberries (*nebes*), figs, &c., unguents and scented oils, heads of bulls and birds, and various kinds of garments, ceremonial apparel, &c. In one relief the list of offerings appears in a tabular form, and under the name of each offering is the character 𓆼, "thousand," which indicates that the deceased prayed that the various kinds of food, drink, and clothing might be given to him by the thousand.[1]

On a wooden panel from the tomb of Ḥesi, which probably dates from the end of the Archaic Period, we find a portion of an inscription in which the deceased prays for incense and for libations of cool water, wine, unguents, bulls, oxen, &c., by the thousand.[2] On a panel of a relief from the tomb of Ḥetep-ḥer-s two tables laden with offerings are represented; on the one are fruit and flowers, and on the other joints of meat and loaves of bread and cakes, and on three lower tables, of similar shape, are two dead geese and the head of a bull. This tomb was built in the reign of

[1] Mariette, *Les Mastaba*, pp. 76-79. [2] *Ibid.*, p. 82.

Khufu.[1] In the tomb of Ptaḥ-khā-mert is a tabulated list of offerings ninety-six in number,[2] and in the tomb of Ānkh-mā-ka, who lived in the reign of User-en-Rā, (Vth Dynasty) are two tabulated lists of offerings, the one containing ninety-six objects, and the other one hundred and four.[3] From the reliefs which decorate the walls of several of the tombs of the Vth and VIth Dynasties it is certain that in addition to the bread, fruit, wine, beer, &c., which were offered to the dead, living animals were brought to the tombs and offered up as sacrifices on their behalf. In the tomb of Ptaḥ-shepses[4] we see among those who bear gifts to the tomb ministrants leading goats, gazelle, calves, and sheep, and in one of the lower registers is depicted the slaughter of two bulls, from each of which a fore-leg is being cut off.

If we compare the lists of offerings given in the various tombs it at once becomes apparent that each list only contains a selection of names of objects; that the man who drafted the inscriptions for the mason to cut on the walls usually included only the most important names, and that the number of these depended upon the space which he had at his disposal. In the case of king Unȧs the various objects named as offerings are more than one hundred and forty in number, and in the pyramid of Pepi II. the number is still greater.

Now in addition to supplying us with the names of the objects which pious men were expected to bring

[1] Mariette, *Les Mastaba*, p. 90.
[2] *Ibid.*, p. 119.
[3] *Ibid.*, p. 215.
[4] *Op. cit.*, p. 383.

to the graves of their dead, the inscriptions on the maṣṭaba tombs and other monuments of the Ancient Empire also tell us the names of the chief festivals of the year, during which they were expected to present their offerings. On the sarcophagus of Khufu-ānkh (IVth Dynasty) the following festivals are mentioned:—

1. Festival of the New Year, .

2. Festival of Thoth, 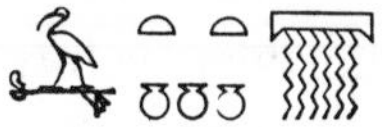 (19th day of Thoth).

3. Festival of the beginning of the year, 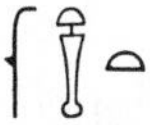.

4. Festival of Uaḳ, 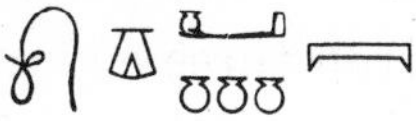 (17th or 18th of Thoth).

5. Great Festival,  (4th of Mekhir).

6. Heat Festival,  (in the month of Mekhir).

7. Appearance of Menu Festival, 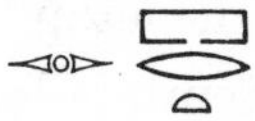 (30th day of Pashons).

8. Festival of Uaḥ-ākh, 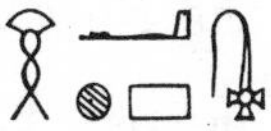 (preparing the fire-altar).

9. Festival of Satch, .

10. Festival of the beginning of the month, .

11. Festival of the beginning of the half month, .

12. Every festival on every day for ever 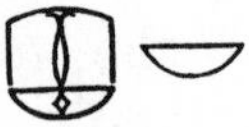
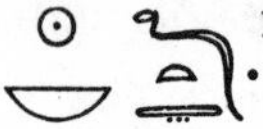[1]

Passing now to the period of the XIIth Dynasty, we find that lists of offerings similar to those on monuments of the Vth and VIth Dynasties are not unknown, and a good example of such is given in the tomb of Ȧmen-em-ḥāt at Beni Hasan. Here on one of the walls is a picture of the deceased seated, with tables and stands loaded with offerings before him, and in the upper registers is a tabulated list containing the names of one hundred and twenty-one offerings.[2] This may for convenience' sake be called the Great List of Offerings. Elsewhere are given three copies of a list containing the names of twenty-two offerings;[3] this may be called the Little List of Offerings. A Great List, containing the names of fifty-four offerings, and a Little List, containing the names of twenty-two, are also found in the tomb of Khnemu-ḥetep.[4] The list of the festivals given in the latter tomb is long, and contains the following:—

1. Festival of the New Year, .
2. Festival of Thoth, .
3. Festival of Pert Menu, 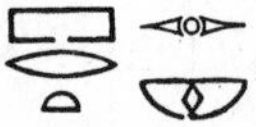.
4. Festivals of Pati, 12 in number, .

[1] Brugsch, *Kalendarische Inschriften*, p. 235.
[2] Griffith and Newberry, *Beni Hasan*, pt. i., pl. xvii.
[3] *Ibid.*, pll. xviii., xix. and xx. [4] *Ibid.*, pll. xxxv., xxxvi.

5. Great Festival, .

6. Festivals of Great Heat and Little Heat, 
.

7. Festivals of the month, 12 in number, .

8. Festivals of the half-month, 12 in number, .

9. Festival of Āḥā- . . . . . ., .

10. Festivals of Saṭ, 12 in number, 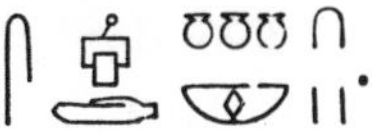.

11. Festival of Khen, .

12. Festival of the Nile Flood, .

13. Festival of the rise of Sothis, 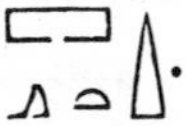.

14. Festival of the rise of Sem, .

15. Festival of Khet ḳerḥ, 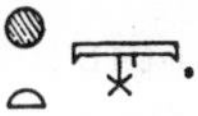.

16. Festivals of the 6th day of the month, 12 in number, 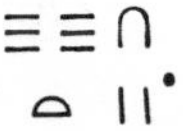.

17. Festival of [Shetchet] shā, 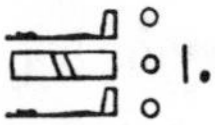.

18. Festivals of the Five Epagomenal Days, 
.

19. Good Festival of him that is on the hill, i.e., Anubis, 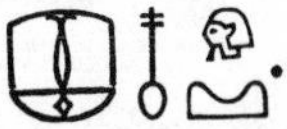.

20. Festival of Uaḳ, 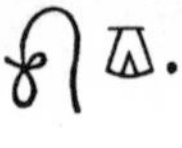.

21. Festival of Thoth, .

22. Great Festival and Little Festival of ......
.

23. Great Festival and Little Festival of the Year,
.

It will be noticed that in the above list some seventy-three festivals are mentioned. The 1st, 6th, 15th, and one other day in each month were fixed festival days, and, if to these we add the other 25 festival days, we find that on an average every fifth day was a day of festival. We are, then, justified in assuming that offerings were made to the dead by well-to-do people about once a week, and at some seasons of the year oftener. In the lists of Festivals given in documents of later periods[1] several other Festivals are mentioned, and during the most flourishing periods of Egyptian history the offerings in the tombs of kings and wealthy folk were renewed, wholly or in part, daily. Thus to feed the spirits of the dead who belonged to him was as much the duty of a pious man as to feed the living who depended upon him, and there is no doubt that, when the country was in a settled state, a regulated portion of the produce of each man's estate was set apart for the dead.

From several Chapters in the Theban Recension of

[1] See the lists given by Brugsch, *Kalendarische Inschriften*, p. 237 ff.

the Book of the Dead many illustrations of the great importance attached to sepulchral offerings may be obtained. In Chapter I. the deceased beseeches the gods "who give cakes and beer to the perfect souls" to give him cakes and beer at the "two seasons," i.e. morning and evening, daily. In Chapter LII. he prays that he may not be made to eat what is an abomination to him. "Filth is an abomination unto me, and let me "not be obliged to eat of it instead of the funerary "cakes which the Kau (or, Doubles) eat. Let it not "touch my body, let me be not obliged to take it in my "hands, and let me not be obliged to walk thereon." And in answer to a question as to what he would live upon before the gods, he replies, "Let me live on the "seven loaves and cakes which are brought before Horus "and Thoth, and let me eat my food under the sycamore "tree of Hathor. Give me authority over my own "fields in Ṭaṭṭu, and over my own crops in Ȧnnu. Let "me eat bread made of white barley, and drink beer "made from red grain." In another place he says, "I "live upon what the gods live upon, and I eat of the "cakes which are in the hall of the lord of sepulchral "offerings" (Chap. LIII.).

In the Papyrus of Nebseni, Chapter CLXXVIII., is a version of a text to which reference has already been made, but in its later form it is so instructive that one or two passages may well be quoted from it. In it Nebseni is made to say: "The Eye of "Horus hath been presented unto thee, and it feedeth "thee with the food of offerings. O Osiris, let him "not suffer thirst before his god, let him suffer "neither hunger nor thirst, and let the god Aḥu carry "them away, and let him do away with his hunger, O "thou that fillest, O thou that fillest hearts. O ye "Chiefs who dispense cakes, O ye who have charge of "the Water-flood (i.e., the Nile), command ye that cakes "and ale be given unto the Osiris Nebseni, even as Rā "himself commanded this thing. Moreover, Rā hath "commanded those who are over the abundance of the "year to take handfuls of wheat and barley and to give "them unto him for his cakes, for behold, he is a great "bull. . . . They shall give cakes and beer unto the "scribe Nebseni, and they shall prepare for him all "good and pure things this happy day, things for "journeying, and things for travelling, things of the Eye "of Horus, things of the Boat, and all things which "enter into the sight of the god. . . . The Eye of Horus "hath ordained these things for the scribe Nebseni, "and the god Shu hath ordered that whereon he shall "subsist, both cakes and beer. . . . The Company of the "gods hath offered incense to the scribe Nebseni, and "his mouth is pure, and his tongue which is therein is "right and true. That which the scribe Nebseni abomi-"nateth is filth, and he hath freed himself therefrom "even as Set freed himself in the city of Reḥiu, and "he set out with Thoth for heaven. . . . Sepulchral "meals have been given unto him by the lord of "eternity, who hath ordered these things for him."

In Chapter CLXXX. the deceased says: "My offer-"ings are in heaven in the Field of Rā, and my "sepulchral meals are on earth in the Field of Ȧaru."

It is unnecessary to multiply extracts from the religious texts of later dynasties, for, so far as the importance and necessity of providing the spirits of the dead with meat and drink are concerned, the same ideas recur, expressed in almost the same words, century after century, and dynasty after dynasty, until the worship of Osiris came to an end throughout the country of Egypt. It will be seen in another part of this book that the list of offerings which were made to Unȧs, a king of the Vth Dynasty, about B.C. 3300, is repeated without many variants in the tomb of Peṭā-Ȧmen-ȧpt, who flourished under the XXVIth Dynasty, some twenty-seven centuries later. Professor Maspero has shown that there are several mistakes in the texts in the Pyramid of Unȧs, due partly to the ignorance of the masons who cut the inscriptions on the walls, and partly to the fact that the scribes who wrote the drafts for them did not always understand the passages which they were transcribing. The variants in the text of Peṭā-Ȧmen-ȧpt may be the result of the difficulties experienced by the scribes of his time in understanding some portions of the text, but there is certainly no ground for thinking that they are due to any authoritative change in the readings of the Ritual of Funerary Offerings.

All the facts we now have tend to show that at some

very early period in the history of Egypt the priests drew up a List of the offerings which it was thought right to offer to the dead, and that they composed a series of formulae which were to be repeated by the officiating priests when they presented the offerings to the dead. This List, with the formulae, was handed down from generation to generation, and was extant in the Roman Period.

In primitive times it is tolerably certain that when the living made offerings to the dead, their sole idea was to provide the spirits with nourishment sufficient to enable them to reach the place where the spirits dwelt in the Other World. As time went on, however, it was thought that the giving of food, and drink, and apparel to the dead, would benefit those who gave them when it was their turn to depart from this world, and proof of this is found in a text cut on the alabaster sarcophagus of Seti I., a king of the XIXth Dynasty. On this fine monument we have an illustrated copy of a "Guide" to the Other World, in which the state and condition of those who dwell there are described. This "Guide" is divided into twelve sections, and the texts tell us what beings live in each, how they live, and how they employ their time. The general deduction to be made from them is that under the XIXth Dynasty the Egyptians believed that the bodies, souls, and spirits of the wicked were destroyed, that those of the good were rewarded with everlasting life and great felicity, and that the offerings made by men in this world went before them and awaited them in that which was to come.

In the Second Division of the Other World (i.e., the Ṭuat) we find a class of beings called "Ḥeteptiu-ṭuau-Rā," and the accompanying description says: "These are they who praised Rā whilst they were upon "earth. They cast spells (or, used words of power) on "[the fiend] Āpep. They presented their offerings, [and] "they made offerings of incense to their gods after their "offerings." The text continues: "They have gained "possession of their libations, they receive their meat-"offerings, and they eat their offerings in the Gate of "him whose name is hidden." And each night when Rā passed through that Division of the Other World he said to them, "Your offerings shall be yours, ye shall "have possession of your libations, your souls shall "never be hacked in pieces, and your food shall never "fail, O ye who have praised [me] and vanquished "Āpep for me."

Now, in addition to helping the souls of the dead to reach their appointed place, offerings were made at the tombs at regular intervals with the express object of bringing the souls of the dead back to this earth to eat the offerings there with the living. The sweet smell of the incense burnt was thought to be grateful alike to the gods and to the souls who were with them, and freshly killed meat, newly baked cakes, fresh fruit, flowers and vegetables, and wine and beer were held to be irresistible attractions to the souls of the departed as they travelled about daily in the country. It is known from many texts that souls journeyed from one great sanctuary to another in Egypt, and that they assisted at all the great national festivals, and expected to receive their due share of the offerings which were brought to the altars. From the Papyrus of Nu (XVIIIth Dynasty) we learn that the deceased expected a house to be provided for him on this earth after his death, to which men and women were to bring offerings and oblations daily. And Osiris ordered that beasts for sacrifice were to be brought to him by the south wind (i.e., cattle from Dâr Fûr), and grain by the north wind, and barley from the ends of the earth.[1]

In the papyrus of Takhart-p-seru-àbṭiu,[2] of the Roman Period, the deceased is addressed in these words: "Thou journeyest upon earth, thou seest those who are "therein, thou inspectest all the arrangements in thy "house, and thou eatest bread there. . . . Thou journeyest "to the city of Nif-urt at the festival of things on the "altar, the night of the festival of the Sixth Day, the "Festival of Ānep. Thou goest to Nif-urt at the Festival "of the Little Heat, thou goest to Ṭaṭṭu during the "Festival of Ka-ḥrà-ka, on the day of setting up the Ṭeṭ."

The same views are very clearly expressed in the "Book of Traversing Eternity,"[3] and we read there

[1] *Book of the Dead*, Chapter CLII.

[2] *British Museum*, No. 10,112.

[3] Ed. Bergmann, *Sitzungsberichte der kaiserlichen Akademie der Wissenschaften*, Bd. 86, Heft 2-3, Vienna, 1877.

that the deceased makes use of his power and freedom in the Other World to explore heaven, earth, and the deep. He visits all the great shrines of Osiris and Rā, holds converse with the gods of every portion of heaven, makes himself acquainted with all their mysteries, and day by day becomes more and more like them. To establish and maintain communication with the spirits of the dead was the heart's desire of pious Egyptians in all ages, and they thought that there was no more certain way of bringing this about than by making offerings to them. By eating the same food as beatified beings, and by drinking the same drink, mortals, they thought, acquired something of the nature of immortals, and the communion of the righteous on earth with the blessed in heaven was effected.

In the foregoing remarks it has been said that funerary offerings were made to the "souls" of the dead, but it must be remembered that the word "souls" (or "spirits") is only used for convenience' sake, and that gifts of food and drink were made in reality to the "Kau" or "Doubles" of the dead. The Ka of a man was his individuality, or personality, to which the Egyptians assigned an independent existence; it took his bodily shape, with all its characteristics, and, when necessary, the form of a mummy. When the body of a man to whom it belonged died, the Ka took up its abode in the portrait statue of the deceased which was provided for it, and well-to-do families were in the habit of appointing priests of the Ka whose duty it was to recite the prayers on behalf of the Kau of the dead, and to attend to the supply of offerings for them. The Ka possessed freedom to move whithersoever it pleased, and it could travel from one end of Egypt to the other, or take up its abode with the gods, or re-unite itself with the mummified body to which it belonged, or remain separted from it. The Ka was provided with a chamber, or special resting-place, in the tomb, and it rejoiced in the smell of the incense which was burnt there, and partook of the meat and drink offerings which were presented to it.

The common Egyptian word for "offering" is Ḥᴇᴛᴇᴘ, , and its primary meaning seems to be "something "given by one being to another with the view of peace-"making or propitiation," in fact, a peace-offering. The word is no doubt connected with *ḥetep* 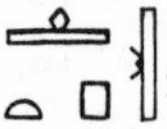, "to be "at peace, to be contented, to be satisfied, to be at rest," etc. *Ḥetep* is often written with the determinative of "bread," 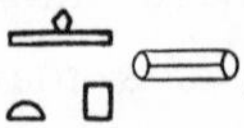, and in the XVIIIth Dynasty the plural is frequently followed by determinatives meaning "cakes," "cattle," "geese," "beer," or "wine," e.g., 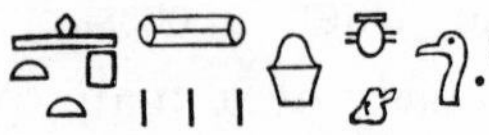.[1] Thus it is clear that the ordinary objects which were offered as funerary gifts are referred

[1] In Unás, l. 203, we have 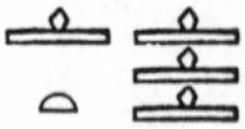, and in Pepi, l. 683 .

to. *Ḥetep* is also one of the words used for the object on which offerings were placed, i.e., altar, which, though usually made of stone, 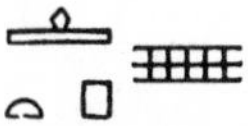, was sometimes made of wood, 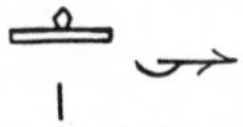, or 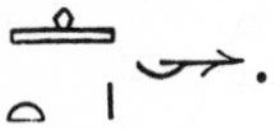.

Yet although *ḥetep* certainly means "offering," it is difficult not to think that in the earliest times the word must have possessed some other signification. If we look at the earliest funerary texts, which are found on the maṣṭabas at Ṣaḳḳârah, we find that many of them begin with the signs

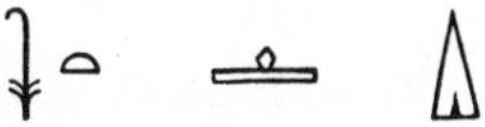

suten *ḥetep* *ṭā*

Now *suten* is the common word for "king," *ḥetep* we have already seen means "offering," and *ṭā* means "to give," and it seems at first sight as if the group of signs must mean something like "May the king give an offering." Frequently, however, these signs are followed by

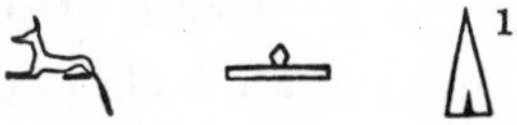[1]

Ȧnpu *ḥetep* *ṭā*

i.e., "May Anubis give an offering." What the king is expected to give is not said, but Anubis is asked, or called upon, to give "a burial in Ȧmenti," and "to "provide the deceased with bread, beer, and cakes at the

[1] See Mariette, *Les Mastaba*, pp. 108, 115, &c.

"festival."[1] Elsewhere we find that the king is asked for the *ḥetep*, and Anubis for the burial, and Osiris is to give the offerings of bread, beer, and cakes, thus:—

, etc.

,[2] etc.

But it is not said of what the *ḥetep* which the king is asked to give is to consist. In another text the king is called upon to give *ḥetep*, and Anubis to give the burial as before, and Osiris of Ṭaṭṭu to make the deceased to advance happily over the beautiful roads of the Other World, and Khenti Ȧmenti is to provide him with the funerary offerings.[3] Still there is no explanation of what the king's *ḥetep* is to consist.

From many passages in texts of the Ancient Empire it is clear that offerings of food were given to the dead, chiefly by Anubis. Thus in Tetȧ, line 387, it is said, "Ȧnpu Khenti Ȧmenti giveth thee an offering, thy "thousands of bread cakes, thy thousands of vessels of "beer, thy thousands of vases of oil, thy thousands "of oxen, thy thousands of changes of apparel, thy "thousands of bulls; one cuts the throat for thee of "the *Smen* goose, one shoots for thee the *Therp* goose."

1 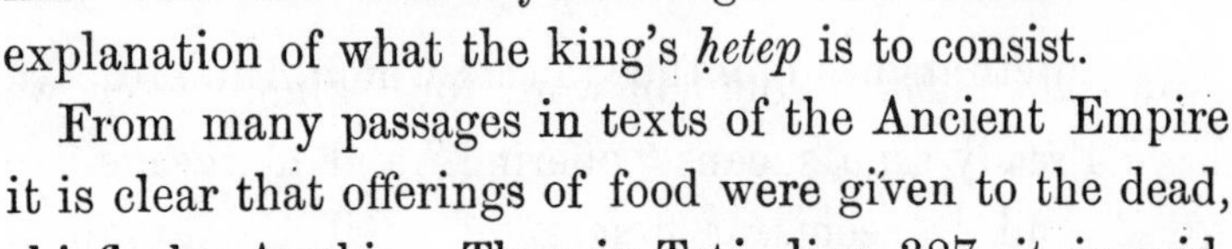

2 Mariette, *op. cit.*, p. 118. 3 *Ibid.*, p. 230.

In Pepi I., line 83, we have: "SUTEN ṬĀ ḤETEP. May "Anubis give an offering: thy thousand bread-cakes, "thy thousand vessels of beer, thy thousand vessels of "purifying fluid which cometh forth from the *Usekh* "chamber, thy thousand pleasant things, thy thousand "oxen, thy thousand things to eat, thy gifts of thy heart. "The palm tree followeth thee, and the mulberry tree "presenteth its head for thee in that which Anubis doeth "for thee." 

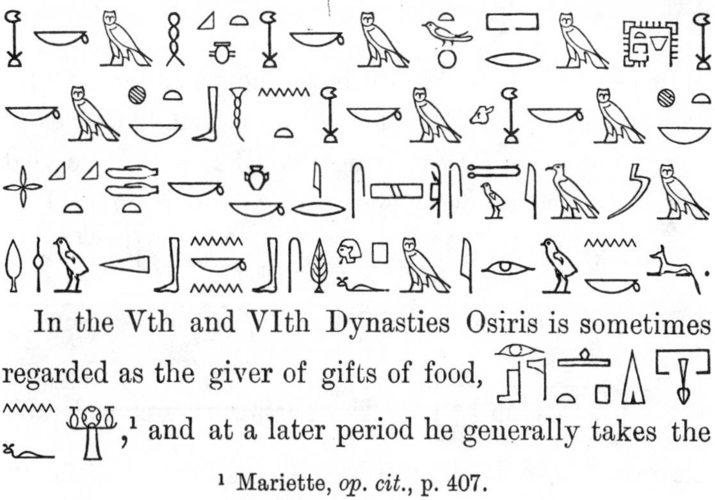

In the Vth and VIth Dynasties Osiris is sometimes regarded as the giver of gifts of food, ,[1] and at a later period he generally takes the

[1] Mariette, *op. cit.*, p. 407.

place of Anubis in the performance of this office. In the text of Tetȧ, line 140, Seb, or Ḳeb, is said to give an offering to the king in his every form and in his every place,  , but when it is remembered that Seb was the great Earth-god, and the lord of all its products, this is not surprising. A few lines further on (line 150) we have: "SUTEN ḤETEP ṬĀ. May Seb give an offering to "this Tetȧ. May he give to thee offerings of all kinds "in sets of four, and a setting forth in abundance of "bread-cakes and vessels of beer, and bread of all kinds "which thou lovest, and which are fair for thee before "the God." 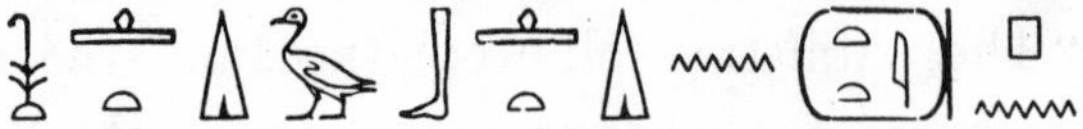

.

In Pepi II., line 680, we have the passage: "SUTEN "ṬĀ ḤETEP. May Seb give these chosen haunches of "beef and *pert-kheru* offerings to all the gods, so that "they may cause every good thing to happen to Pepi "Nefer-ka-Rā." 

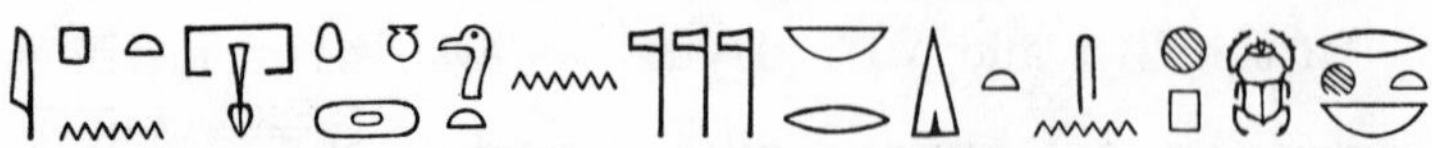

. This passage is of considerable interest, for in it the words 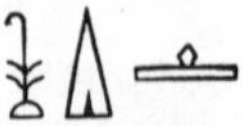 occur, although

the offerings are to be made by Seb, not to a dead man, but to the gods.

In a tomb at Ṣakkârah[1] we have the usual 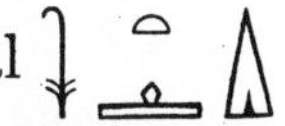 , followed in the second line by  *suten ḥetep ṭā pert kheru*, from which it might be gathered that the *ḥetep* which the king was asked to give consisted of *pert kheru.*

Now it is quite clear that  means "offerings" because the signs are followed by the determinatives of bread, beer, or wine, and cakes. This fact was pointed out by Dr. Birch as far back as 1858,[2] and Egyptologists generally have accepted his rendering of the words *pert kheru.* Professor Maspero has treated the words with his usual skill in his article "Sur l'Expression 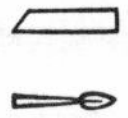 mâ-khrôou,"[3] and shown that the primary meaning of *pert kheru* is the appearance of offerings which "come forth at [the sound of] the voice," and gives the reasons for his opinion thus. The ministrant who performed the ceremony of making funerary offerings called out the names of the objects which were to be offered from a list which he had with him. Having called out a name his assistants brought the object referred to and set it before the statue, or mummy, of the deceased. As each object was presented,

[1] Mariette, *op. cit.*, p. 176.
[2] *Mémoire sur une patère Égyptienne*, p. 72.
[3] *Études de Mythologie*, i., p. 113.

the ministrant recited over it a short formula which contained words similar in sound to the name of the offering, in fact he played on the words, or punned. By means of these formulae the offerings were consecrated, and then they "came forth" on the table of offerings, or on the altar of the god, who was supposed to give a portion of them to the dead. As this "coming forth" only took place after the words had been uttered by the ministrant, the offerings became known as *pert kheru,* or "things which come forth at the voice."

On the other hand *pert kheru,* or *pert er kheru,* may have another meaning, as we see from a passage in the Biography of Paḥeri (l. 42). This official addresses those who live upon earth, and declares that they shall hand on their exalted positions and dignities to their children, provided that they say on his behalf, "SUTEN ṬĀ ḤETEP!" according to the things which are written in the Books, and "PERT ER KHERU," according to the saying of the men of olden time, "like unto the PERRT "(i.e., the things which come forth) from the mouth of "the god."

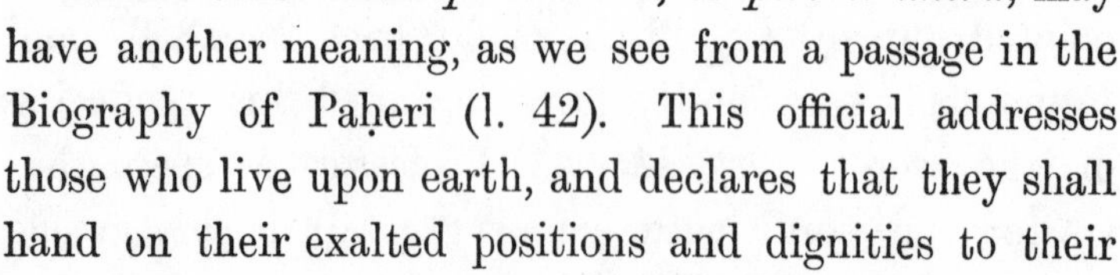

From this we see at once that the words *suten ṭā*

ḥetep have become a mere formula, and that this formula was to be recited because it was found in the sacred books. Next, it is clear that the words *pert er kheru* (i.e., "things which come forth at the word") were also a formula, which was to be recited because the men of olden time had been in the habit of reciting it. But the text goes on to say that the *pert er kheru* were to be "like the *perrt* from the mouth of the god," and its meaning is plain. When the god of creation made the world and the things in it, he merely uttered the names of the things which he wished to make, and these things came into being. Paḥeri wished the people whom he addressed to say *pert er kheru mȧ perrt em re en neter*, so that the things which came forth might be like the things which appeared after the god had uttered their names. In other words, the mere utterance of the words of the formula by the living would cause offerings of every kind to appear in abundance, just as the utterance of the words *suten ṭā ḥetep* would produce a "royal offering." It was unnecessary to place offerings in the tomb, for these would appear as a matter of course as a result of the recital of the formulae.

The meaning of *pert kheru* has also been discussed by Mr. Griffith,[1] who thinks that *pert kheru* and *pert er kheru*, , undoubtedly represent the old form 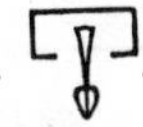. Other authorities who accept the general

[1] *Proc. Soc. Bibl. Arch.*, 1896, p. 199.

meaning of "offerings" for *pert kheru* are Virey,[1] Amélineau,[2] and Erman.[3]

It now remains to consider how the words  *suten ḥetep ṭā,* were understood by the Egyptians. It is true that they occur on almost every sepulchral monument known to us, but there are cases in which they are omitted. To one of these Mr. Griffith has called attention, namely the inscription of Methen, which begins with the words *Ȧnpu ḥetep ṭā* 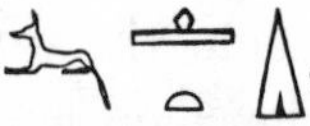, "May Ȧnpu give an offering," and makes no mention of the *ḥetep* of the king. Another is found in the work of Mariette, *Les Mastaba,* p. 116, where we have   "May the great god give an offering," and no mention is made of the king. Both examples come from monuments which are not later than the IVth Dynasty, and it is clear that there was a time in Egypt when men invoked the god and made no mention of the king. It is quite possible, and very probable, that the king sent gifts or offerings when his friends among the nobles, or highly meritorious officials, were laid to rest in their tombs, and a proof of this is perhaps furnished in a text published by Mariette (*op. cit.*, p. 396) where we have the following :—

[1] *Tombeau de Rekhmara* (*Mémoires*, v., 101, note 7).
[2] *Un Tombeau Égyptien* (*Revue de l'histoire des Religions*, 1891).
[3] *Egyptian Grammar*, p. 50*.

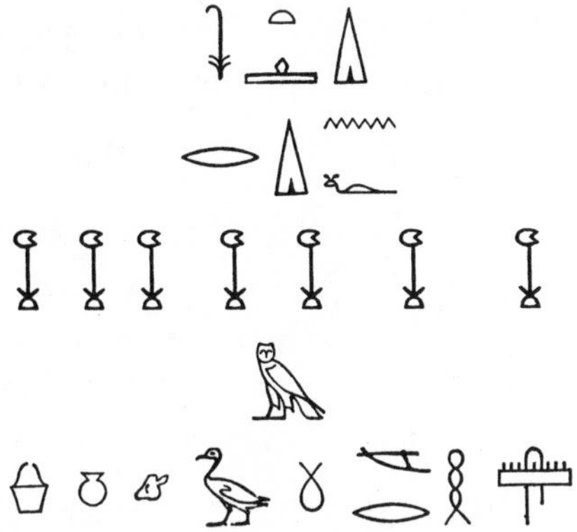

"May the king give an offering! May he give 1000 "loaves, 1000 [vessels of] wine (or beer), 1000 oxen "(or, bulls), 1000 geese, 1000 swathings, 1000 [vessels "of] oil, 1000 linen garments."

On the other hand, it is possible to regard 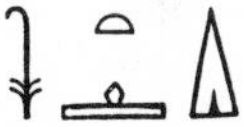 merely as a formula of pious import, which is not intended to be understood literally, and to translate  by "may one give." The Egyptians were an eminently practical people, and, however great and powerful they thought their kings, they must have perceived that it was impossible for them to send funerary gifts to the tombs of each and all their subjects. It may be argued that the king was held to be god as well as man, and that he was therefore able to supply every dead person with offerings, like Seb, or Ȧnpu, or Osiris, or Khenti Ȧmenti, but there seems to me to be no evidence in the texts which would support this view. Moreover, there is a passage in the text of Pepi II. which makes it impossible. In line 680 a prayer is made that Seb will give *pert kheru*, 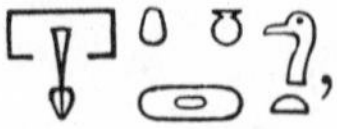, to all the gods, provided that they give to the king all good things, and make "this pyramid, this work," 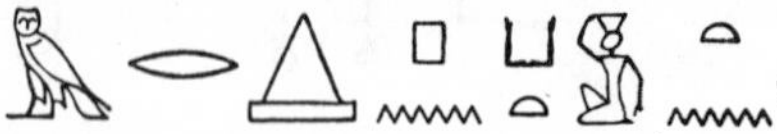, endure for ever. So long as the gods do this, provision shall be made for them, they shall be adored, they shall possess both soul and vital power , "there shall be given unto them a *ḥetep ṭā suten* of "cakes, bread, beer, oxen, geese, linen garments, and "unguent," 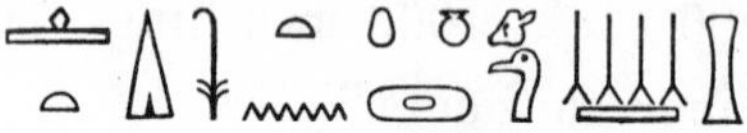, they shall receive their divine offerings, 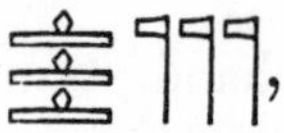, choice animals and geese shall be slain for them, festal (?) offerings, 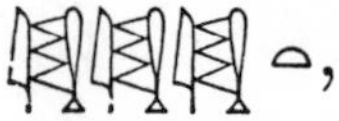, shall be made for them, and they shall take possession of the Urerit crown like the Great and Little Companies of the gods. In this passage, it seems to me, the words 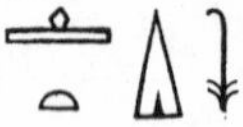 must mean something like a "royal offering," and Professor Maspero's rendering "offrande royale," or "proscynème royale," is no doubt correct,[1] that is to say, it represents the meaning which the Egyptians attached to them in the time of king Pepi II.

The almost universal occurrence of 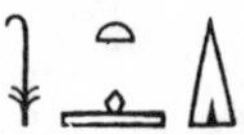 before

[1] See also his renderings of Tetȧ, l. 150, and Pepi I., l. 83.

the prayer to Anubis and other gods for funerary offerings proves that these words were believed to benefit the dead in some way, but it seems that their exact meaning was forgotten in very early times, and that their appearance on sepulchral monuments of the later periods is due entirely to the respect shown by the Egyptians for ancient tradition, and to their religious conservatism. With the dynastic Egyptians they expressed, I believe, the hope that the offerings made at their tombs would, in number and abundance, resemble those made to a king, in fact, a "royal offering," and many Egyptologists have translated them by these or similar words. Thus Birch rendered  by "a royal oblation";[1] Bergmann by "eine königliche Opfergabe";[2] Dümichen by "königlich Gnade (wie es ein "König thut, wie es eines Königs würdig est)";[3] Brugsch by "die Königliche Gabe eines Opfertisches";[4] Baillet by "don de royale offrande";[5] Maspero[6] and de Horrack by "royale offrande";[7] Pierret by "oblation";[8] &c. As an alternative rendering Brugsch gives, "der König gewährt einen Opfertisch,"[9] and Birch gives, "act of homage";[10] and Ledrain,[11] and Piehl give "Proscy-

[1] *Egyptian Texts*, p. 30. [2] *Recueil*, ix., p. 35.
[3] *Der Grabpalast des Patuamenap*, i., p. 6.
[4] *Wörterbuch*, p. 1007. [5] *Recueil*, xii., 53.
[6] Tetà, l. 150; Pepi II., l. 683.
[7] Chabas, *Mélanges*, Sér. iii., tom. 2, p. 204.
[8] *Vocabulaire, s.v.* [9] *Wörterbuch*, p. 1008.
[10] *Trans. Soc. Bibl. Arch.*, viii., p. 148.
[11] *Recueil*, i., p. 92.

nème"[1] (προσκύνημα). The view recently put forward that we must translate 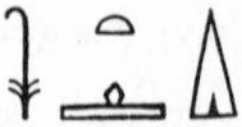 by "May the king give an offering," is practically a revival of Brugsch's rendering, "der König gewährt einen Opfertisch," which was published in 1868.

It is well known that among all African peoples, when a man of importance dies, all his kinsfolk and friends send gifts to swell the amount of food which is intended to be consumed at the funeral feast. In primitive times in Egypt, the king also probably sent gifts of food when his officials were buried, and at a later period it is possible that certain portions or articles of food were described as the "royal offering," whether they were given by the king or not. In fact, no funeral feast was considered to be complete without its "royal offering." This view seems to me to be supported by a vignette on plate xii. of Dümichen's *Grabpalast*, Abth. ii., which contains the version of the Book of Opening the Mouth found in the tomb of Peṭā Ȧmen-ȧpt. In this we see a ministrant "preparing the royal offering," 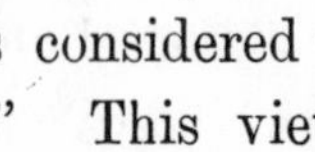, whilst the Sem priest stands behind him sprinkling water from a libation vase. Here there is no mention of the king giving the offering, and it is clear that the "royal offering" was only one of many which were given to the dead.

[1] *Recueil*, i., p. 133.

CHAPTER II.

The Liturgy of Funerary Offerings Described.

The religious literature of all periods of Egyptian history proves that the Egyptians believed in a resurrection and in immortality, and that from the earliest to the latest times they performed ceremonies at, or in, the tomb, and recited formulae, which were part incantations and part prayers, with the view of assisting the dead to renew their life, to enjoy their existence in the Other World, and to escape from "dying a second time." We have already seen that so far back as the beginning of the IVth Dynasty, about B.C. 3800, it was customary to offer series of gifts of food, and drink, and raiment to the dead, and there is every reason to think that the presentation of such gifts was made by priests, who recited over them forms of words which were believed to sanctify the things offered, and to make them to become suitable for the needs of the dead. We know that certain kinds of food and drink were offered in certain quantities, and in a definite order, and that every detail of the ceremonies connected with their presentation was performed according to a system which had then been in use for a very long time. The ceremonies and formulae of the liturgy of funeral sacrifice in their oldest forms belong, no doubt, to the earliest period of Egyptian civilization, and it is very probable that many of them were in existence in the Predynastic Period.

Among the oldest of the ceremonies which were performed for the benefit of the dead is that called the "Opening of the Mouth," and its object is explained by its name. The Egyptians realized at a very early period that it was useless to load the tables for offerings in the tombs with bread, beer, meat, fruit, and vegetables unless the dead could in some way partake of them, and the priests invented a series of ceremonies and composed formulae which were intended to bring about this desirable result. The belief in the importance of "Opening the Mouth" for the dead has long been known to Egyptologists, in fact ever since the publication of the text of the Saïte Recension of the *Book of the Dead* by Lepsius in 1842. In the Saïte Recension, as in the Theban, the XXIIIrd Chapter is devoted to the opening of the mouth of the deceased, and in the Vignette a priest is seen standing before a statue of the deceased, to which he addresses certain words. In his left hand he holds a vase of unguent, which played a prominent part in the ceremony performed by the priest whilst he uttered the prescribed formula.

The XXIst and XXIInd Chapters were written with the view of "giving a mouth to a man in Neter

Khert," or the Other World, and in the Vignette the priest is seen standing and holding the Ur-ḥekau instrument in his right hand, and a vase in his left. He holds out the instrument towards the face of the deceased, and is, as we know from other sources, about to touch his mouth. In the text of the XXIIIrd Chapter the deceased says, "Ptaḥ hath opened for me "my mouth with his instrument of iron wherewith he "opened the mouth of the gods." This is an important statement, for it shows that in the Ptolemaïc Period a legend was extant that at some time during their existence the mouths of the gods needed opening, that the origin of the ceremony of "Opening the Mouth" was divine, and that it was performed in the mythological period.

The illustrated papyri which contain the Theban Recension of the *Book of the Dead* supply further details of the ceremony, and in the papyrus of Ani, in the Vignette of Chapter XXIII., we see a SEM priest, clad in a panther's or leopard's skin, performing one portion of it on a figure of the scribe Ani. In front of him are a sepulchral box for holding unguents, three  instruments, and the instrument 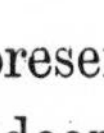. In another Vignette in the same papyrus is a representation of the performance of the ceremony at the door of the tomb. The mummy of Ani is held upright by Anubis, and three priests are officiating; two hold the instruments to the face of the mummy, and the third reads the formulae from a roll of papyrus in his hands. Between the mummy and the priests is a table loaded with offerings, and on the ground round about are the various objects which are used in the performance of the ceremony. Behind the priests are the cow and calf for sacrifice, and an assistant is seen bringing a leg of beef.

In the Papyrus of Hunefer this scene is repeated with some modifications and fuller details; these are illustrated by the accompanying block. In the upper register one priest presents to the face of the mummy four vases, and another holds in one hand the instruments , and presents with the other the Ur-ḥekau instrument, the head of which is in the form of that of a ram. The SEM priest stands behind holding a libation jar in his right hand, and a censer in his left. In the lower register are the cow and calf for sacrifice, two ministrants, the one bearing the heart and the other the leg of a bull, a sepulchral coffer, a table of offerings, and a stand on which are spread out a panther's skin or leopard's skin, and the instruments, vases, &c., which were used in the performance of the ceremony. Above these scenes are several short lines of text, which are entitled, "The Chapter of performing the Opening of the Mouth of the statue" [of the deceased]. This chapter contains two extracts from the "Liturgy of Funerary Offerings."

The merit of discovering the "Liturgy of Funerary Offerings" belongs to Sig. Ernesto Schiaparelli, who in 1877 was able to prove that the contents of Papyrus

No. 3155 in the Louvre were identical in a large number of places with the text on the coffin of Butehai-Åmen, 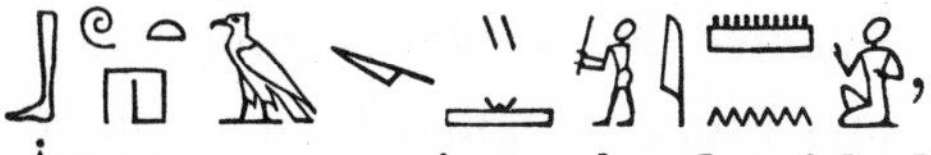, in Turin. Butehai-Åmen was a priest who flourished under the XXth Dynasty, and he caused a copy of the Book of Opening the Mouth to be written upon the two covers of his coffin in red and black ink. Devéria had examined this papyrus many years before, and he stated in his *Catalogue des Manuscrits Égyptiens* (Paris, 1881, p. 171) that it "contained a liturgical text entirely "different from the ordinary funerary works, and that "it was noteworthy by reason of the mention in it of "the priests of different orders who officiated, and the "description of the part which each individual per-"formed in the funeral ceremony." In a valuable paper entitled "*Le Fer et l'Aimant en Égypte*,"[1] he translated about a page and a half of the papyrus, and Sig. Schiaparelli believes that he cherished the thought of publishing the complete work.

The papyrus was written for a priestess called SAIS, 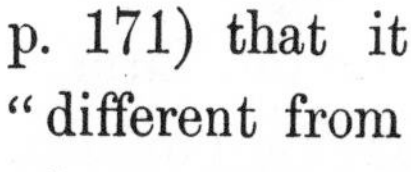. The lower portions of the first few leaves are wanting, and the writing is in places very difficult to read. Being convinced of the importance of the text, Sig. Schiaparelli spent a winter in copying it, and he devoted himself to the preparation of an edition of the text on the coffin in Turin, which dates from the

[1] *Mélanges d'Archéologie Égyptienne*, tom. i., p. 45.

XXth Dynasty, and that of the Paris papyrus, which was written probably between A.D. 50 and 150. Neither text is accompanied by Vignettes, and many parts of them it is impossible to understand without illustrations. About this time, fortunately, his attention was called to a series of drawings of scenes in the tomb of Seti I. at Thebes which Champollion [1] had made and published. In these priests are represented performing ceremonies on the statue of the king, and the short texts which accompany them were quickly seen by Sig. Schiaparelli to resemble passages in the Liturgy of Funerary Offerings. From a paper by Professor Naville [2] he was able to identify a passage in the text on the coffin of Butehai-Åmen, and with the help of the careful copy of all the scenes and texts in the tomb of Seti I., with which Professor Naville supplied him, he was at length able to give a rendering of the whole text, and to describe the ceremonies which were there illustrated.

The first part of his work,[3] i.e., the plates, appeared in 1881, and the two volumes of text in 1882 and 1890 respectively. In 1882 Professor Maspero published in his *Recueil* (tom. iii., p. 171 ff.) the first part of the texts from the Pyramid of Unås, which contains the oldest known form of the Liturgy of

[1] *Monuments*, plates 237, 243-248.

[2] *Aeg. Zeitschrift*, Bd. xi., 1873, p. 29 ff.

[3] *Il Libro dei Funerali degli antichi Egiziani tradotto e commentato da* E. S., Rome, 1881-90.

Funerary Offerings, with a French translation of a portion of it. Another copy of this early form is found in the Pyramid of Pepi II. Nefer-ka-Rā, and this Professor Maspero published, with a translation of the whole, in a later volume of the same work, and in his complete edition of the "Pyramid Texts" entitled, "Les Inscriptions des Pyramides de Saqqarah," Paris, 1894. In 1884-5 Dr. J. Dümichen published the first two parts of his monograph[1] on the tomb of Peṭā-Åmen-åpt, a high priestly official who flourished under the XXVIth Dynasty, containing copies of the scenes and texts with descriptions, translations, &c., in German. The first part contains the complete text of the Liturgy of Funerary Offerings, and the second a version of the Book of Opening the Mouth; both works have Vignettes.

A year later appeared the first volume of the great French work on the Royal Tombs of Thebes,[2] containing all the scenes and texts in the Tomb of Seti I. Among these were accurate copies of the texts of the Liturgy of Funerary Offerings, as they are found in the tomb of Seti I. at Thebes, and the Book of Opening the Mouth. In 1887 Professor Maspero published a valuable paper in the *Revue de l'Histoire des Religions*, tom. xv., pp. 159-188, in which he treated the Book of Opening the Mouth at con-

[1] *Der Grabpalast des Patuamenap*, Leipzic, 1884-5.

[2] *Les Hypogées Royaux de Thèbes*, by Bouriant, Loret, and Naville (*Mémoires de la Mission au Caire*, tom. ii., Div. i., Paris, 1886).

siderable length, and explained the Vignettes and the texts of the version in the tomb of Seti I. Since that time the texts of several tombs at Thebes have been published, and the material available for the study of the texts and Vignettes has been greatly increased.

The principal versions of the Liturgy of Funerary Offerings and the Book of Opening the Mouth may now be summarized. For the Liturgy there are two copies of the period of the Ancient Empire, one in the Pyramid of Unȧs, and one in the Pyramid of Pepi II. Nefer-ka-Rā. Several Lists of offerings, more or less complete, from the maṣṭaba tombs at Ṣaḳḳârah are also available. Of the XIXth Dynasty there are the Lists in the tomb of Seti I. at Thebes and in his temple at Abydos. Of the XXth Dynasty there is the List on the covers of the coffin of Butehai-Ȧmen; of the XXVIth Dynasty the List of Peṭā-Ȧmen-ȧpt; and of the Roman Period the List in the Papyrus of Sais, the priestess, in Paris. For the Book of Opening the Mouth there are: a copy, with Vignettes, in the tomb of Rekhmȧrā at Thebes, of the XVIIIth Dynasty; a copy, with Vignettes, in the tomb of Seti I. at Thebes, of the XIXth Dynasty; a copy, without Vignettes, written for Butehai-Ȧmen on the covers of his coffin, of the XXth Dynasty; a copy, with Vignettes, in the tomb of Peṭā-Ȧmen-ȧpt, of the XXVIth Dynasty; a copy, without Vignettes, written for the priestess Sais in the Roman period.

The reader who will take the trouble to compare

the various versions of the Liturgy and the Book of Opening the Mouth will find that, in all essentials, they remained unchanged from the IVth Dynasty to about the end of the first century of the rule of the Romans in Egypt. The Vignettes, though we owe them to the funerary artists of the XVIIIth, XIXth, and XXVIth Dynasties, illustrate faithfully ceremonies which had been performed for many centuries before they were drawn, and the evidence which they afford may be used as a sure guide in determining the exact meaning of many obscure points in the rubrical directions and texts.

We may now give an account of the Liturgy of Funerary Offerings, derived from the texts in the Pyramid of Unȧs and the tomb of Peṭā-Ȧmen-ȧpt. The Liturgy was recited in a chamber of the tomb called "Ṭuat," 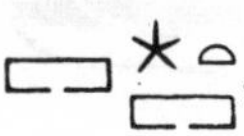, and when the offerings had been brought there, the table for the offerings, or altar, was purified for the KA, or Double, of the deceased, and the service began. The formulae were recited by the Kher ḥeb priest, who held in his hands a roll of papyrus, on which was written a copy of the service, and who directed the assistant priests; the ceremonies were performed chiefly by the SEM, or SMER, priest, assisted by one or more ministrants. In the earliest times the ceremonies were probably performed over the mummy, but at a later period a statue of the deceased was substituted.

The First Ceremony.

To cleanse and purify the statue so that it might become a suitable and permanent dwelling-place for the Ka was the object of the first ceremony. The Sem priest took up a vessel filled with clean water, ,

The Sem priest pouring water from a libation vase into a libation bowl held by a ministrant.

in which salt or soda had been dissolved, and poured it into a bowl which was held in the hands of an assistant. He next walked round the statue four times, sprinkling the salted water on it on all sides, or perhaps washing portions of it, and meanwhile the Kher heb said four times:—

"O Osiris, everything which is hateful in Unȧs hath "been carried away for thee; for that which was "uttered in his name of evil hath Thoth come, and he "hath carried it away to Osiris. I have brought that "which was spoken in the name of Unȧs of evil, and "have placed it in the palm of thy hand. The SA "shall not be separated from thee, and thou shalt not "be separated from it."

From the way in which Osiris is mentioned in this passage it is clear that the cult of this god was general in Egypt when this Liturgy was drawn up, and that he was already recognized as the god of the dead. The effect of the sprinkling of water over the statue, or the washing of it with water, was to remove the sins of the deceased from him, and to cleanse his body and Ka. There can be no doubt that the Egyptians in all periods attached very great importance to the use of water ceremonially, and there is good reason for believing that they regarded it as one of the principal sources of life, since the gods were created from water, and Nu, the great god of the celestial deeps, was the father of the gods. They believed that water possessed a mysterious power which made itself manifest under the form of life, and it may be noted in passing that, in the scenes in which Thoth and Horus are pouring out water over the heads of kings, the water is indicated by series of *ānkh* signs ☥☥☥, i.e., "life, life, life." Dümichen has already in this connection pointed out the fact that in the "Tale of the Two Brothers," Ȧnpu put the heart of his younger brother Bata into a vessel of water; when the heart had absorbed all the water it came to life. Water not only washed away sin, but gave new birth and life to the dead.

The Gnostics, who preserved many ancient Egyptian beliefs, attached great importance to the use of water ceremonially, and, according to Irenaeus (*Haeres*, 1, 2, § 5), they threw oil and water over the heads of the dying to make them invisible to the powers of darkness. The ancient Egyptians certainly dissolved salt, or soda in some form, in their "holy water," and it is probable that they pronounced some formula over it before sprinkling it upon the dead. The sprinkling of the dead was the first and most important of burial ceremonies among the Egyptians for thousands of years, and it is probable that it was adopted, under the name of baptism of the dead, by many sections of the Christian Church. For centuries certain Christians actually baptized the dead, and they continued to do so in spite of the prohibitions of many Councils.

The exact meaning which is to be attached to the word *ṭu* or "evil" is not quite clear;[1] it was certainly connected with the words of Unȧs, but whatever it was this "evil" was carried to Osiris by Thoth. Here we see Thoth acting as a sort of advocate for Unȧs with Osiris, and playing his part as the "lord of divine words," and author of holy books, with which we are familiar from the texts of the Theban Recension of the

[1] Maspero renders it by *Mauvais*.

Book of the Dead. In the Judgment it was he who "weighed words," and who weighed the heart of the dead man in the Great Balance, and reported the result to Osiris. It is the "words" of Unȧs which are in question here, and in Egypt both gods and men judged a man by his "words." The sprinkling of the water caused Thoth to carry the words of evil uttered by Unȧs, and place them in the hand of the god.

The words which were said by the Kher ḥeb here, as in many other places in the Liturgy, were to be repeated *four times.* The Egyptians divided the earth into four quarters, over each of which a god presided, and in order to secure for the dead permission to move about freely through these quarters of the world, formulae, whether of blessing or of banning, were repeated four times, once for each god, and certain offerings were made in quadruplicate. The gods of the four quarters of the world at the time when this Liturgy was drawn up were Horus, Set, Thoth, and Sep, and they were probably the gods of the four cardinal points also. Later, however, their places seem to have been taken by the four sons of Horus, Mesthȧ, Ḥāpi, Ṭuamutef and Qebḥsennuf, each of whom presided over one of the four pillars that held up the sky. The priest by walking round the mummy or the statue four times, and sprinkling water as he went, bestowed upon the Ka the power to journey into all parts of heaven and earth, and made him a pure being in respect of the four gods of the four quarters of the earth.

At the end of the first formula quoted above come the words, "The *Sa* shall not be separated from thee, "and thou shalt not be separated from it." By the word *Sa*  or , the Egyptians understood that mysterious energy and life-giving power which existed in the gods, and which for want of a better name we may call the "fluid of life." Its source was the Sun-god, by whatever name he is called, Horus or Rā, and Rā in the text of Unȧs[1] is said to be "Sovereign of the "divine *Sa*" 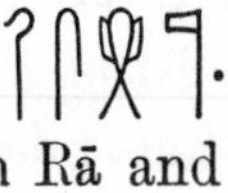. The gods and goddesses received this *Sa* from Rā and communicated it to those whom they loved upon earth. According to M. Moret,[2] the fluid of life could be transmitted from the being who possessed it to the person to whom it was desired to transfer it, by embracing that person and by making "magnetic passes" along the back. M. Maspero also describes the *Sa* as a sort of "magnetic fluid," or "aura," which could be transmitted to a person by laying hands on him, or by making passes over the nape of the neck or the spinal column. The phrase *setep sa* 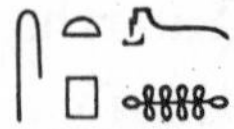, means something like to "make passes." The *Sa* was transmitted to a king from the statue of a god by placing the arms of the statue round him, and by laying one of its hands on the nape of his neck as he knelt before it.[3]

[1] Line 562, *Suzerain de la vertu divine.* Maspero.

[2] *Le Rituel du Culte divin journalier*, Paris, 1902, p. 99.

[3] *Contes Populaires*, p. 165.

When the statue had exhausted the store of the power which was in it, it was able to obtain a fresh supply from the Other World. The object of making passes before the statue of the dead, or his mummy, was to give a place in the fore-front of the company of the KHU, or "Spirits," in the Other World. This is certain from a passage in the text of Pepi I., wherein it is said, "The "passes by which he obtaineth the fluid of life having "been made over him by [Rā] and Horus, he is at the "head of the KHU" (l. 695).

THE SECOND CEREMONY.

The ceremony of the sprinkling of water having been completed, the second ceremony begins. The SEM priest, or one of his assistants, took in his hand a censer in which incense has been placed, and having set fire in it, and made the incense to burn, he walked with it four times round the statue or mummy, and censed it, whilst the Kher ḥeb recited the following four times:—

"Let him that advanceth advance with his KA.
"Horus advanceth with his KA.
"Set advanceth with his KA.
"Thoth advanceth with his KA.
"Sep advanceth with his KA.
"Osiris advanceth with his KA.
"Khenti-maati[1] advanceth with his KA.

[1] Dümichen, "the dweller in the town of Sekhem (Letopolis)."

"Thy Ṭeṭ shall advance with thy KA.
"Hail, Unȧs! The arm of thy KA is before thee.
"Hail, Unȧs! The arm of thy KA is behind thee.
"Hail, Unȧs! The leg of thy KA is before thee.
"Hail, Unȧs! The leg of thy KA is behind thee.
"O Osiris Unȧs! I have given unto thee the Eye

The Sem priest carrying the censer of burning incense.

"of Horus, and thy face is filled therewith, and the "perfume of the Eye of Horus is to thee."

This formula begins with an address to the statue, or mummy, which is bidden to advance, just as do Horus, Set, Thoth, Sep, Osiris, and Khenti-maati, i.e., the dweller without eyes (the Horus of the dark night when neither sun nor moon is visible). These gods are not separated from their KAU, and the KA of Unȧs, as the equal of their KAU, shall be with him. With his KA, however, shall come his *Tcheṭ*, or *Ṭeṭ*, 𓆓𓂧𓊽, or 𓊽𓂧, i.e., his backbone, or pillar which supports the backbone. The 𓊽, as Prof. Maspero has shown, represents the tree-trunk which was worshipped at Mendes in connection with Osiris; it was animated by Osiris, and was all-powerful in supporting the dead because of the presence of the god in it. Under the Middle and New Empires the 𓊽 is often seen painted on the bottoms of the insides of coffins, and when coffins were intended to stand on their feet, the 𓊽 was generally painted on the back outside. Thus when lying down the mummy rested on his 𓊽, and when standing up was supported by it. The KA of the deceased comes with him because it is supported by Osiris, and it comes with one leg and one arm before him, and one leg and one arm behind him. The exact signification of these expressions is unknown, but about the translation of the words there is no doubt.

We next see that the incense with which the mummy is censed represents the Eye of Horus, or the Sun, and the use of the expression dates from the time when Horus was the greatest of the gods of heaven, and the sun was regarded as his eye. The sun was, of course, the source of heat and light, and therefore of all life, and "Eye of Horus" was a synonym for everything which was beneficial for the living and the dead. The hot fumes of the incense surrounded the mummy or statue and gave warmth to it, the smoke rose up before its face, which it covered with a sort of layer, and the general effect of the ceremony was to make the deceased pure and warm. The first ceremony removed sin from the new dwelling-place of the KA, and the second continued its purification, and gave to it the quickening heat which was derived from the Eye of Horus. The pungent smell of the incense formed a sort of atmosphere for the dead, and was pleasant to them.

THE THIRD CEREMONY.

The third ceremony of purification was performed by means of water, in which two different kinds of incense had been dissolved. The rubric in the text of Unȧs mentions "two balls" of incense, but that of the text of Peṭā-Ȧmen-ȧpt says that one ball shall be of incense of Shet pet, i.e., of the incense prepared from the salt found in the Natron Valley, and the other of the salt which is found near the city of Nekheb, or Eileithyiapolis. Shet pet was a portion of the Sekhet-Ḥemam, or "Field of Salt," known to-day as the "Wâdî an-Naṭrûn," which lies about forty-five miles to the north-west of Cairo, and the incense made from the salt deposits here was called "Incense of the North." The incense made from the salt deposits near Nekheb was called "Incense of the South." The KA whose statue had been purified by incense from each place was free to journey through the North and South of Egypt, and in a sense it made him "lord of the Two Lands," i.e., of all Egypt. The priest, having dissolved the balls of natron in the water in the vessel, , poured it out into

The Sem priest pouring water from a libation vase into a libation bowl held by a ministrant.

a bowl held by an assistant. He then took the bowl, and, going round the statue four times, sprinkled it with the water of the natrons of the South and North, whilst the Kher ḥeb repeated the following words four times:—

"This libation is for thee, O Osiris, this libation is

"for thee, O Unȧs; it cometh forth from thy son, it "cometh forth from Horus.

"I have come and I have brought unto thee the Eye "of Horus, that thy heart may be refreshed therewith. "I have brought it [and placed it] under thee, [under] "thy sandals, and I have presented unto thee that "which floweth forth from thee. Whilst it is with "thee there shall be no stoppage of thy heart, and it "shall be with thee with the things (or, persons) which "came forth at the [sound of the] voice."

The libation now poured forth represents the moisture which Horus sends forth from himself and from his Eye, and is intended to take the place in the body of the deceased of that which flowed forth from him before death, or during the process of mummification. The deceased is identified with Osiris, and Horus therefore becomes his son. This fluid of Horus will make the heart of the deceased to live again, just as the water in which the heart of Bata was placed in the Tale of the Two Brothers, having been absorbed, made it to live. So long as a supply of it exists in the body of the deceased his heart shall not stop, and this supply was provided among the "things which come forth at the voice," i.e., the offerings. We have already seen that *pert kheru* is a name given to offerings, because they were believed to appear when the deceased, or the priest, ordered them to appear, and it is clear that the words *perthȧ nek kheru* in the text here refer to the offerings. The Egyptians attached great importance to spoken words, and they regarded the power of speech and the gift of the voice as mighty weapons, both for the living and the dead. The KAU, or Doubles, of the dead who had learned to utter words correctly, and who knew the proper tones to employ in uttering them, were in a position to go where they pleased and to do what they liked, for no god, spirit, fiend, or devil, and no inanimate object, could help obeying the commands which they uttered. The order for food or water having been given by them, food or water appeared forthwith.

In the passage translated above are the words "that which floweth forth," which I have used as the equivalent of the Egyptian word *erṭu*, , or . The exact meaning of the word is "effluxes," or "outflowings," and the determinatives show that by *erṭu* we are to understand the strong-smelling liquid which exudes from a dead body. Several passages in the *Book of the Dead* support this view, as the following examples will prove. In Chapter LXIIIB. 2, we have, "I have lifted up the "efflux from Osiris," 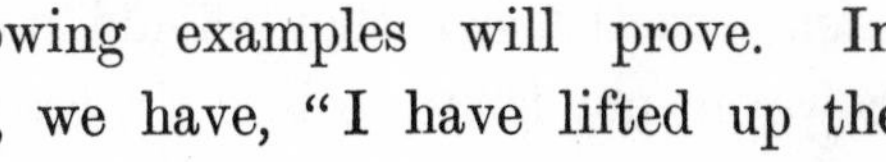; in Chapter CXIX., "Pure are the effluxes which are "borne away from thee," 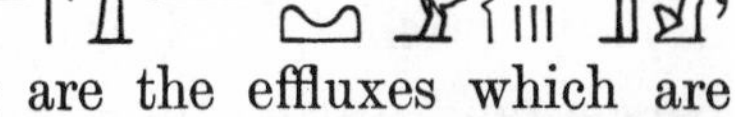 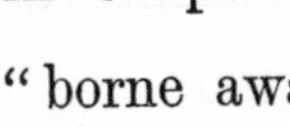; in Chapter CXLVII. 6, "I have come unto "thee, Osiris, pure one of effluxes," 

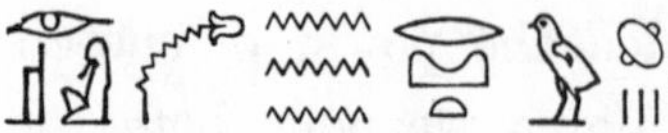; in Chapter CXLIX. (Åat XIII.), "Like the stream from the effluxes coming forth "from Osiris,"  ; and in Åat XIV. of the same Chapter, "I "shall not be destroyed by the effluxes which come "forth from Osiris,"  . The effluxes of Osiris here referred to are undoubtedly the humours which were believed to have drained out of the body of Osiris when Horus and his "sons" were embalming it. From the above passages it is clear that the Egyptians regarded these humours as pure or holy, for they represented the very essence of the god. Now the Egyptians were not the only people in the world who attached mystic power and importance to the fluid which ran out from the dead, but though the texts make it certain that they did, we cannot learn from them exactly *why* they should do so. The reason is, however, not far to seek. Mr. Crawley tells us (*Mystic Rose*, p. 287) that communion with the dead is most exactly reached, and the identity of eating with a person and eating him most clearly shown, in the common Australian practice in which mourners drink the humours of the decaying corpse, or eat its flesh. The Kurnai anoint themselves with decomposed matter from the dead. It is done in the Kingsmills to "re-

member him." So in Timorlaut mourners smear themselves with the fluids of the corpse. The Aru islanders drink them "to effect union with the dead man." Some of the liquid is kept in order to injure enemies. The object of drinking the liquid is, clearly, to obtain the qualities of the dead man, his strength, and, perhaps, his vital power, and it is possible also that those who indulged in such practices did so with the idea of avoiding injury from the departed spirit. What the Egyptians did with the humours of the dead is unknown, but in the case of great and holy men, that which drained from their bodies was certainly turned to some good account by the living. The custom of draining the dead body of its moisture is common enough among modern peoples of Central Africa, as we may see from the account of a great Baluba chief's death quoted by Sir H. Johnston (*Grenfell and the Congo*, ii., p. 655). "When an important Luba chief "expires, every one, great and small, must mourn in a "subdued tone; the members of all the brotherhoods "come before the house where the body lies to perform "dances; the women violently strike their hatchet and "hoe against each other. This deafening hubbub lasts a "day. . . . During this time a young slave is obtained, "his neck is broken by a heavy blow, and he is laid "by the corpse for two days. He is the chief's boy "attendant. His wives, squatting near him, do not "cease their lamentations. Some days pass in this way "without other incidents, after which the stiffened limbs "are forcibly bent, and the body placed in the wicker "coffin. In the house two stages are raised, one above "the other; on the upper one is placed the coffin, on the "lower one a large earthen pot. The body decomposes; "a noxious liquid infested with maggots escapes from it "and falls into the receptacle; it is left there for several "weeks." The Belgian missionary who describes the chief's burial does not tell us what was done with the "noxious liquid," but, as human flesh and bones form an important element in the "medicines" which are prescribed by medicine men in Central Africa, we are probably justified in assuming that the liquid was used in the same way.

THE FOURTH CEREMONY.

The first ceremony removed evil or sin from the body of the deceased, the second gave it warmth, and the third restored to it the humours which had been expressed from it. For the fourth ceremony the SEM priest dissolved five grains of incense made from the salt deposits near the city of Nekheb, i.e., "Incense of the South," in a libation vase of water, and, having poured it into a vessel, walked with it four times round the mummy or statue, and sprinkled it each time. The name given to this libation water is "Semmȧn," , and of the five grains of salt, or alum, which it contained, one was for Horus, one for Set, one for Thoth, one for Sep, and one for Osiris, that is, for the deceased himself. Whilst the SEM priest walked round the statue the Kher ḥeb said the following words four times:—

"[Here is] *Semmàn!* [Here is] *Semmàn!*

"Open thy mouth, O Unȧs, and taste thou the taste "thereof in the halls of the god, for *Semmàn* is the "emission of Horus, for *Semmàn* is the emission of Set,

The Sem priest pouring water from a libation vase into a libation bowl held by a ministrant.

"for *Semmàn* is the stablisher of the heart of the two "Hawk-gods (i.e., Horus and Set). Thou art cleansed "with *ḥesmen* (natron), and thou art like unto the "followers of Horus."

The libation thus poured out either represented the essence of Horus and the essence of Set, which was the source of the strength of their hearts, and the substance which gave them life, or was believed to be transmuted into that essence through the words of power spoken by the Kher ḥeb. The power of the *Semmàn* water was great, for as soon as it touched the face of the deceased his mouth was opened, and he was able to taste the emission, or life essence, of Horus and Set. Having tasted it, his whole being was changed, and he became a new creature, and henceforth he was a counterpart of the *Shemsu Ḥeru* , or "Followers of Horus." The Horus here referred to must not be confounded with the twin-brother of Set. The Horus who is always associated with Set is "Horus the Great," or "Horus the Elder," the Haroeris of the Greeks, but the Horus mentioned in the Liturgy in connection with "Followers" is "Horus, the son of Isis."

The "Followers of Horus" were a group of beings who were closely connected with Osiris, and having "followed" him in this world they passed after him into the Other World, where they became his ministrants and messengers, partaking of his immortal nature, and sharing his life. Horus the Elder was "followed" by a group of beings also, but these were of a totally different character, for they were called "Mesentiu," 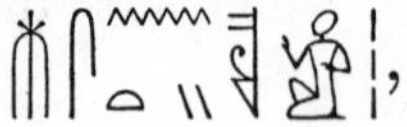, i.e., "workers in metal," or "blacksmiths." In some texts the followers of Horus, the son of Isis, are identified with the metal-workers of

Horus the Elder, and it is possible that this is the case in the Liturgy. On the other hand, the deduction to be made from our text seems to be that the essence of Horus and Set introduced into the body of the deceased changed his nature into theirs, while the cleansing with natron made him a counterpart of the followers of Horus, the son of Isis. He thus possessed the nature of Horus, the oldest god of heaven, and the nature of a "follower" of the son of the man Osiris, who rose from the dead and became the ever-living god and judge of the dead.

THE FIFTH CEREMONY.

The next ceremony continued the process of assimilating the deceased with the gods. The priest, having dissolved five grains of incense made from the salt deposit in a place in the Natron Valley called "Shet pet," 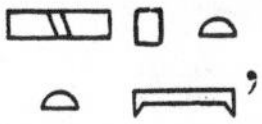, or "Lake of Heaven," in a libation vase of water, and poured it into a vessel, walked with it four times round the mummy and sprinkled it each time. As he did so the Kher ḥeb said the following words four times:

"Thou art purified with natron, and Horus is purified "with natron.

"Thou art purified with natron, and Set is purified "with natron.

"Thou art purified with natron, and Thoth is purified "with natron.

"Thou art purified with natron, and Sep is purified "with natron.

"Thou art purified with natron, and thou art "stablished among them.

"Thy mouth is the mouth of the sucking calf on the "day of his birth."

It is possible to translate "Thou art purified with

The Sem priest pouring water from a libation vase into a libation bowl held by a ministrant.

"natron as Horus is purified with natron," &c., as did Dümichen, but it seems better to render the passage without the addition of "as" in each member, for it is clear that the salted water was offered as much to the deceased as to each god. The effect of this sprinkling was to give the deceased power to take his place with the gods of each of the four quarters of heaven, and to make him their equal. In the last line of the passage, "Thy mouth is the mouth of the sucking-calf on the "day of his birth," we appear to have an allusion to the calf figured in the Vignettes to Chapter CIX. of the *Book of the Dead*, which is entitled "The Chapter of "knowing the Souls of the East." In the Theban Recension we see the deceased standing in adoration before Rā-Harmachis, between whom and the deceased is a spotted calf. In the Saïte Recension the deceased stands in adoration before the Boat of Rā, which is about to pass between the two "Trees of Emerald" into the sky. In the Boat are: 1. Rā-Harmachis, with the sign for wind above his disk, . 2. The deceased. 3. A calf with a star above his back. The text tells us that the Souls of the East are Rā-Harmachis, the Calf of the goddess Kherȧ (?),[1] and Neter-ṭuai, or the planet Venus. The "Sucking-calf" must therefore be the name of a morning star which was associated with the rising sun, and with Isis as a morning star. It seems clear, then, that the passage in the Liturgy signifies that the deceased is identified in it with the star which was born in the sky at sunrise; as its mother was Isis the star was a form of Horus, son of Osiris and Isis, and the deceased is therefore the son of Osiris, that is, Horus.

[1] Theban, 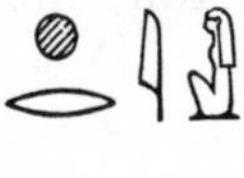 (?); Saïte, .

The Sixth Ceremony.

In the next ceremony the Sem priest continues the purification of the deceased, and on this occasion he takes in his hand a ball of incense and lifts it up before the face of the mummy, or statue. We may assume that he does this four, or even five, times, and offers four balls of incense, one for Horus, one for Set, one for

The Sem priest presenting a ball of incense.

Thoth, and one for Sep. Meanwhile the Kher ḥeb says:—

"Thou art purified with natron, and Horus is purified "with natron.

"Thou art purified with natron, and Set is purified "with natron.

"Thou art purified with natron, and Thoth is purified "with natron.

"Thou art purified with natron, and Sep is purified "with natron.

"Thou art purified with natron, and thy KA is "purified with natron.

"Thou art purified with natron,

"Thou art purified with natron,

"Thou art purified with natron,

"Thou art purified with natron,

"O thou who art stablished among thy brethren the "gods.

"Thy head hath been censed for thee, thy bones have "been cleansed thoroughly for thee, and thou art filled "with that which belongeth unto thee. O Osiris, I "have given unto thee the Eye of Horus, and thy face "is filled therewith, and it spreadeth its odour about "thee."

CHAPTER III.

The Seventh Ceremony.

DESCRIPTION OF THE OFFERINGS.

THE ceremonies of purification are now ended. The new body in which the KA is to dwell has been made by means of them. Its bones, and head, and mouth have been brought into a state of ceremonial purity, it contains the fluid of life, and all its humours, and

The Sem priest holding the "Kef-pesesh."

warmth, and its face is enveloped with an emanation from the Eye of Horus, and the odour of purity has been restored to it. It is not, however, prepared to enjoy the offerings which are about to be presented to it, because its jaw-bones, which have been pressed out of their places under the process of mummification, have no freedom of movement. To "establish" the jaw-bones was the next thing. The SEM priest took in his hands the instrument called "KEF PESESH," 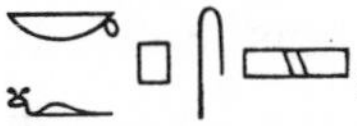, i.e., "the overcomer of the divisions," the shape of which was , and presented it before the face of the mummy, or touched it with it. Meanwhile the Kher ḥeb said these words:—

"O Unȧs, thy two jawbones which were separated "have been established."

As the result of these words the jawbones resumed their former positions, and power was given to them to masticate food. It is interesting to note that a specimen of this instrument is preserved in the British Museum (Third Egyptian Room, Table-case M, No. 888). It is made of flint, and was found near Abydos with large numbers of flint knives and tools of the Neolithic Period. If the object be a KEF PESESH, and there is no reason to doubt it, it forms an important proof which connects this ceremony with the Predynastic Period. Compare also another example of this amulet, which is surmounted by the head of a goddess, in the British Museum (Table-case F, Fourth Egyptian Room, No. 505).

THE EIGHTH CEREMONY.

The SEM priest next presented before the face of the mummy two objects of the shape , or , made of iron of the South and iron of the North respectively, and the Kher ḥeb said twice :—

"O Unȧs, the two gods have opened for thee thy "mouth."

The "two gods" are, of course, Horus and Set. It will be noted that in the text of Unȧs the two iron objects which represent Horus and Set are in the form of axe-heads attached to handles, 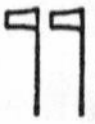, and that in the

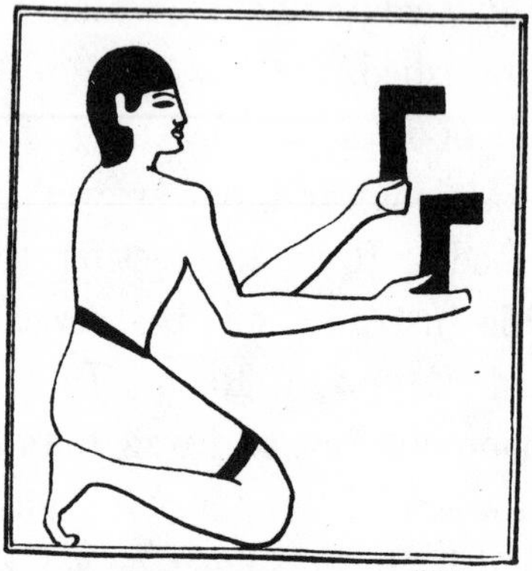

The Sem priest presenting .

text of Peṭā-Ȧmen-ȧpt they are in the form 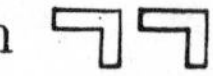. Amulets in both forms are known, for, as Professor Maspero has pointed out, small axes, with heads of metal and handles of wood, have been found in the tombs, and also small angles of haematite, of which many examples exist in our museums.[1] The application of these objects to the mouth of the mummy was, no

[1] E.g., British Museum, Table-case F, Fourth Egyptian Room, Nos. 510–520.

doubt, intended to supplement the presentation of the KEF PESESH.

THE NINTH CEREMONY.

The first object presented to the mummy after the opening of the mouth was *sel*, or *ser*, , which has been translated both by "butter" and "cheese." The Vignette represents the SEM priest offering a vessel with four balls, or round cakes, of some substance in it,

The Sem priest presenting cheese.

, and, when we remember that the Egyptians have never made butter in our sense of the word, we are justified in accepting Dümichen's rendering of "cheese."[1] Whilst the four cakes of cheese were being offered, the Kher ḥeb said the following words :—

"O Unȧs, the Eye of Horus hath been presented

[1] The Egyptian is probably the original of the Coptic ⲥⲁⲓⲣⲉ; compare Genesis xviii. 8 (ed. Ciasca, p. 18).

"unto thee, and with it the god passeth (or, cometh);
"I have brought it unto thee: place thou it in thy
"mouth."

THE TENTH CEREMONY.

The SEM priest next brought in a vessel four balls, or round cakes, called *shȧku* 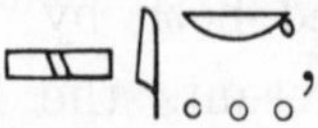, and whilst he presented these the Kher ḥeb said:—

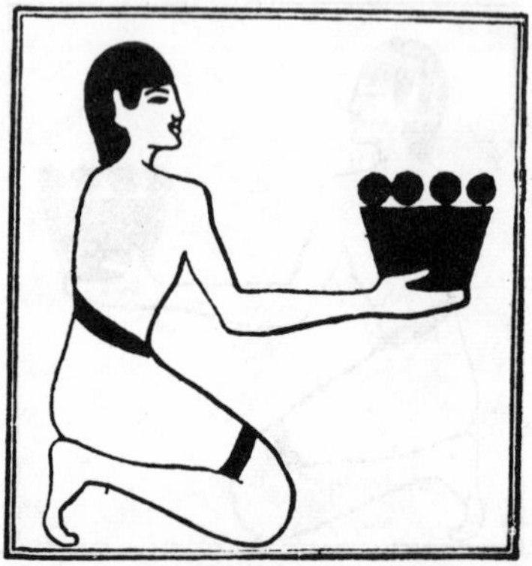

The Sem priest presenting shȧku.

"O Unȧs, the SHȦKU of Osiris have been presented "unto thee, the SHȦKU from the top of the breast of "Horus, of his body hast thou taken to thy mouth."

The exact meaning of the word *shȧku* is unknown, but it seems clear that the object symbolized the nipples on the breast of Horus, or the nipples on the breast of his mother Isis, which the god had taken into his mouth.

The Eleventh Ceremony.

In the next ceremony the Sem priest offered a vessel of milk and a vessel of whey (?), and whilst he did so the Kher ḥeb said:—

"[That which is] from the breast of thy sister Isis, "the emission of thy mother, thou hast taken possession "of for thy mouth."

The Sem priest presenting a vessel of milk and a vessel of whey (?).

The text of Peṭā-Ȧmen-ȧpt is somewhat fuller, and reads:—

"[That which floweth] from the breast of Horus, and "is of his body, hath been presented unto thee for thy "mouth. That which cometh from the breast of thy "sister Isis, the emission of thy mother, hath been "seized by thee for thy mouth, and thou openest thy "mouth by means of it."

The Twelfth Ceremony.

The ceremonies symbolizing the nursing of Horus by Osiris having been performed, the Sem priest took libation vases of pure water of the north, i.e., from the Delta, not water with natron dissolved in it, and went

The Sem priest pouring water from a libation vase into a libation bowl held by a ministrant.

round the mummy, sprinkling it on all sides as he went, whilst the Kher ḥeb said four times:—

"This libation is for thee, O Osiris, this libation is "for thee, O Unȧs; it cometh forth from thy son, it "cometh forth from Horus.

"I have come and I have brought unto thee the Eye "of Horus, that thy heart may be refreshed therewith.

"I have brought it [and placed it] under thee, [under] "thy sandals, and I have presented unto thee that "which floweth forth from thee. Whilst it is with "thee there shall be no stoppage of thy heart, and it "shall be with thee, with the things (or, persons) which "come forth at the [sound of] the voice."

The powers which the deceased enjoyed upon earth having now been bestowed upon him once more, or upon his KA, he is in the position of being able to

The Sem priest presenting a vessel of white wine and a vessel of black.

partake of the symbolic offerings which are about to be made to him, and to assimilate them after they have been transformed into spiritual meat and drink by the words of the Kher ḥeb.

THE THIRTEENTH CEREMONY.

The SEM priest took in his hands two vessels, 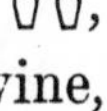, one filled with white and the other with black wine, each holding one *hathes* measure, and as he presented them to the deceased, the Kher ḥeb said:—

"Thou hast taken possession of that which hath "flowed forth from the Eyes of Horus, and when they (i.e., "the wines) are in front of thee they illumine thy face."

The white and the black wine were not intended to be drunk, but to be poured over the head and forehead of the deceased, so that the strength in them might be transmitted to his face. The wines, being regarded as emanations from the Eyes of Horus, the White and the Black, contained the divine power which existed in the Eyes of the god, and they transferred to the deceased the might of the Day and the Night.

THE FOURTEENTH CEREMONY.

In the next ceremony the SEM priest offered a bread-cake, of the kind called "Ḥem," , which was presented for the "lifting up of the face" of the deceased. This name is followed by the word *tchaut*, the exact meaning of which is not easy to say. In the "Ḥem"-cake Dümichen[1] thought he saw the original of a cake in use among the Egyptians which was stamped with a figure of a vanquished hippopotamus; this beast was the symbol of Set, or Typhon, as we know from the texts, and from Plutarch,[2] who says that he was chained. In the pictures of the chained hippopotamus[3] the head of the monster is

[1] *Grabpalast*, i., p. 23. [2] *De Iside*, Cap. 50.
[3] Naville, *Mythe d'Horus*, pll. 3 ff.

"turned back," i.e., he is looking behind him, and it is possible that the name "Ḥem," which means "to turn back," was given to cakes because they were stamped with a figure of the animal in this attitude. The words *pat tchaut* Maspero renders by "Gâteau de passage," and Dümichen by "Hem-Brod wohlschmeckendes (?)"; the former rendering gives the better sense. The "Gâteau de passage" is the equivalent of the round bread-cake which is common all over Egypt and the

The Sem priest presenting the Ḥem cake.

Sûdân at the present day, and it is the first thing with which the native provides himself when he is about to set out on a journey. Whilst the Sem offers the *ḥem* cake the Kher ḥeb says:—

"Day hath made an offering unto thee in the sky.

"The South and the North have caused an offering "to be made unto thee.

"Night hath made an offering unto thee.

"The South and the North have made an offering "unto thee.

"An offering is brought unto thee. An offering thou "seest, of an offering thou hearest.

"There is an offering before thee, an offering behind "thee, an offering with thee."

THE FIFTEENTH CEREMONY.

The offering of "bread for the journey" is followed

The Sem priest presenting a ball of incense.

by that of onions. The SEM priest presented five onions to the deceased whilst the Kher ḥeb said:—

"Osiris Unȧs, the white teeth of Horus are presented "unto thee that they may fill thy mouth."

THE SIXTEENTH CEREMONY.

The Vignette which illustrates the next ceremony shows us the SEM priest kneeling before a small table on which rests a bread-cake, which is called "the Uṭen-"cake, for the lifting up of the face." Whilst this bread-cake is being offered, the Kher ḥeb said, according to the text of Unȧs, four times:—

"SUTEN ḤETEP ṬĀ to the KA of Unȧs."

These words were followed by:—

"Osiris Unȧs, the Eye of Horus hath been presented "unto thee—the bread which thou eatest."

The Sem priest offering the Uṭen cake.

According to the text of Peṭā-Ȧmen-ȧpt the Uṭen-cake is to be divided into two equal parts, and the words "Suten ḥetep ṭā to the KA of Peṭā-Ȧmen-ȧpt" are to be said four times in connection with each half. Whilst the SMEN priest offers these the Kher ḥeb says four times:—

"Osiris, the Eye of Horus hath been presented unto "thee—the bread which thou eatest, and thy mouth "hath been opened thereby."

It has been said above (p. 21) that, though the words

suten ḥetep ṭā may at one time have been intended to mean "May the king give an offering," it is clear they had already lost this meaning when the funerary texts were inscribed on the maṣṭabas at Ṣaḳḳârah. The passage from the text of Unȧs is an important proof that such is the case, for it is quite clear that the king is not entreated to give to Unȧs an offering. Here the words *suten ḥetep ṭā* occur some forty lines from the beginning of the Liturgy, where, in the ordinary course of things, we should expect them to appear. From the fact that they are ordered to be recited four times in one text, and eight times in the other, we are fully justified in believing that they are the opening words of a formula which was composed in primitive times and recited by priests and relatives on behalf of the dead, and that they were used by pious folk, as Dümichen first pointed out, in much the same way as "Pater-noster" and "Ave Maria" are used in our own times. It may be noted too in passing that the passage from the Liturgy under consideration presents us with one of the oldest examples of the use of the formula "*suten* "*ḥetep ṭā en ka en*," "May there be a royal offering to "the KA of," which is so common on stelae from the XIIth Dynasty downwards.

THE SEVENTEENTH AND EIGHTEENTH CEREMONIES.

In the next two ceremonies the SEM priest offers two vessels of wine to the deceased, each containing a Hathes measure; one vessel is made of some white material, and the other of black. Whilst the former is being offered the Kher ḥeb says:—

"Osiris Unȧs, the Eye of Horus hath been presented "unto thee; it hath been snatched from the hand of "Set, and thou hast taken possession of it for thy "mouth, and thou hast opened thy mouth therewith."

And whilst the latter is being offered he says:—

"Osiris Unȧs, thy mouth is opened by that which

The Sem priest presenting a white vessel of wine.

"floweth (?) from thee." The words "Eye of Horus which "hath been snatched from the hand of Set" refer to the belief that it was Set, the god of darkness, who swallowed the sun and moon during eclipses, and devoured the moon piecemeal after it was fourteen days old. The Eye of Horus was restored to him sometimes by Shu, who snatched it out of the hand of Set,[1] but more

1  Lefébure, *Le Mythe Osirien*, p. 87; Moret, *Rituel*, p. 84.

frequently by Thoth, who is often represented in the form of an ibis-headed man carrying the Eye of Horus, 𓂀, before him in his hands. As the Eye of Horus was the abode of disembodied souls and spirits, the presentation of this eye to the mummy, or statue, was equivalent to restoring to it the soul of the deceased. In this passage, and throughout the Liturgy generally,

The Sem priest presenting a white vessel of wine.

the fundamental idea of the presentation of objects which are symbolic of the Eye of Horus is to bring back to the deceased his KA and BA, i.e., soul and the various members of his spiritual and mental economy.

The wine in the black vessel is declared to be the fluids or humours which ran out of the deceased before death, or during the process of preparing him for the tomb. They are here restored to him in the form of wine, the nature of which is changed by the words of the Kher ḥeb.

The Nineteenth Ceremony.

The process of restoring to the deceased the fluid of his body is continued in the next ceremony, wherein the Sem priest presents to him a black stone vase, ▽, containing *ḥent* beer. Whilst he is doing this the Kher ḥeb says:—

"Osiris Unȧs, there hath been presented unto thee

The Sem priest presenting a black stone vessel of Ḥent beer.

"that which hath been pressed out of theė, which hath "come forth from thee."

The Twentieth Ceremony.

After the presentation of the wine and beer the Sem priest took in his hands a small table, or stand, on which were placed several bread-cakes of different shapes and kinds, called "Tchesert," , i.e., "the holy table." With this he advanced to the deceased, and whilst he offered it to him the Kher ḥeb said: —

"O Rā, may the worship which thou hast in heaven "and all the worship which is offered to thee be to "Unȧs, and may everything which is offered to thy "body be offered to the KA of Unȧs; and may every- "thing which is offered to his body be thine."

The Sem priest presenting the holy table of offerings.

From this passage we learn that the deceased is identified with Rā, and that it was expected that he would share with Rā the praises, and worship, and offerings which were dedicated to him. The offerings made to the deceased were intended for Rā, upon whom devolved the duty of feeding him with a portion of them. The bread-cakes of earth were transmuted into the "bread of everlastingness," and the wine into the "wine of eternity," whereon Rā lived.

The Twenty-First Ceremony.

In the next ceremonies the various kinds of bread and cakes on the "Tchesert" table were offered one by one. The first was the *ṭept,* and as the Sem priest presented it the Kher ḥeb said:—

"Unȧs, the Eye of Horus hath been presented unto "thee for thy tasting."

The Sem priest presenting the Ṭept cake.

Here there is a play on the words *ṭept,* a "kind of bread," and *ṭep,* "to taste."

The Twenty-Second Ceremony.

The next offering was the *aḥ* 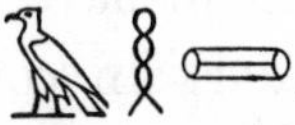, which according to Dümichen was not a bread-cake, but a lump of cooked meal, like the *Puls* of the Romans and the *Polenta* of the modern Italians. According to Maspero, it was a flat cake mixed with fat, and perhaps sweetened, and folded like a pancake. Whilst the Sem priest presents this the Kher ḥeb pronounces a formula, which in the Unȧs text seems to mean,

"The darkness (or, the night) becometh denser and "denser," and in the text of Peṭā-Ȧmen-ȧpt,

"The *aḥ* food is spread out before thee like a field."

It is clear that in the one text there is a play of words in *aḥaḥ* and *ȧkkȧ*, and in the other in *aḥaḥ* and *aḥ*, but the exact meanings of the sentences are unknown because we do not understand the allusions.

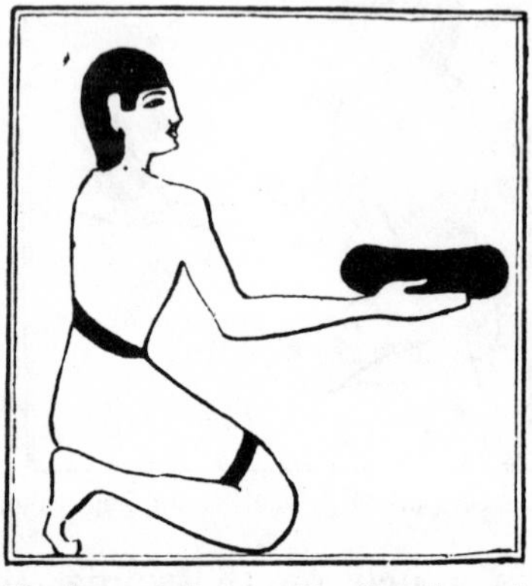

The Sem priest presenting the Aḥ meal.

Dümichen thought that the word *ȧkkȧ*, i.e., "darkness" or "night," referred to the *colour* of the *aḥ*-cake, and that it might have been baked to a brown colour which was so dark in comparison with the *ṭept* cake that it appeared to be black.

The Twenty-Third Ceremony.

In this ceremony the Sem priest offered the breast of some animal, and as he did so the Kher ḥeb said:—

"Ụnȧs, the Eye of Horus hath been presented unto "thee so that it may embrace thee (or, be united unto "thee)."

The breast naturally symbolized the act of embracing, which was in itself an important ceremony. When Horus embraced the deceased, the act of embracing him "smote Set," and when he had snatched his Eye out of the hand of the god of evil, "he gave to the "deceased his heart, and the power which was therein."[1]

The Sem priest presenting the breast.

When, in the Tale of the Two Brothers, Ȧnpu restored to Batau his heart, "each embraced the other."[2] Life

[1] See Tetȧ, l. 173.   , and Moret's excellent remarks in *Rituel*, p. 88.

[2] Papyrus D'Orbiney, pl. xiv., ll. 3, 4.

was given to a statue by embracing it, and when a living person, priest, or relative embraced a mummy, his, or her, object was to reunite the bones, to knit together afresh the flesh, and to give order to the members of the body, which in primitive times had been dislocated, like the body of Osiris, and then put together, piece by piece, to form a complete whole.[1] As to the breast itself, we may note in passing that in the Levitical law it was ordered that the breast of a

The Sem priest presenting a stone vessel of wine.

ram should be waved for a wave offering before the Lord (Leviticus vii. 30).

The Twenty-Fourth Ceremony.

The next four ceremonies deal with the offering of wine and three kinds of beer. The SEM priest presented

[1] Moret, *Rituel*, p. 89.

a white vessel of wine to the deceased, and as he did so the Kher ḥeb said:—

"Unȧs, the Eye of Horus hath been presented unto "thee, which was snatched from the hand of Set, and "was rescued for thee, and thou dost open thy mouth "with it."

The Twenty-Fifth Ceremony.

He next offered a black vessel containing a *ḥent* measure of beer,[1] while the Kher ḥeb said:—

The Sem priest presenting a stone vessel of beer.

"Unȧs, there hath been presented unto thee that "which hath been pressed out and cometh forth from "Osiris."

The Twenty-Sixth Ceremony.

This was followed by an offering of an iron vessel

[1] Or, "a vessel containing a *ḥent* measure of black beer."

containing one *ḥent* measure of beer,[1] and at the same time the Kher ḥeb said:—

"Unȧs, the Eye of Horus hath been presented unto "thee, which was rescued for thee; there is no iron "therein, and it belongeth to thee."

In the "iron vessel" we may probably see an allusion to the iron spear with which Horus defended himself against the attack of Set. If this be so we are to understand from the text that the strength of the iron

The Sem priest presenting an iron vessel of beer.

weapon is transferred to the vessel, which in turn transfers it to the beer. From the beer the deceased obtains the magical power of Horus which will enable him to repulse any attack made upon him by Set.

THE TWENTY-SEVENTH CEREMONY.

The SEM priest then offered a *ḥetemet* vessel con-

[1] Or, "a vessel containing a *ḥent* measure of iron beer."

taining one *ḥent* measure of beer,[1] and as he did so the Kher ḥeb said:—

"Unȧs, the Eye of Horus hath been presented unto "thee that thou mayest be filled therewith."

At this point in the service the SEM priest paused in his presentation of offerings to the deceased, and made ready to pour out further libations to him. Having dissolved three cakes of natron in pure water, he took four vases of the solution, and walked round the

The Sem priest presenting a stone vessel of beer.

mummy, or statue, and sprinkled it on all sides, whilst the Kher ḥeb recited the following words four times:—

"This libation is for thee, O Osiris, this libation is "for thee; it cometh forth from thy son, it cometh "forth from Horus.

"I have come and I have brought unto thee the Eye "of Horus that thy heart may be refreshed thereby. I

[1] Or, "a vessel containing a *ḥent* measure of *ḥetemet* beer."

"have brought it to thy feet, and have presented unto "thee that which hath flowed and come forth from "thee. Whilst it is with thee there shall be no "stoppage of thy heart, and it shall be with thee, with "the things (or, persons) which come forth at the "[sound of] the voice."[1] (The Vignette is a duplicate of that given on page 42.)

The Twenty-Eighth to Thirty-Fourth Ceremonies.

These seven ceremonies deal with the anointing of the mummy, or statue, with seven kinds of unguents, which are called:—

1. Seth ḥeb, 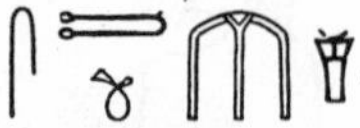.
2. Ḥekenu, .
3. Sefth, 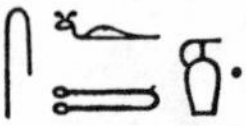.
4. Neshnem, .
5. Tuatu, .
6. Ḥātet āsh, .
7. Ḥātet Theḥennu, 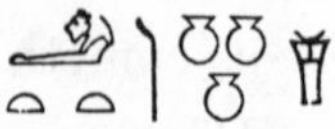.

[1] From indications given in the text of Pepi II. it is clear that at this place in the series of ceremonies articles of apparel and jewellery were offered one by one to the deceased, and that appropriate words of dedication were recited during their presentation. See Maspero, *Pyramides de Saqqarah*, p. 361.

The SEM priest offered a vessel of the Seth ḥeb unguent, and the Kher ḥeb said four times:—

"Osiris Unås, I have filled thine eye for thee with "*metchet* oil."

He next offered a vessel of Ḥekenu unguent, and the Kher ḥeb said:—

"Osiris Unås, there hath been presented unto thee

THE SEVEN UNGUENTS.

Ḥātet Theḥennu. Ḥātet āsh. Tuatu. Neshnem. Seft. Ḥekenu. Seth ḥeb.

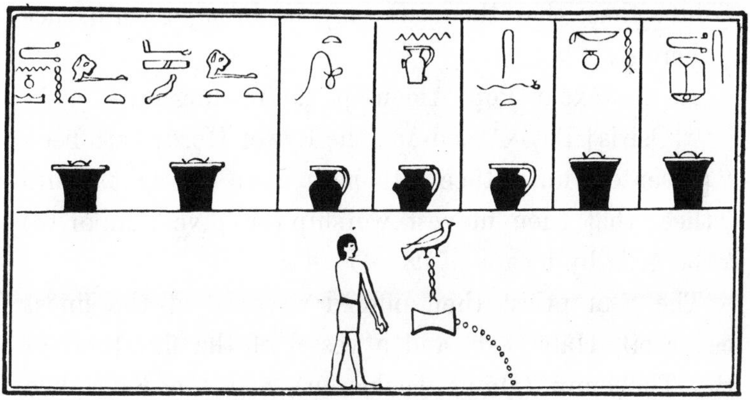

The Sem priest pouring out libations.

"that which hath been pressed out from thy "face."

He next offered a vessel of Seft unguent, and the Kher ḥeb said:—

"Osiris Unås, the Eye of Horus hath been presented "unto thee, and [Set] hath been made weak in respect "of thee thereby."

The Seft unguent was dark in colour, and symbolized Set, the god of darkness, and as it represented the greasy emanation of his face this god was supposed to suffer through its absence.

The SEM priest next offered a vessel of Neshnem unguent, and the Kher ḥeb said:—

"Osiris Unȧs, the Eye of Horus hath been presented "unto thee, that it may unite itself unto thee."

He next offered a vessel of Tuatu unguent, and the Kher ḥeb said:—

"Osiris Unȧs, the Eye of Horus hath been presented "unto thee, that the gods may be brought unto thee "thereby."

In the text of Peṭā-Ȧmen-ȧpt the reading is:—

"[Osiris] Peṭā-Ȧmen-ȧpt, the Eye of Horus hath been "presented unto thee. It hath been brought [unto "thee] that thou mayest worship (or, give thanks to) "the gods by means of it."

The SEM priest then offered a vessel of the finest cedar oil, Ḥātet āsh, and a vessel of the finest oil of the Theḥennu (Ḥātet Theḥennu), and the Kher ḥeb said:—

"O ye Oils, O ye Oils, which are on the forehead "of Horus [place ye yourselves on the forehead of the "Osiris Unȧs, make ye him to smell sweet in possessing "you], make ye him to become a KHU (i.e., Spirit) "through possessing you, make ye him to have his "SEKHEM (i.e., Vital Power) in his body, make ye him "to have openings before his eyes, and let all the KHU "(i.e., Spirits) see him, and let them all hear his name. "Behold, Osiris Unȧs, the Eye of Horus hath been "brought unto thee, for it hath been seized that it may "be before thee."

THE THIRTY-FIFTH CEREMONY.

In this ceremony the materials with which the eyes of the deceased are to be painted are offered. The SEM priest took a bag of Uatch and a bag of Mesṭemet, and as he offered them the Kher ḥeb said:—

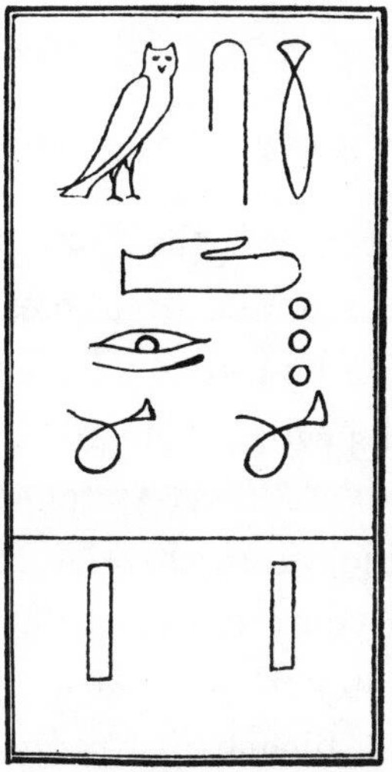

A bag of Uatch and a bag of Mesṭemet.

"Osiris Unȧs, I have painted for thee the Eye of "Horus with Mesṭemet so that there may be health "to thy face."

The eye-paint called Uatch was first used as a medicine for the eyes, and only later as an ornament; it was a preparation of copper. The eye-lids were first smeared with oil or some unguent, and the powder was applied to them by means of a short, thin stick made of wood, bone, or metal, which among the Arabs is called a "needle." The eye-paint Mesṭemet, which appears in Coptic under the form ⲥⲑⲏⲙ, or ⲥⲧⲏⲙ, was made from antimony, and its use was general; it was used daily, and was believed to protect the eye against ophthalmia. In modern times preparations of lead, black oxide of manganese, the lamp-black of burnt almonds, &c., are commonly used as "Koḥl," or eye-paint.

The Thirty-Sixth Ceremony.

In the next ceremony the Sem priest offered two linen bandlets, or scarves, or sashes, called *unkhu* to the deceased, and as he did so the Kher ḥeb said:—

"Watch thou in peace. The goddess Tȧat watcheth "in peace, the goddess Tȧat watcheth in peace. The "Eye of Horus which is in the city of Pe-Ṭep watcheth "in peace. The Eye of Horus which is in the temple-"houses of Net watcheth in peace. Receive thou the "milk-[white] and bleached bandlets of the goddess "Ur-ā. Cause ye, O bandlets, that the Two Lands "may submit to this Unȧs, even as they bow down "before Horus, and make ye the Two Lands to be in "awe of Unȧs, even as they are terrified before Set. "Tarry ye before Unȧs in his divinity. Open ye his "way at the head of the Khu (or, Spirits), and let him "stand at the head of the Spirits. O Ȧnpu-Khenti-"Ȧmenti, forwards, forwards, to the Osiris Unȧs."

The two bandlets are assumed to have been made by the goddess Tȧat, who presided over the apparel of the deceased, and provided them with raiment made by her own hands; as she wove the bandlets she wove into them her magical protection, which not only preserved their wearers from the discomforts of nakedness, but assured to them the respect of the gods and spirits who

The Sem priest presenting two bandlets.

saw them. One bandlet also carried with it the protection of the Horus-god who dwelt in the city of Pe-Ṭep, or Buto, and the other the protection of the Horus-god who dwelt in the city of Net (Neith). Horus of Pe-Ṭep was the son of Isis-Uatchit, and Horus of Saïs was the son of Net, the goddess to whom the invention of the art of weaving was attributed. The city of Saïs was famous in all ages for the production of textile fabrics, and here was situated "Ḥet-menkh," the "Temple of woven stuffs."[1] The opening lines of this passage in the Liturgy are differently translated by Dümichen and Maspero. In his translation of the text of Unȧs Maspero rendered the signs 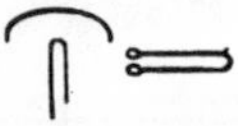 by "Vêts-toi," "clothe thyself," but later he came to the conclusion that  is not the equivalent of , and that it is to be read *res*, i.e., "Watch," or "Keep vigil." Thus his renderings are :—

Vêts-toi en paix! Vêts ton vêtement en paix! Que Taït se vête—*Vêtements de fête, deux*—en paix! Œil d'Hor dans Doup, en paix! Œil d'Horus dans les demeures de Nit, en paix! Reçois le linge blanc! Donne qu'elles se courbent pour cet Ounas, les deux terres, &c.

Veille en paix! veille Tait en paix, veille Taitit en paix! Œil d'Hor qui est dans Dopou en paix, veille Œil d'Hor qui est dans les *Châteaux de Nit* en paix! La plus brillante (?) des nourrices (?), celle qui orne le maître du tombeau (?), donne que les deux terres se courbent devant ce Pepi Nofirkerî, &c.[2]

The rendering of Dümichen agrees with the older rendering of Maspero as far as "Nit, en paix!" but

[1] De Rougé, *Géographie*, p. 26.
[2] *Pyramides de Saqqarah*, p. 362.

for the following words he has "Nimm in Empfang "die milchfarbige und die gebleichte von der Göttin "Ur-ā. Bewirket, dass sich in Ehrfurcht beugen die "Länder," &c.[1]

At this stage in the service an interval appears to have been allowed to the deceased to absorb the meat and drink offerings which had been presented to him, and to take possession of the bandlets, &c. In the temples the presentation of offerings to the god was nearly always accompanied by a burning of incense,[2] for the gods rejoiced in the mingled odours of the objects offered and the burning incense.

THE THIRTY-SEVENTH CEREMONY.

The SEM priest next burned incense, and as he was doing this the Kher ḥeb said four times:—

"Let him advance! Let him advance with his KA! "Horus advanceth with his KA, Set advanceth with "his KA, Thoth advanceth with his KA, Sep advanceth "with his KA, Osiris advanceth with his KA, Khenti-"Maati advanceth with his KA, thy backbone, 𓊽 "advanceth with thy KA.

"Hail, Unȧs! The arm of thy KA is before thee.
"Hail, Unȧs! The arm of thy KA is behind thee.
"Hail, Unȧs! The leg of thy KA is before thee.
"Hail, Unȧs! The leg of thy KA is behind thee.

[1] *Grabpalast*, i. 28.
[2] Moret, *Rituel*, p. 119.

"Osiris Unȧs, I have given unto thee the Eye of "Horus, and thy face is filled therewith, and the "perfume of the Eye of Horus spreadeth itself over "thee."

The Sem priest presenting burning incense.

THE THIRTY-EIGHTH CEREMONY.

This censing of the mummy, or statue, was followed by another set of libations. Whilst the SEM priest was sprinkling the deceased with water in which two grains, or caḳes, of incense had been dissolved, the Kher ḥeb said four times:—

"This libation is for thee, O Osiris, this libation is

"for thee, O Unȧs; it cometh forth from thy son, it "cometh forth from Horus.

"I have come and I have brought unto thee the Eye "of Horus, that thy heart may be refreshed therewith. "I have brought it [and placed it] under thee, [under

The Sem priest pouring water from a libation vase into a libation bowl held by a ministrant.

"thy sandals,] and I have presented unto thee that "which floweth forth from thee. Whilst it is with "thee there shall be no stoppage of thy heart, and it "shall be to thee with the things (or, persons) which "come forth at the [sound of] the voice."

CHAPTER IV.

THE LITURGY DESCRIBED.

WITH the pouring out of the last series of libations the first series of ceremonies at or in the tomb came to an end. In the text of Unȧs there is no break in the text to indicate this fact, but in the text of Peṭā-Ȧmen-ȧpt at this place come the following words:—

"Here shall be set forth the food, and the drink, and "the things which are to be placed on the altar, and "one shall enter with the 'suten ḥetep' (i.e., 'royal "offering')."

This rubrical direction indicates that the ceremonies which have already been performed on the mummy, or statue, have opened the mouth of the deceased, and given him power to speak, and eat and drink, and that they have provided the KA with a pure statue wherein to dwell. The offerings up to this point were intended for the deceased only, and one of the chief objects in presenting them was to prepare the KA for partaking of the funeral feast which was to follow. The relatives of the deceased wished his KA to eat and drink with them, because it enabled them to establish and maintain communion with a being who had taken upon himself the nature of the gods. By eating the same food and drinking the same drink the souls of the living and the dead were joined in a bond which brought solace, consolation, and comfort to the living, and destroyed the feeling of separation from their beloved ones which death brought in its train. The funeral feast, that is, the eating of food together by the living and the KA, produced identity of substance, and as the KA was divine by virtue of the ceremonies which had been performed over him and the formulae recited during the presentation of offerings, his living kinsfolk became divine, and they became, for the time being at least, as gods. Since these ideas existed in connection with the funeral feast, there is small reason for wonder at the insistence in funerary texts on the necessity for a regular and constant supply of offerings in the tombs. It must also be remembered that the nature of the material offerings presented to the dead was changed during the act of offering by the sacred formulae which the Kher ḥeb recited over them. The bread and meat, and wine and beer, were transmuted into the essence and substance of Horus, the great god of heaven. When these were eaten and drunk in a place ceremonially pure, which for the time being represented heaven, both the spirits of the dead and of the living ate and drank their god in the form of the spiritual natures of the material offerings, which the living absorbed into their material bodies, provided that such bodies were also ceremonially pure.

THE THIRTY-NINTH CEREMONY.

The second series of ceremonies began with the bringing in of the *pert kheru*, or offerings of meat and drink, which were to be placed upon the altar, and a

The altar on which the offerings are placed.

ministrant came with the *suten ḥetep*, or "royal offering." Whilst this was being done the Kher ḥeb said:—

"Thoth returneth bringing it with him, he appeareth "with the Eye of Horus."

"He hath given the Eye of Horus, and he is content "therewith."

It has already been said that the Eyes of Horus, or the sun and moon, suffered eclipse at times through the agency of Set, and that the moon after the fourteenth day was devoured by him piecemeal each month. The souls of the dead who lived in the Eyes of Horus shared these calamities with the god, and thus it fell out that when the time had come to make the soul of the deceased to enter his body, the soul would be found to have disappeared with the solar or lunar Eye. Sometimes Horus went to look for his Eyes, and sometimes he sent one of them to look for the other; in every case the Eye was "found" and restored to the god. Occasionally Shu "found" the Eye in the hand of Set, and having rescued it from him he gave it back to Horus.

The god, however, to whom Horus was most often indebted for his Eye was Thoth, who presided over the stars, and knew the times of their appearances and disappearances, and regulated their courses. Thoth was called the "Heart of Rā," , that is to say, he took possession of the soul of the god, and it was he who gave back the soul to the deceased, or to a god.[1] In the present case the mummy, or statue, of the deceased is ready to receive back his soul, and the Kher ḥeb announces, as we have seen above, that Thoth hath returned with the Eye of Horus, which he had sought for, and that he hath given it to the deceased, who is content therewith. The deceased,

[1] See Dümichen, *Grabpalast*, p. 29; Moret, *Rituel*, p. 84.

having once more regained his soul, is now able to enjoy the funeral feast.

The Fortieth Ceremony.

The Sem priest next offered two *suten ḥetep* cakes, or "royal offering cakes," and the Kher ḥeb said:—

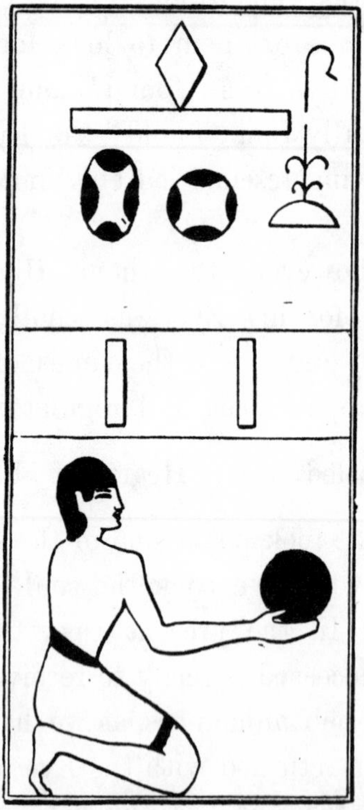

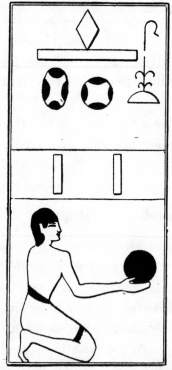

The Sem priest presenting the two "royal offering" cakes.

"Osiris Unȧs, the Eye of Horus hath been presented "unto thee, and he is content therewith."

The Forty-First Ceremony.

The offering of two vessels of beer in the *usekh* hall [1] followed, and the Kher ḥeb said :—

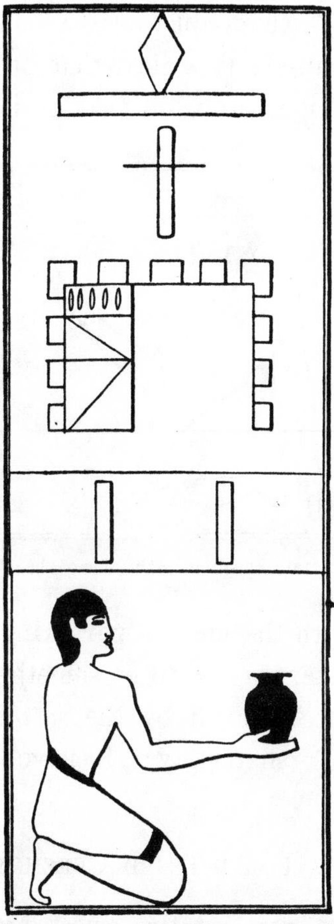

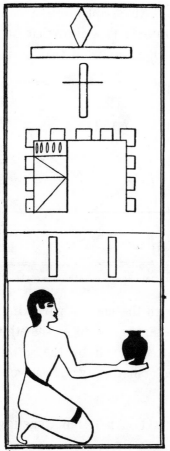

The Sem priest presenting two vessels of beer.

"Osiris Unȧs, the Eye of Horus hath been presented "unto thee, and he is content therewith."

[1] Dümichen, *Grabpalast*, p. 30.

The Forty-Second Ceremony.

The next line of the Liturgy is difficult to translate, for there are variants in the text. In the Vignette in the tomb of Peṭā-Åmen-åpt we see a man kneeling, with his left hand raised; it is clear that he is not making an offering, but it is probable that he is "seated" near

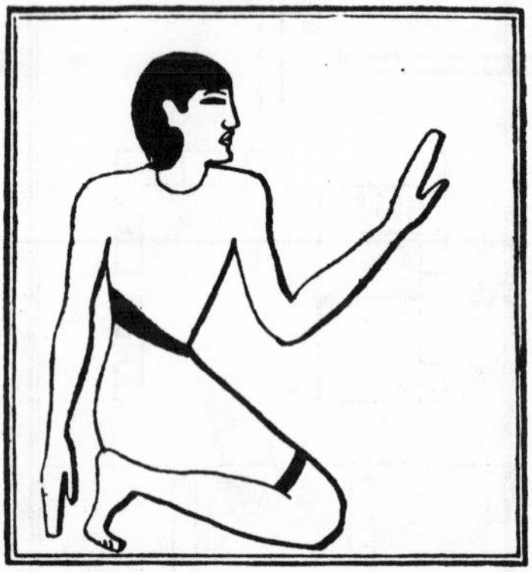

A ministrant kneeling by the side of the offering.

the offerings, with the view of partaking of them. The meaning of the text seems to be something like:—

"He who sitteth down by the *suten pert kheru* (or "royal offering) shall say: I have seated myself "with it."

The Forty-Third Ceremony.

In the next ceremony the priest presented for the *ush* (?) offering a Ṭua cake and a Shens cake, whilst the Kher ḥeb said:—

"Osiris Unȧs, the Eye of Horus hath been presented

"unto thee, and it hath been made to approach thy "mouth for thee."

The Sem priest presenting the Ṭua and Shens cakes.

THE FORTY-FOURTH CEREMONY.

A Tut cake was next presented, and the Kher ḥeb said:—

The Sem priest presenting the Tut cake.

"Osiris Unȧs, the Eye of Horus hath been presented "unto thee for the smiting down of Set."[1]

[1] The Unȧs text seems to be corrupt in this place.

THE FORTY-FIFTH CEREMONY.

A Reṭhu cake was next offered, and the Kher ḥeb said:—

"Osiris Unȧs, the Eye of Horus, which was chained "up [by Set], hath been presented unto thee."

The Reṭhu cake was round, and on it was probably

The Sem priest presenting the Reṭhu cake.

stamped a figure of a hippopotamus, symbol of Set, in fetters.

THE FORTY-SIXTH CEREMONY.

A vessel of Tchesert drink was next presented, and the Kher ḥeb said:—

"Osiris Unȧs, the Eye of Horus hath been presented "unto thee, the little one, which became the food of "Set (or, which entered into Set)."

The "little" Eye of Horus here referred to seems to be the moon, which, as already mentioned, was devoured piecemeal by Set after the fourteenth day each month.

The passage in the Liturgy suggests that Set must, on one occasion, have found the new moon in the sky,

The Sem priest presenting a vessel of drink.

when he was roaming through the night, and swallowed it.

The Forty-Seventh Ceremony.

A vessel of Khenemes beer was next offered, and the Kher ḥeb said:—

The Sem priest presenting a vessel of beer.

"Osiris Unȧs, the Eye of Horus, which hath been "smitten for thy mouth, hath been presented unto "thee."

The Forty-Eighth Ceremony.

In the next ceremony a bread-cake and a vessel of beer were placed on a small table, and "lifted up" before the mummy, whilst the Kher ḥeb said:—

The Sem priest presenting a bread cake and a vessel of beer.

"Osiris Unȧs, the Eye of Horus hath been presented "unto thee, and it hath been lifted up for thee to thy "face. There shall be lifting up to thy face, there shall "be lifting up to thy face, O Osiris. Hail, Unȧs! let "thy soul advance.

"Lift up thy face, O thou Unȧs, and look afar off, "and fix thy gaze intently upon that which cometh "forth from thee. That which was corruptible in thee "hath been washed away, O Unȧs, and thy mouth hath "been made holy for thee by the Eye of Horus."

The Forty-Ninth Ceremony.

In the next ceremony there were presented as a *Shebu* offering a Ṭua cake and a Shens cake, and the Kher ḥeb said:—

"Let there be praise to thee and to thy Ka, O Osiris,

The Sem priest presenting the Ṭua cake and the Shens cake.

"which hath been cut away from the hand of him that "doeth violence to the dead. O Unȧs, thou hast re-"ceived these thy bread-cakes, which are from the Eye "of Horus.

"Osiris Unȧs, the Eye of Horus hath been presented "unto thee, [that is to say,] that which hath been "mixed together for thee by it, so that thou mayest be "filled with that which hath been pressed out and hath "come forth from thee." This sentence was recited four times.

The presentation of the following offerings then took place; each object was offered to the mummy (or,

The Sem priest presenting the Sut joint.

statue) four times, and each formula was recited by the Kher ḥeb four times.

The Fiftieth Ceremony.

The Sut joint, , with the formula:—

"Osiris Unȧs, the Sut joint hath been presented unto "thee [as] the Eye of Horus."

The Fifty-First Ceremony.

Two vases of water, ▽▽, with the formula :—

"Osiris Unȧs, the water which is in these hath been "offered unto thee."

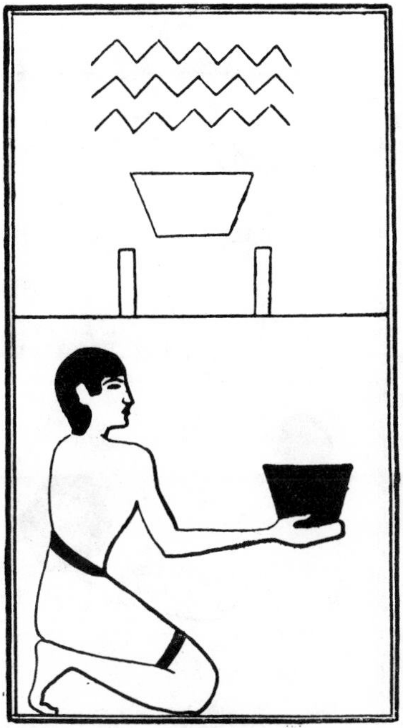

The Sem priest presenting two vessels of water.

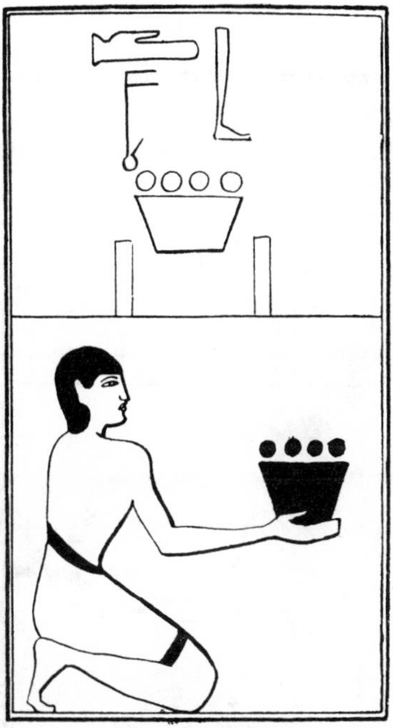

The Sem priest presenting two vessels of Beṭ incense.

The Fifty-Second Ceremony.

Two vessels of Beṭ incense, , with the formula :—

"Osiris Unȧs, the Eye of Horus hath been presented "unto thee that it may purify for thee thy mouth."

THE FIFTY-THIRD CEREMONY.

A Tua cake and a Shens cake as an *Ush* offering, with the formula:—

"Osiris Unȧs, the Eye of Horus hath been presented "unto thee, and it hath been offered unto thee for thy "mouth."

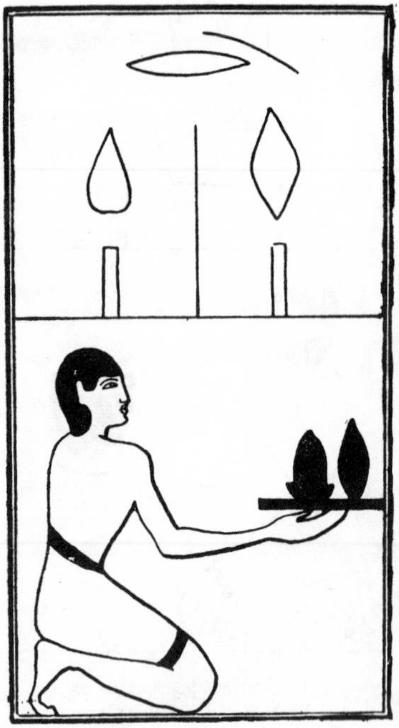

The Sem priest presenting the Ṭua cake and the Shens cake.

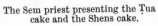

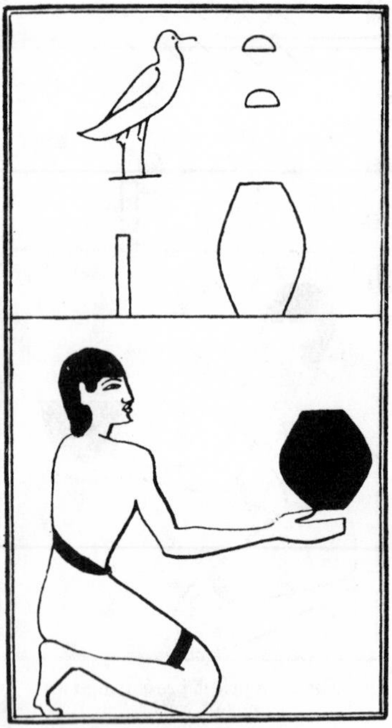

The Sem priest presenting two Tut cakes.

THE FIFTY-FOURTH CEREMONY.

Two Tut cakes, with the formula:—

"Osiris Unȧs, the Eye of Horus hath been presented "unto thee, which struck down Set."

THE FIFTY-FIFTH CEREMONY.

A Reṭhu cake, , with the formula :—

"Osiris Unȧs, the Eye of Horus, which was put under "restraint by him (i.e., by Set), hath been presented "unto thee."

The Sem priest presenting a Reṭhu cake.

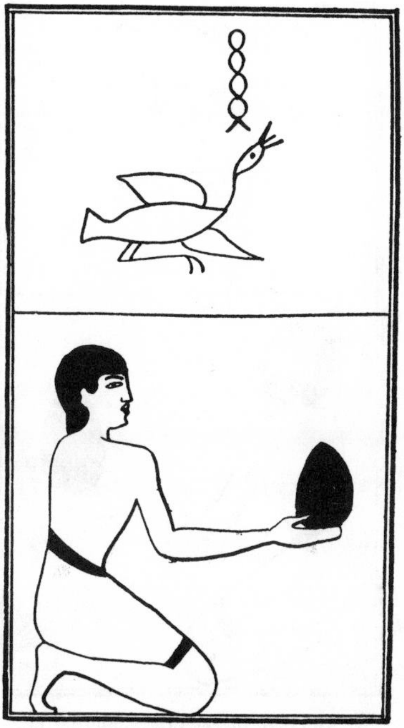

The Sem priest presenting two Ḥeth cakes.

THE FIFTY-SIXTH CEREMONY.

Two Ḥeth cakes, , with the formula :—

"Osiris Unȧs, the Eye of Horus hath been presented "unto thee, that thou mayest seize it for thy mouth."

THE FIFTY-SEVENTH CEREMONY.

Two Neḥrȧ cakes, , with the formula:—

"Osiris Unȧs, the Eye of Horus hath been presented "unto thee, and there hath been brought unto thee that "which is intended for thy mouth."

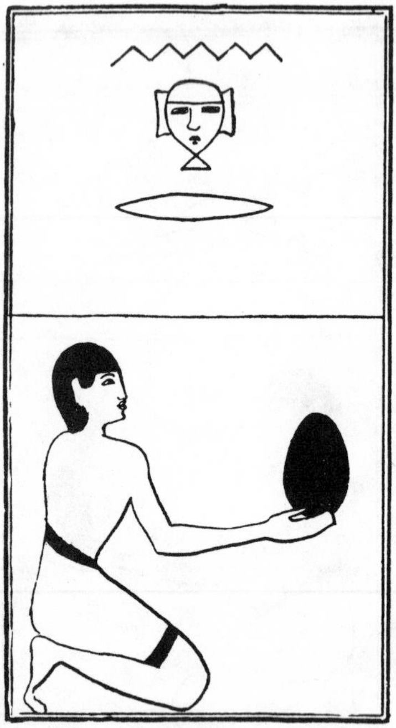

The Sem priest presenting two Neḥrȧ cakes.

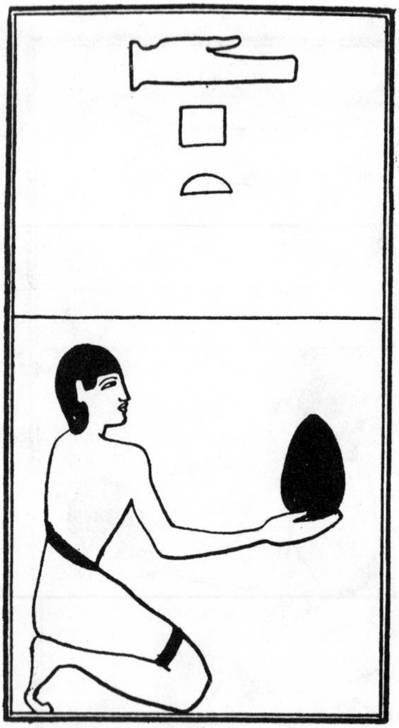

The Sem priest presenting Ṭept cakes.

THE FIFTY-EIGHTH CEREMONY.

Four Ṭept cakes, , with the formula:—

"Osiris Unȧs [, the Eye of Horus hath been presented "unto thee], and hath been given unto thine Eye for "thee to taste."

The Fifty-Ninth Ceremony.

Four Peṭen cakes, , with the formula:—

"Osiris Unȧs, the Eye of Horus hath been presented "unto thee, the glorious one; [these cakes] have been "baked thereby."

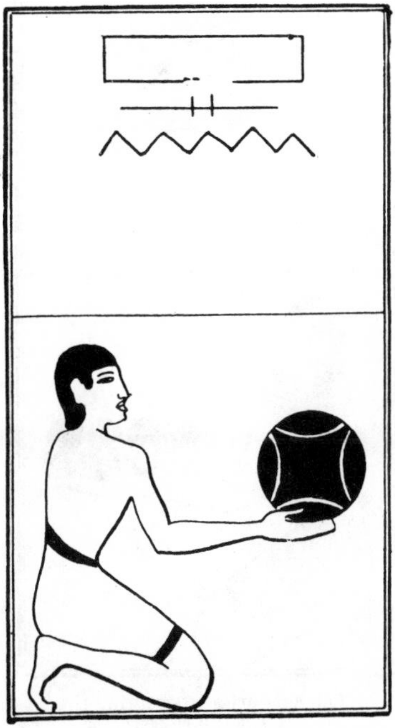

The Sem priest presenting the Peṭen, or Pasen, cakes.

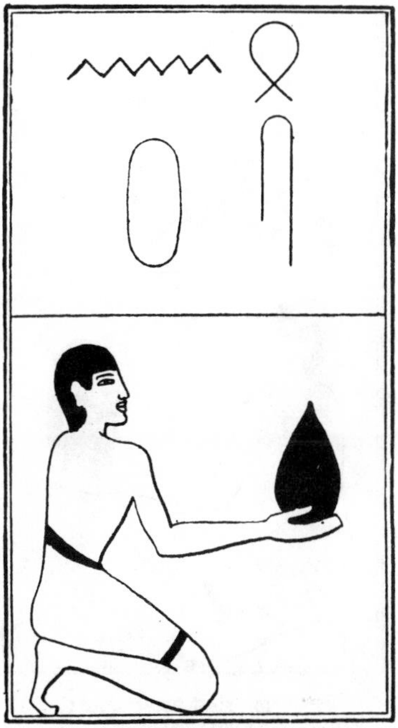

The Sem priest presenting the Shens cakes.

The Sixtieth Ceremony.

Four Shens cakes, 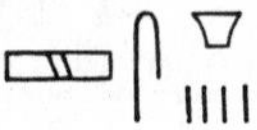 (or Shens, ), with the formula:—

"Osiris Unȧs, thou hast received thy head."

The Sixty-First Ceremony.

Four Åmta cakes, , with the formula:—

"Osiris Unȧs, thine eye hath been presented that "thou mayest take possession of it."

The Sem priest presenting the Am-ta cakes.

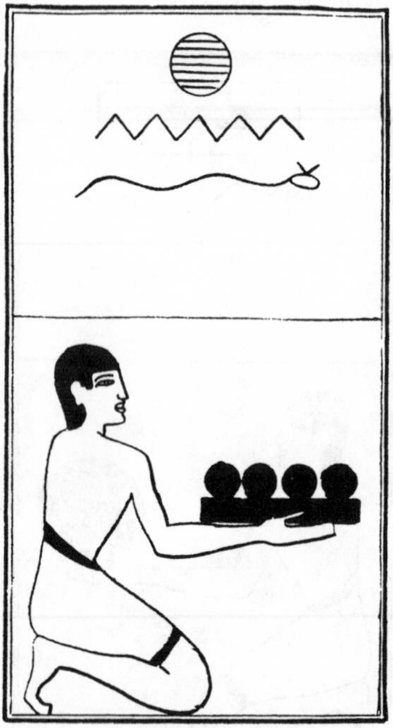

The Sem priest presenting the Khenfu cakes.

The Sixty-Second Ceremony.

Four Khenfu cakes, , with the formula:—

"Osiris Unȧs, the Eye of Horus, which hath been "made in the form of fish-scales for thee, hath been "presented unto thee."

THE SIXTY-THIRD CEREMONY.

Four baskets of Ḥebennet cakes (?), 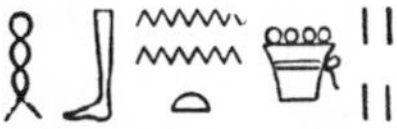,
with the formula :—

"Osiris Unȧs, the Eye of Horus hath been presented unto thee, that it may well up with water (?) [before thee]."

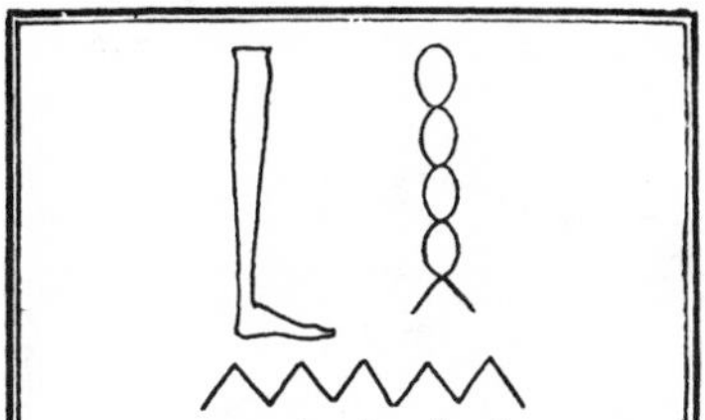

The Sem priest presenting the Ḥebennet cakes.

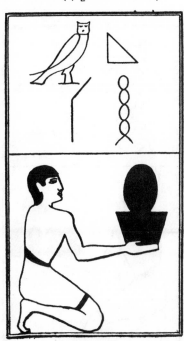

The Sem priest presenting the cakes of Qemḥ.

THE SIXTY-FOURTH CEREMONY.

Four cakes made of fine, white flour (*qemḥ*  = Arab قمح), with the formula :—

"Osiris Unȧs, the Eye of Horus, which was fettered by him [i.e., by Set], hath been presented unto thee."

The Sixty-Fifth Ceremony.

Four Åṭet cakes, 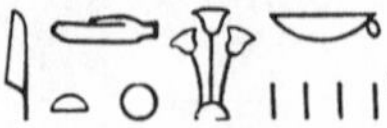, with the formula:—

"Osiris Unås, the Eye of Horus hath been captured "and placed for thee in thy mouth."

The Sem priest presenting the Åṭet, or Åṭent, cakes.

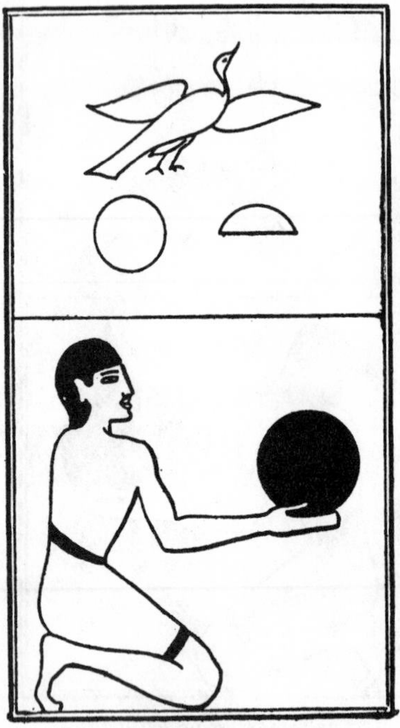

The Sem priest presenting the Pat cakes.

The Sixty-Sixth Ceremony.

Four Pat cakes, , with the formula:—

"Osiris Unås, the Eye of Horus hath been presented "unto thee; [it is] thy cake which thou eatest."

THE SIXTY-SEVENTH CEREMONY.

Four Ashert cakes, 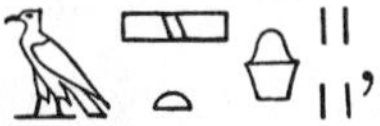, with the formula:—

"Osiris Unås, the Eye of Horus, which was put under "restraint by him [i.e., by Set], hath been presented "unto thee."

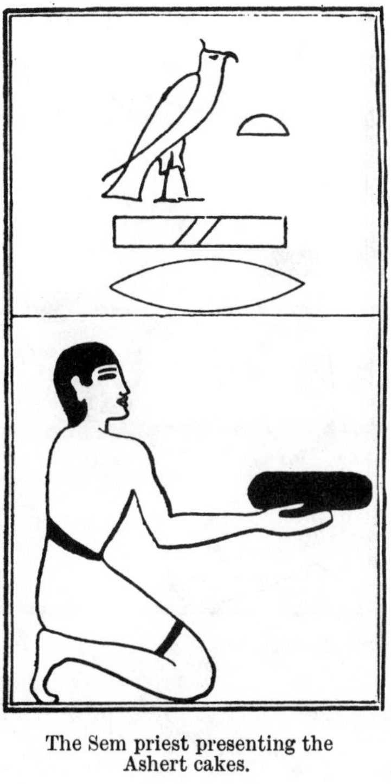

The Sem priest presenting the Ashert cakes.

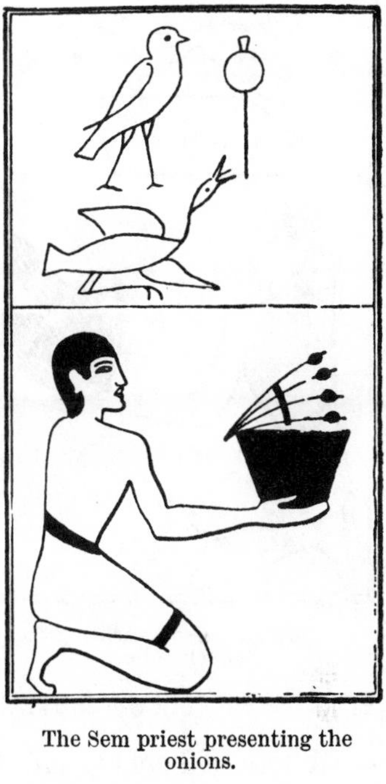

The Sem priest presenting the onions.

THE SIXTY-EIGHTH CEREMONY.

Four onions, or bunches of onions, with the formula:—

"Osiris Unås, his [i.e., Horus's] teeth, which are "white and health-giving, have been brought unto thee."

The Sixty-Ninth Ceremony.

A haunch of beef, with the formula :—

" Osiris Unȧs, accept (?) the haunch of beef [as] the " Eye of Horus."

The Sem priest presenting the haunch of beef.

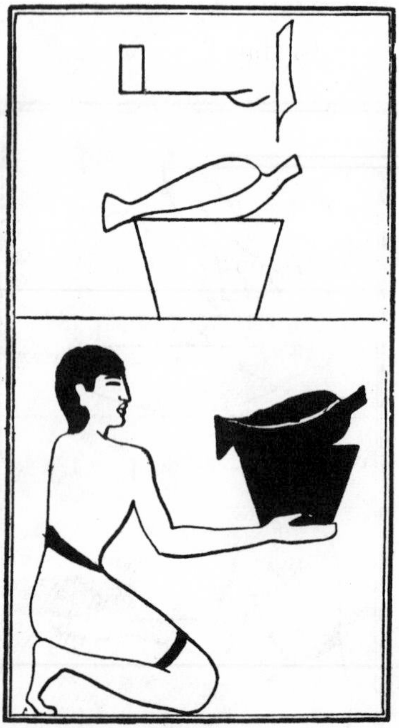

The Sem priest presenting the loin of beef.

The Seventieth Ceremony.

A loin of beef (?), *Ȧā* , with a formula, two versions of which are extant. The rendering of one is :—

" Osiris Unȧs, [here is] the marked piece of flesh and " bone from which Seb cuts not off the *ȧāu* joint," [1]

[1] Maspero, " Osiris, le marqué, de la chair duquel Sibou ne " retranche pas chair."

and of the other :—

"[Osiris] Peṭā-Ȧmen-ȧpt, the mark of that which is "abominable (or, the abominable one) is burnt into the "*ȧā* joint."[1]

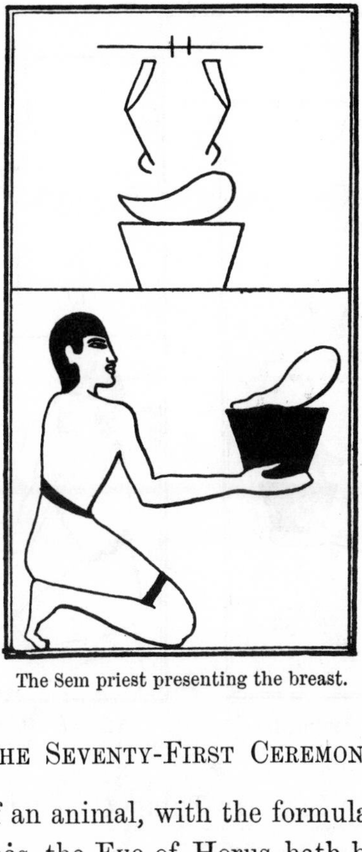

The Sem priest presenting the breast.

The Seventy-First Ceremony.

A breast of an animal, with the formula :—

"Osiris Unȧs, the Eye of Horus hath been presented "unto thee, so that it may embrace thee."

[1] Dümichen, "O Obercherheb Petamenap, das Malzeichen des Schändlichen ist eingebrannt an der Lende."

The Seventy-Second Ceremony.

The Sut joint, , with the formula :—

"Osiris Unȧs, the Sut joint hath been presented unto "thee as the Eye of Horus."

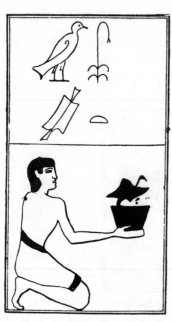

The Sem priest presenting the Sut joint.

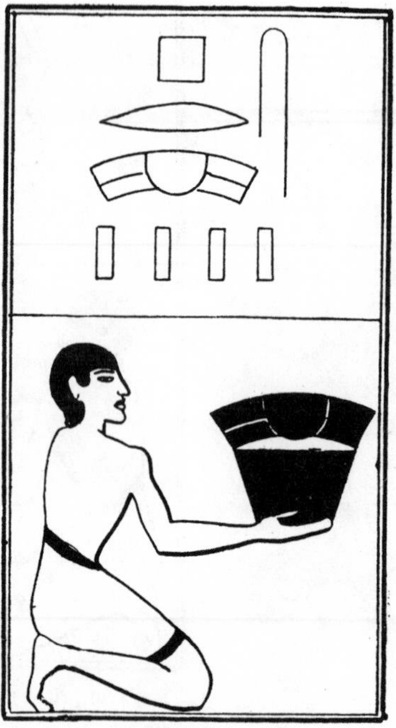

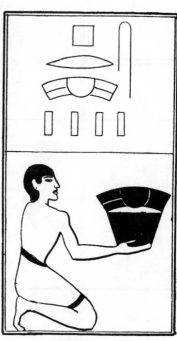

The Sem priest presenting four ribs of beef.

The Seventy-Third Ceremony.

Four ribs of beef (?), with the formula :—

"Osiris Unȧs, the enemies have been presented unto "thee [for they are thine, and thou hast smitten "them]."

THE SEVENTY-FOURTH CEREMONY.

[Four] pieces of roasted flesh, with the formula :—

" Osiris Unås, the things which are ordained for thee " have been presented unto thee."

The Sem priest presenting four pieces of roast meat.

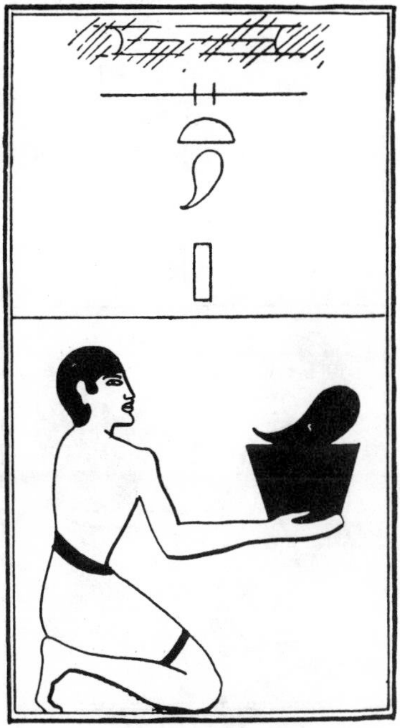

The Sem priest presenting a liver.

THE SEVENTY-FIFTH CEREMONY.

A liver, 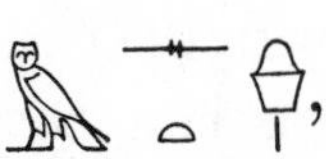, with the formula :—

" Osiris Unås, the Eye of Horus hath been presented " unto thee, so that thou mayest journey with it."

THE SEVENTY-SIXTH CEREMONY.

A spleen, with the formula:—

"Osiris Unås, the Eye of Horus hath been presented "unto thee, so that thou mayest go (?) with it."

The Sem priest presenting a spleen.

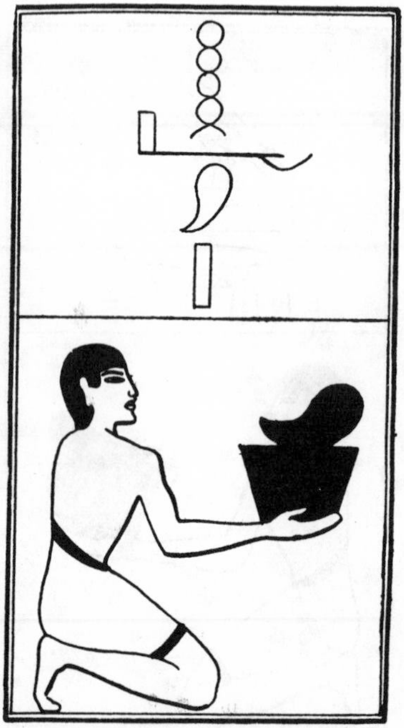

The Sem priest presenting a fore-quarter of beef.

THE SEVENTY-SEVENTH CEREMONY.

A fore-quarter of an animal, with the formula: —

"Osiris Unås, the Eye of Horus hath been presented "unto thee in the form of his fore-quarter [i.e., the fore-"quarter, or shoulder, of Set]."

THE SEVENTY-EIGHTH CEREMONY.

Slices of meat from the fore-quarter, with the formula:—

"Osiris Unȧs, accept (?) the Eye of Horus, which is "in the form of the fore-quarter of Set."

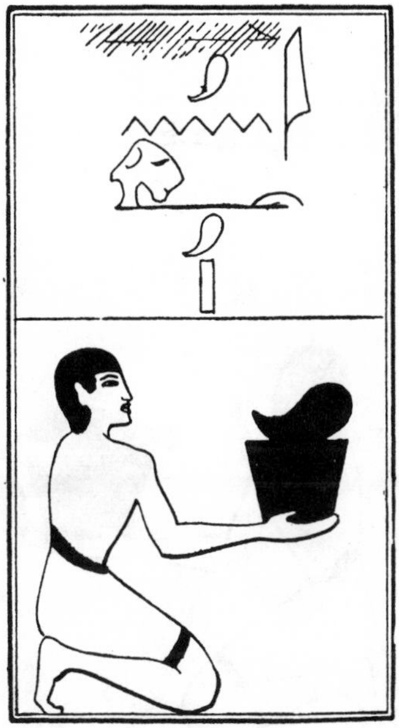

The Sem priest presenting joints from the fore-part of a bull.

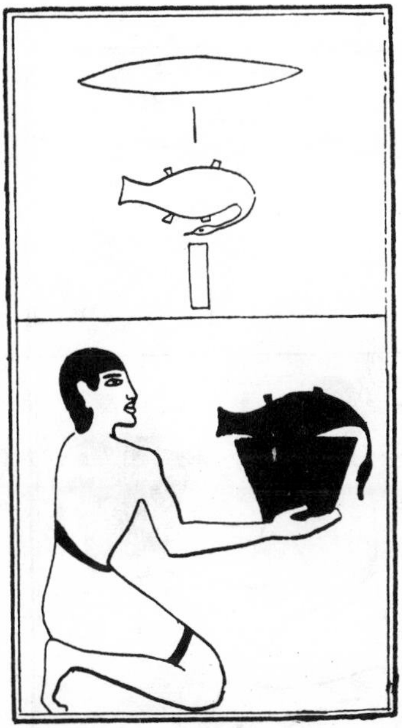

The Sem priest presenting a Re goose.

THE SEVENTY-NINTH CEREMONY.

A Re goose, with the formula:—

"Osiris Unȧs, the heads of the followers of Set have "been presented unto thee [in the form of this] Serȧ "goose."

THE EIGHTIETH CEREMONY.

A Therp goose, with the formula :—

"Osiris Unȧs, this [goose] hath been presented unto "thee according to thy heart's desire."

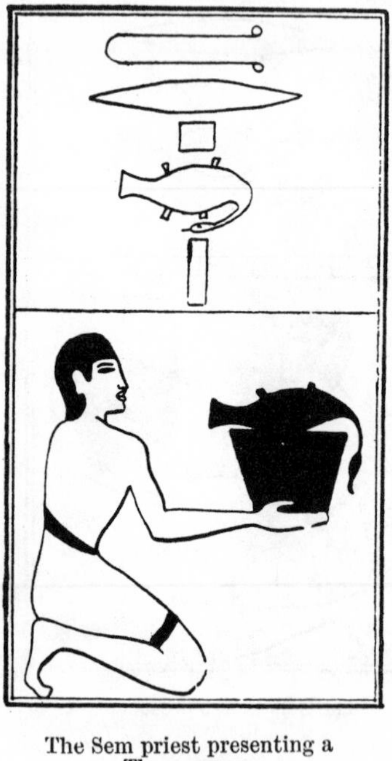

The Sem priest presenting a Therp goose.

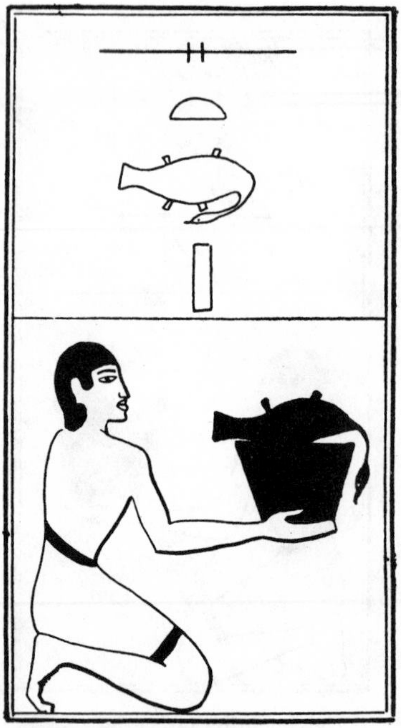

The Sem priest presenting a Set goose.

THE EIGHTY-FIRST CEREMONY.

A Set goose, with the formula :—

"Osiris Unȧs, the Eye of Horus hath been presented "unto thee, and it is carried unto thee."

THE EIGHTY-SECOND CEREMONY.

A Sert goose, with the formula :—

" Osiris Unås, the Eye of Horus hath been presented " unto thee [in the form of] the things which come for " thee."

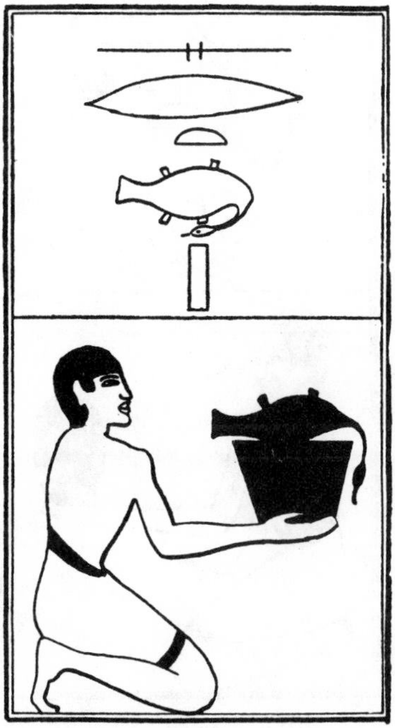

The Sem priest presenting a Sert goose.

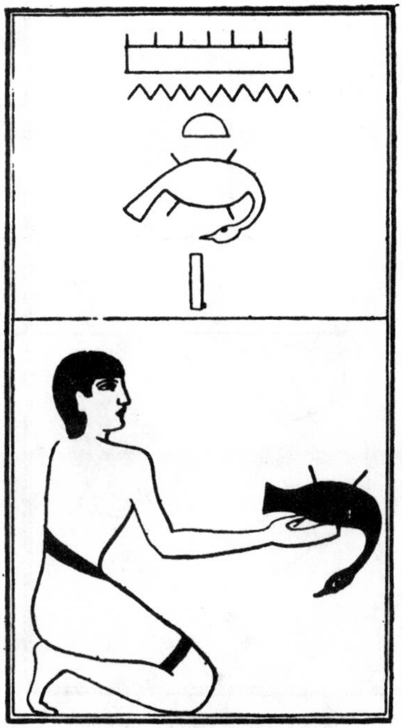

The Sem priest presenting a dove.

THE EIGHTY-THIRD CEREMONY.

A dove, with the formula :—

" Osiris Unås, the Eye of Horus hath been presented " unto thee, the glorious one, the dove which is thine."

THE EIGHTY-FOURTH CEREMONY.

A Sȧf cake, [hieroglyphs], with the formula :—

" Osiris Unȧs, the Eye of Horus, which was put under " restraint by him [i.e., by Set], hath been presented " unto thee."

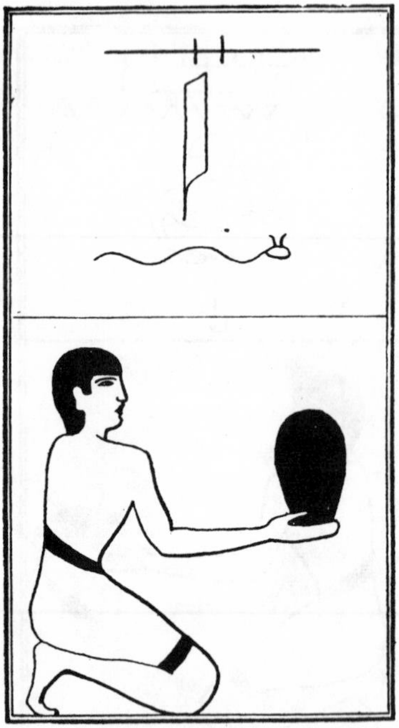

The Sem priest presenting a Sȧf cake.

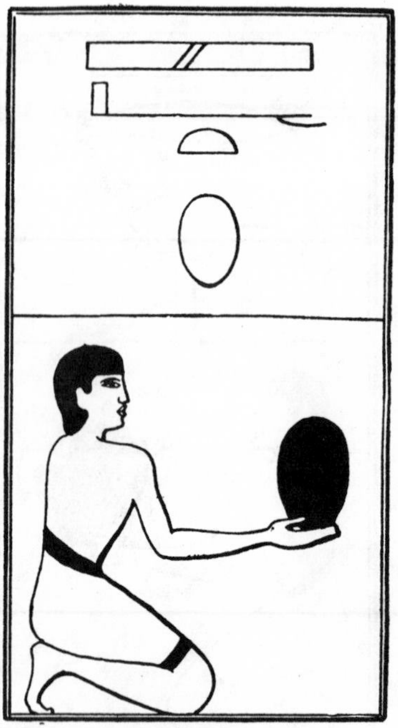

The Sem priest presenting two Shāt cakes.

THE EIGHTY-FIFTH CEREMONY.

Two Shāt cakes, [hieroglyphs] (or, honey-cakes), with the formula :—

" Osiris Unȧs, the Eye of Horus hath been presented un- " to thee, and it shall not be cut off from him by thee (?)."

THE EIGHTY-SIXTH CEREMONY.

Two baskets of Nepat grain, with the formula :—

"Osiris Unȧs, the Eye of Horus, which hath been "counted[1] (or reckoned up), hath been presented unto "thee."

The Sem priest presenting two baskets of Nepat grain.

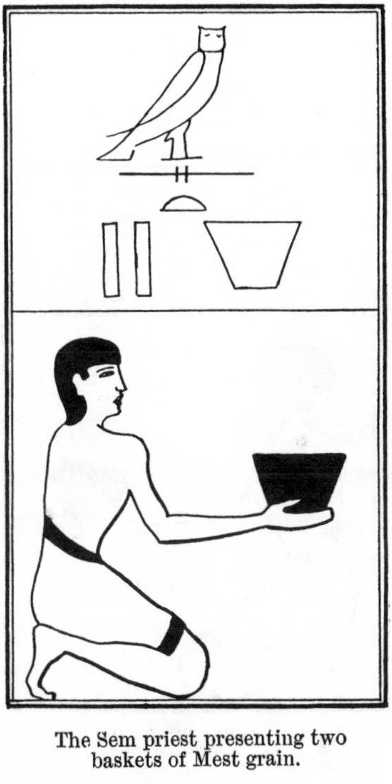

The Sem priest presenting two baskets of Mest grain.

THE EIGHTY-SEVENTH CEREMONY.

Two baskets of Mest grain, with the formula :—

"Osiris Unȧs, the Eye of Horus hath been taken, and "the water which is in it hath been made to be with thee."

[1] I.e., restored to its master Horus.

THE EIGHTY-EIGHTH CEREMONY.

Two vessels of Tchesert drink, with the formula :—

"Osiris Unȧs, the Eye of Horus hath been presented "unto thee, the little one which became the food "of Set."

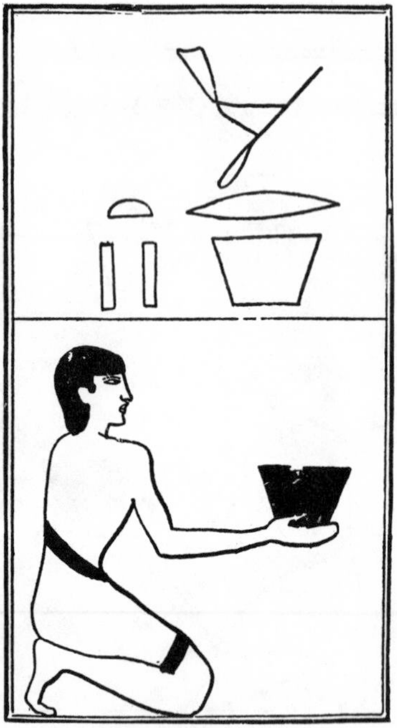

The Sem priest presenting two vessels of Tchesert drink.

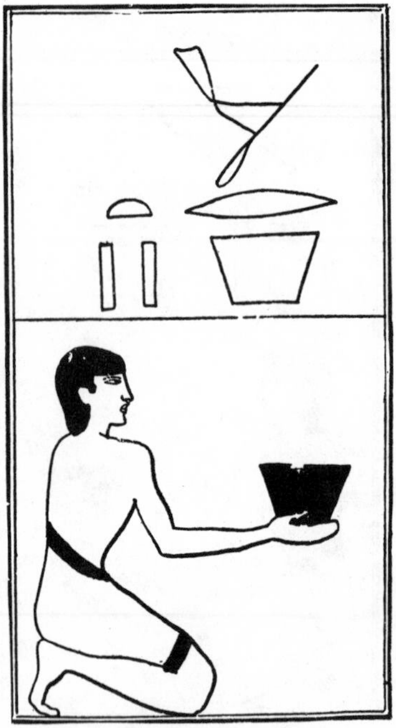

The Sem priest presenting two vessels of Tchesert drink.

THE EIGHTY-NINTH CEREMONY.

Two vessels of Tchesert drink, with the formula :—

"Osiris Unȧs, the Eye of Horus hath been presented "unto thee [, and there is power to it in thine hand]." [1]

[1] The words in brackets are from the text of Peṭā-Ȧmen-ȧpt.

THE NINETIETH CEREMONY.

Two vessels of Khenemes drink, with the formula :—

"Osiris Unȧs, the Eye of Horus hath been presented "unto thee, and the fire of wrath rageth in him [i.e., "Set] against thee."

The Sem priest presenting two vessels of Khenemes drink.

The Sem priest presenting two vessels of beer.

THE NINETY-FIRST CEREMONY.

Two vessels of Ḥeqt beer, with the formula :—

"Osiris Unȧs, thou art filled with that which hath "been pressed out and hath come forth from thee."

The Ninety-Second Ceremony.

Two vessels of Sekhpet grain, with the formula :—

"Osiris Unȧs, thou art filled with that which hath "been pressed out and hath come forth from thee."

The Sem priest presenting two vessels of Sekhpet grain.

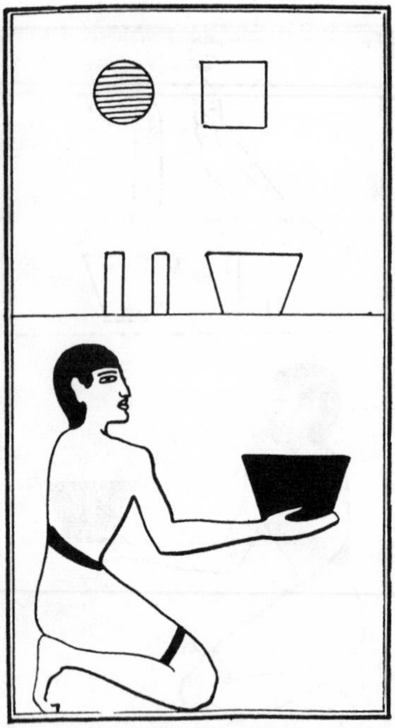

The Sem priest presenting two vessels of Pekh grain.

The Ninety-Third Ceremony.

Two vessels of Pekh grain, with the formula :—

"Osiris Unȧs, thou art filled with that which hath "been pressed out and hath come forth from thee."

THE NINETY-FOURTH CEREMONY.

Two vessels of Nubian beer, with the formula :—

"Osiris Unȧs, thou art filled with that which hath "been pressed out and hath come forth from thee."

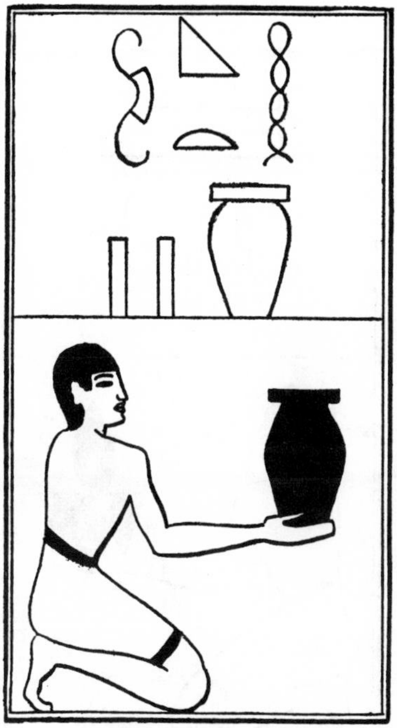

The Sem priest presenting two vessels of Nubian beer.

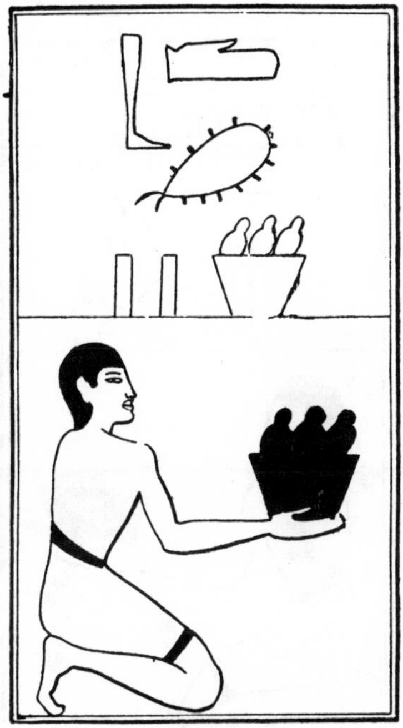

The Sem priest presenting two baskets of figs.

THE NINETY-FIFTH CEREMONY.

Two baskets of figs, with the formula :—

"Osiris Unȧs, the breast of Horus hath been pre-"sented unto thee, and the gods eat of it together with "thee."

THE NINETY-SIXTH CEREMONY.

Two vessels of wine of the North, with the formula:—
"Osiris Unȧs, [there hath been presented unto thee "that which filled thy father, and][1] thy mouth hath "been opened thereby."

The Sem priest presenting two vessels of wine of the North.

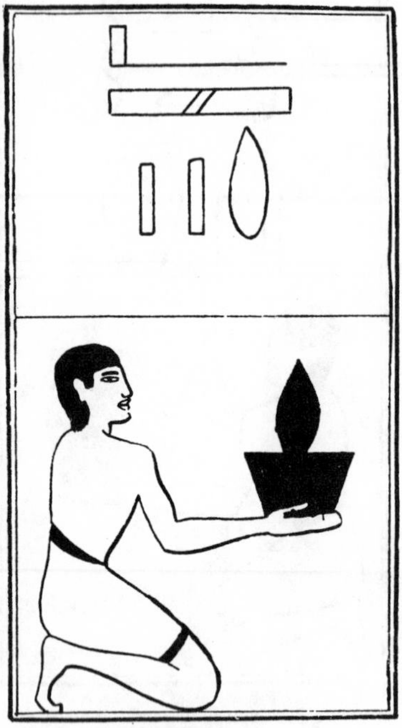

The Sem priest presenting two vessels of white wine.

THE NINETY-SEVENTH CEREMONY.

Two vessels of white wine, with the formula:—
"Osiris Unȧs, the Eye of Horus, the glorious one,

[1] The words in brackets are from the text of Peṭā-Ȧmen-ȧpt.

"which he [i.e., Set] devoured and afterwards vomited,[1] "hath been presented unto thee."

The Ninety-Eighth Ceremony.

Two vessels of Amt (?) wine, or wine of Pelusium, with the formula:—

"Osiris Unȧs, the child which is in the Eye of Horus

The Sem priest presenting two vessels of Amt wine.

"hath been presented unto thee, and thy mouth hath "been opened thereby."

[1] According to the *Book of the Dead*, Chapter CVIII., Rā drove an iron harpoon into Set, and he vomited all that he had eaten,

By the words "child which is in the Eye,"  , we are to understand "pupil of the eye," or "apple of the eye," i.e., that which is guarded as the most precious thing. The same idea exists in

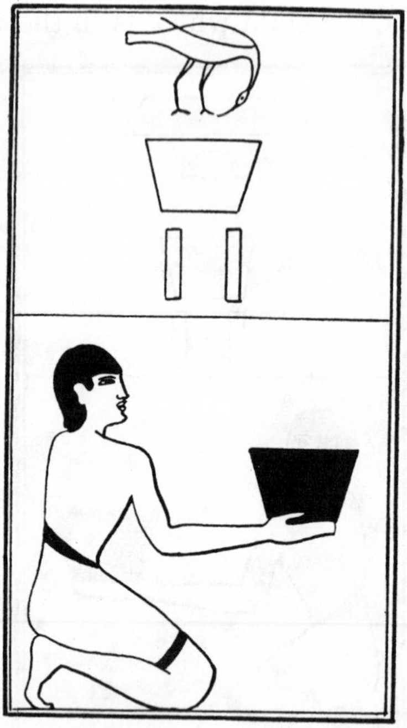

The Sem priest presenting two vessels of Qem wine.

Hebrew, compare אִישׁוֹן, the "little man" of the eye (Deut. xxxii. 10; Proverbs vii. 2), and in Arabic, compare انسان العين. We have also "daughter of the eye," בַּת־עָיִן, in Psalm xvii. 8, in Arabic بنت العين, and in Ethiopic ብንት ፡ ዐይን ፡ = Greek *κόρη* (Deut. xxxii. 10; Psalm xvi. 9; Proverbs vii. 2).

THE NINETY-NINTH CEREMONY.

Two vessels of Qem wine, or wine of Mareotis, with the formula:—

"Osiris Unås, the Eye of Horus which was snared in "a net hath been presented unto thee, and thy mouth "hath been opened thereby."

The Sem priest presenting two vessels of Senu wine.

THE ONE HUNDREDTH CEREMONY.

Two vessels of Senu wine, or wine of Syene, or Aswân, and the formula:—

"Osiris Unås, the Eye of Horus, which hath no like, "hath been presented unto thee, and it is to thee."

THE ONE HUNDRED AND FIRST CEREMONY.

Two vessels of Hebnent wine, with the formula:—

"Osiris Unȧs, the Eye of Horus hath been presented "unto thee, and it hath overthrown them [i.e., the "companions of Set]."

The Sem priest presenting two vessels of Ḥebnent wine.

The Sem priest presenting two baskets of Khenfu cakes.

THE ONE HUNDRED AND SECOND CEREMONY.

Two vessels, or baskets, of Khenfu cakes, with the formula:—

"Osiris Unȧs, the Eye of Horus hath been presented "unto thee, which hath been made in the form of these "scale-shaped cakes for thee."

THE ONE HUNDRED AND THIRD CEREMONY.

Two vessels of Åsheṭ fruit, with the formula:—

"Osiris Unås, the Eye of Horus, which hath been "snatched out of the hand of Set, hath been presented "unto thee."

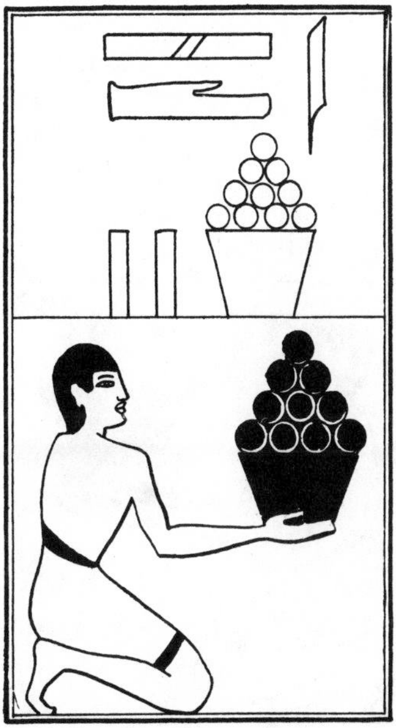

The Sem priest presenting two vessels of Åsheṭ fruit.

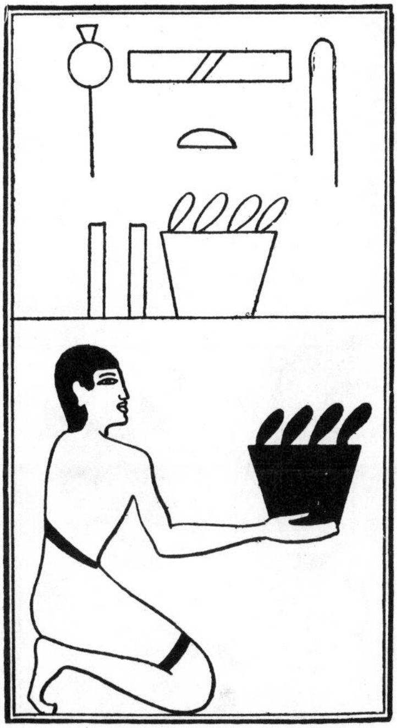

The Sem priest presenting two vessels of Seshet grain.

THE ONE HUNDRED AND FOURTH CEREMONY.

Two vessels of White Seshet grain, with the formula:—

"Osiris Unås, the Eye of Horus hath been presented "unto thee, the White One, the Glorious One, and it "shall serve for thy food."

THE ONE HUNDRED AND FIFTH CEREMONY.

Two vessels of Green Seshet grain, with the formula:—

"Osiris Unȧs, the Eye of Horus hath been presented "unto thee, the Green One, the Glorious One, and it "shall serve for thy food."

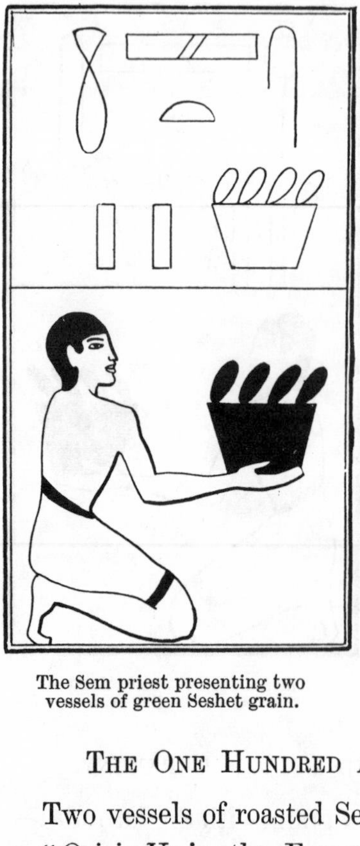

The Sem priest presenting two vessels of green Seshet grain.

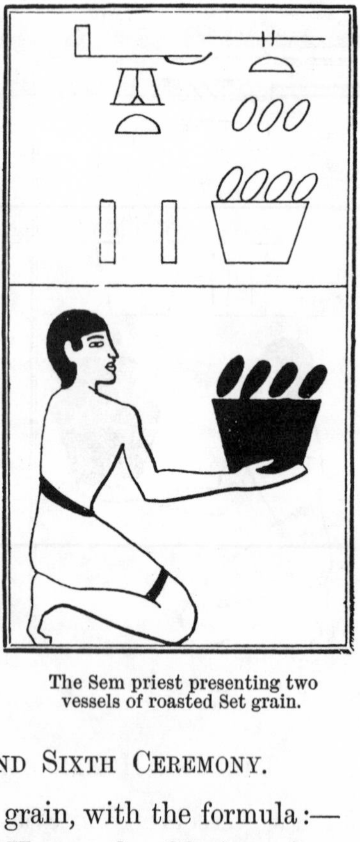

The Sem priest presenting two vessels of roasted Set grain.

THE ONE HUNDRED AND SIXTH CEREMONY.

Two vessels of roasted Set grain, with the formula:—

"Osiris Unȧs, the Eye of Horus, the Glorious One, "which shall turn back [the fiends of Set], hath been "presented unto thee."

THE ONE HUNDRED AND SEVENTH CEREMONY.

Two vessels of roasted Set grain, with the formula :—
"Osiris Unȧs, the Eye of Horus hath been presented "unto thee, the Glorious One, which shall turn back "[the fiends of Set]."

The Sem priest presenting two vessels of roasted Set grain.

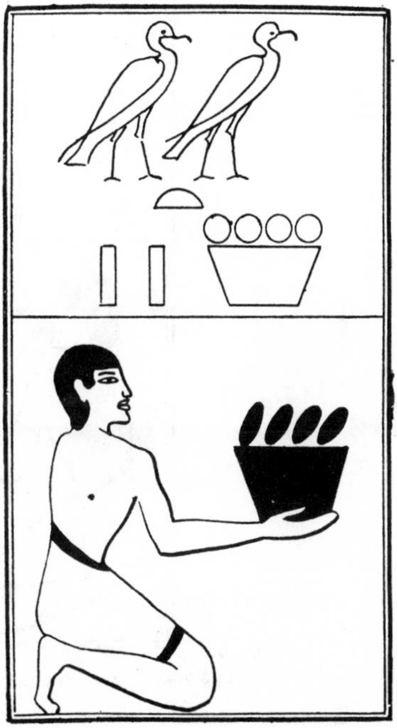

The Sem priest presenting two vessels of Babat fruit.

THE ONE HUNDRED AND EIGHTH CEREMONY.

Two vessels of Babat fruit, with the formula :—
"Osiris Unȧs, the Eye of Horus hath been presented "unto thee, and behold, it is from Baba (?)."

Dümichen thought that Baba was a name of Set, but it seems more probable that the Baba mentioned here is 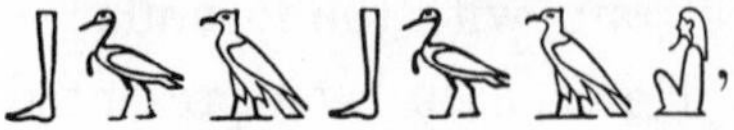, or , the first-born son of Osiris.

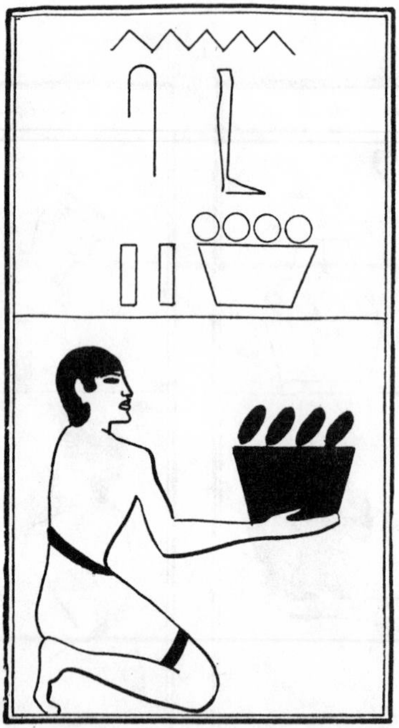

The Sem priest presenting two vessels of mulberries.

The One Hundred and Ninth Ceremony.

Two vessels of Nebes fruit (mulberries ?), with the formula :—

" Osiris Unȧs, the Eye of Horus, which burneth with " fire against them [i.e., the enemies of Set], hath been " presented unto thee."

The One Hundred and Tenth Ceremony.

Two vessels of Nebes cakes, with the formula:—

"Osiris Unȧs, thine eyes have been made to open, "and thou seest with them."

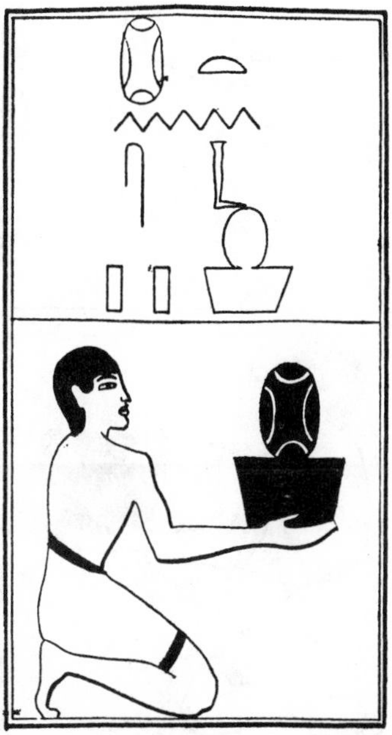

The Sem priest presenting two vessels of mulberry cakes.

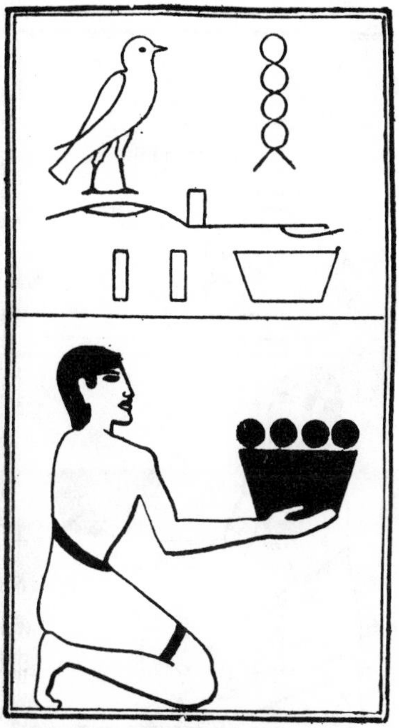

The Sem priest presenting two vessels of Ḥuā grain.

The One Hundred and Eleventh Ceremony.

Two vessels of Ḥuā grain, with the formula:—

"Osiris Unȧs, the Eye of Horus hath been pre-"sented unto thee, the Glorious One, who was in his "throat (?)."

The One Hundred and Twelfth Ceremony.

Two measures of sweet things of all kinds, with the formula :—

"Osiris Unȧs, the Eye of Horus hath been presented "unto thee, the sweetness of which followeth thee."

The Sem priest presenting sweet things of all kinds.

The Sem priest presenting spring fruit, flowers, &c.

The One Hundred and Thirteenth Ceremony.

Two baskets of spring fruit, flowers, and vegetables, with the formula :—

"Osiris Unȧs, the Eye of Horus hath been presented "unto thee, and thou hast had experience thereof."

The One Hundred and Fourteenth Ceremony.

Gifts of every kind, with the formula:—

"Osiris Unȧs, behold, thou hast swallowed the things "which were [intended] for thee."

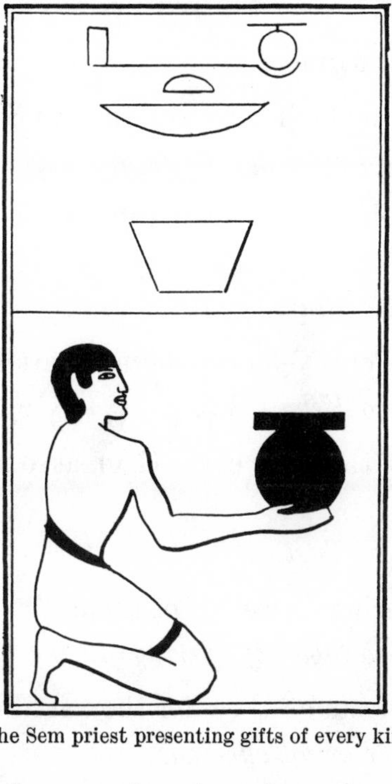

The Sem priest presenting gifts of every kind.

The following section is taken from the text of Pepi II. Nefer-ka-Rā, and is not found in the ordinary copies of the Liturgy of Funerary Offerings:—

"1. May Seb give a royal offering to Pepi Nefer-"ka-Rā!"

"2. I have given unto thee gifts of every kind, and

" set forth there bread and drink of every kind, which " thou lovest and which are good for thee, before the " god for ever and for ever."

" 3. Osiris Pepi Nefer-ka-Rā, Horus hath come, and " he hath made offerings to thee, because thou art his " father,

Present Abt grain.

" 4. and he maketh thee to return to Seb,

Present two vessels of Besen grain.

" 5. and Seb giveth thee thy two eyes that thou " mayest rest."

Present one altar.

" 6. Osiris Pepi Nefer-ka-Rā, thou art his Double."

Present two Keḥa cakes.

" 7. Accept the two eyes, O great one, Osiris Pepi " Nefer-ka-Rā."

Present two Turt cakes.

" 8. An offering on behalf of them!"

Present two tables of offerings in the Usekht hall.

" 9. Horus rests on thee, for thou art his father."

Present one bread offering.

" 10. Accept the crop of the Eye of Horus, which I " have gathered, and Horus hath given unto thee."

Present two vessels of Bat grain.

" 11. Accept the crop of the Eye of Horus, which I " have gleaned, and Horus hath given unto thee."

Present two vessels of Bes grain.

"12. Accept the Eye of Horus, which I have cultivated, and Horus hath given unto thee."

Present two vessels of Aḥā grain.

"13. Hath been presented unto thee that which hath been pressed out and come forth from Osiris."

Present two jugs of beer.

"14. Osiris Pepi Nefer-ka-Rā, accept the water which was in thee and Horus hath given unto thee."

Present two jugs of Thenem drink.

"15. Osiris Pepi Nefer-ka-Rā, I have presented unto thee the Eye of Horus, and have opened thy mouth with it."

Present two vessels of Wine of the North.

"16. Osiris Pepi Nefer-ka-Rā, accept the Eye of Horus which I have taken for him, which Horus hath given unto thee."

Present two vessels of Uatch Wine.

"17. Accept the Eye of Horus, which welleth up with water, and Horus hath given unto thee."

Present two vessels of Ḥebent drink.

"18. Accept the Eye of Horus, which I have seized for him and he hath given unto thee."

Present two vessels of Kheri-Khenfu drink (?).

"19. Accept the Eye of Horus, the White One, which I have bound up for him and he hath given unto thee."

Present two vessels of White Seshet grain.

"20. Accept the Eye of Horus, the Green One, which "I have bound up for him and he hath given unto "thee."

Present two vessels of Green Seshet grain.

"21. Accept the Eye of Horus, which I have counted "for Horus and he hath given unto thee."

Present two vessels of Nepat grain, or cakes.

"22. Accept the Eye of Horus, which I have pursued "for him and he hath given unto thee."

Present an Ȧāt joint.

"23. Osiris Pepi Nefer-ka-Rā, the Eye of Horus "hath been presented unto thee that thou mayest "taste it."

Present two vessels of Ṭeben grain, or fruit.

"24. Hail, Osiris Pepi Nefer-ka-Rā, the Eye of Horus "hath been presented unto thee, it is sweet to the taste, "and it followeth thee."

Present two vessels of fruit of all kinds.

"25. I count them for thee."

Present two vessels of spring fruit, flowers, and vegetables.

"26. Behold they have been swallowed by thee."

Present two tables of offerings.

"27. Osiris Pepi Nefer-ka-Rā, this is the Eye of "Horus, it germinateth in thee, in thee in thy name of "'Spearer of the Enemy.'"

Present offerings the whole year.

"28. Osiris Pepi Nefer-ka-Rā, Horus hath filled thee "wholly with his Eye."

Present offerings at the Festival of Uaḳ.

"Rejoice[1] and dance, O Pepi Nefer-ka-Rā, for standing up and sitting down thou hast thousands of vessels "of beer, and joints of meat, and thy *sheba* offerings are "from the house of the [divine] block. . . . As the god "is filled with his divine offerings of bread, and cakes, "and ale, so shall Pepi Nefer-ka-Rā be filled with his "bread. Come to thy son, Osiris, the Spirit among the "Spirits, the Sekhem in his places, whom the gods who "are in the House of the Prince adore. Hail, Pepi "Nefer-ka-Rā, I make thee to approach, and I lead "thee to the tomb and to the funeral hall, that I may "give unto thee the Eye of Horus, which I have "counted for thee. Hail, thou hast swallowed that "which was before thee. Hail, Pepi Nefer-ka-Rā, thou "hast stood up and received the bread which is thine "from my hand."

Recite four times.

"Hail, Osiris Pepi Nefer-ka-Rā, thou art at the "door (?), thou restest [there] (?), O Pepi Nefer-ka-Rā, "and remainest, O Pepi Nefer-ka-Rā, thou passest on. "Thou utterest words to the regions of Horus, and thou "passest on. Thou utterest words to the regions of Set, "and thou passest on. Thou utterest words to the "regions of Osiris, [and thou passest on]. A royal offer-

[1] See Unås, l. 295 ff.; Tetå, l. 141 ff.

"ing [to thee] in all thy forms. Thou puttest on thy "loin-cloth, and thy panther skin, and thy girdle with "a jackal's tail. Thou advancest with thy two vessels "[for the blood], thou slaughterest the bull, thou "advancest in the boat Uatch-ān, in all thy forms, in "all thy places. Thy mace is at the head of the living, "and thy word is at the head of the Spirits. Ȧnpu, "president of the region of the West, and Āntchet, "who is at the head of the nomes of the East, make "offerings unto thee of the things which are thine. "Hail, Pepi Nefer-ka-Rā, thou art a counterpart of the "gods thy brethren, ... thy son. Thou art endued "wholly with the fluid of life in the earth. Attire "thou thy body when thou comest into their presence."

Recite four times.

THE LITURGY OF FUNERARY OFFERINGS.

I. From the Pyramid of Unȧs.

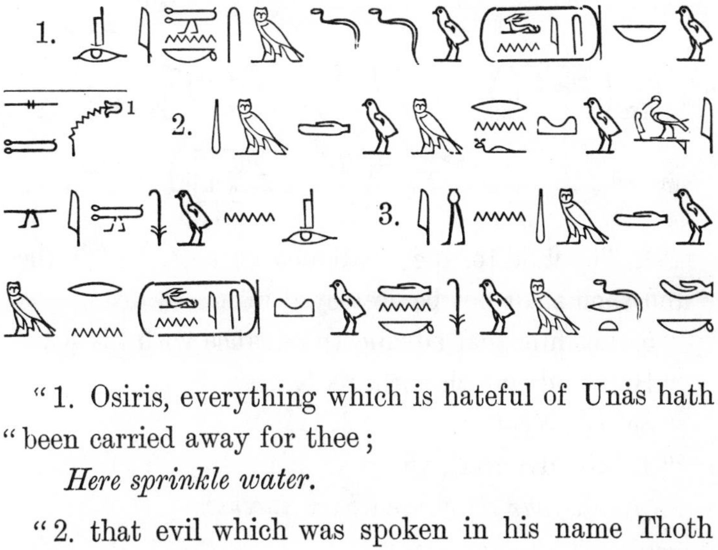

"1. Osiris, everything which is hateful of Unȧs hath "been carried away for thee;

Here sprinkle water.

"2. that evil which was spoken in his name Thoth "hath advanced and carried it to Osiris. 3. I have "brought the evil which was spoken in the name of "Unȧs, and I have placed it in the palm of thy hand "for thee.

Recite four times.

[1] Var., 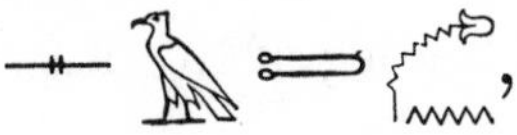, line 350.

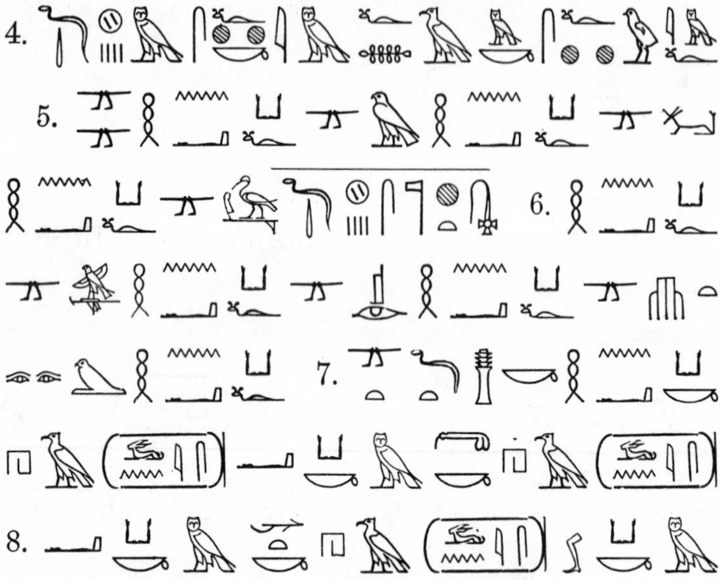

"4. The fluid [of life] shall not be destroyed in thee, "and thou shalt not be destroyed in it.

"5. Let him that advanceth advance with his KA.

"Horus advanceth with his KA.

"Set advanceth with his KA.

"Thoth advanceth with 6. his KA.

Recite four times, and burn incense.

"Sep advanceth with his KA.

"Osiris advanceth with his KA.

"Khent-maati advanceth with his KA.

"7. Thy *Tcheṭ* (backbone) shall advance with thy KA.

"Hail, Unȧs! The arm of thy KA is before thee.

"Hail, Unȧs! 8. The arm of thy KA is behind thee.

"Hail, Unȧs! The leg of thy KA is before thee.

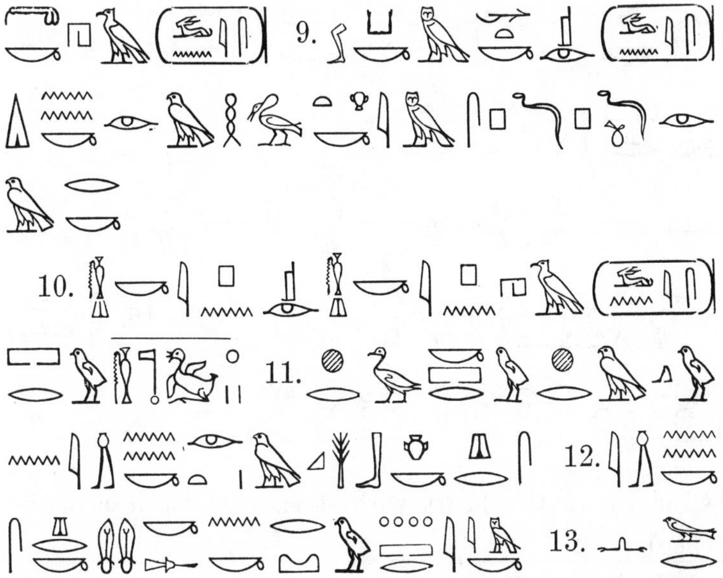

"Hail, Unȧs! 9. The leg of thy Ka is behind thee.

"Osiris Unȧs, I have given unto thee the Eye of "Horus, and thy face is filled therewith, and the per- "fume of the Eye of Horus is to thee.

"10. This libation is for thee, Osiris, this libation is "for thee, O Unȧs, coming forth

Here pour out a vessel of water in which two grains of incense have been dissolved.

"11. before thy son, coming forth before Horus. I "have come and I have brought unto thee the Eye of "Horus, that thy heart may be refreshed therewith.

"12. I have brought it under thee, [under] thy "sandals, and I have presented unto thee the efflux "which cometh forth from thee. 13. There shall be no

"stoppage to thy heart with it (i.e., whilst it is with "thee),

Recite four times.

"and there shall be a coming forth to thee [of things, "or persons] through the word which is spoken (or, "through the voice), and there shall be a coming forth "to thee [of things, or persons] through the word which "is spoken (or through the voice).

"14. [Cleansing by] SEMMÅN! [Cleansing by] SEM-"MÅN!

"Open thy mouth, O Unås,

Here offer five grains of Nekheb incense from the city of Nekheb.

"15. and taste thou the taste thereof in the halls of the

16. [hieroglyphs]

17. [hieroglyphs]

18. [hieroglyphs]

19. [hieroglyphs]

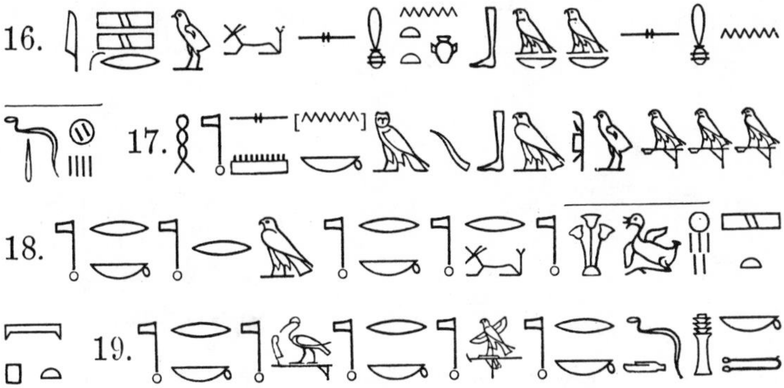

"god. An emission of Horus is SEMMÁN, 16. an
" emission of Set is SEMMÁN, the stablisher of the heart
" of the two Horus-gods is SEMMÁN.

Recite four times.

" 17. Thou art cleansed with *ḥesmen* (natron), and art
" like unto the Sheshu (or, Shemsu)-Ḥeru (i.e., the
" Followers of Horus).

" 18. Thou art purified with natron, and Horus is
" purified with natron.

Thou art purified with natron, and Set is purified
" with natron.

*Here offer five grains of natron of the North from
Shet-pet.*

" 19. Thou árt purified with natron, and Thoth is
" purified with natron.

" Thou art purified with natron, and Sep is purified
" with natron.

" Thou art purified with natron, and thou art stablished

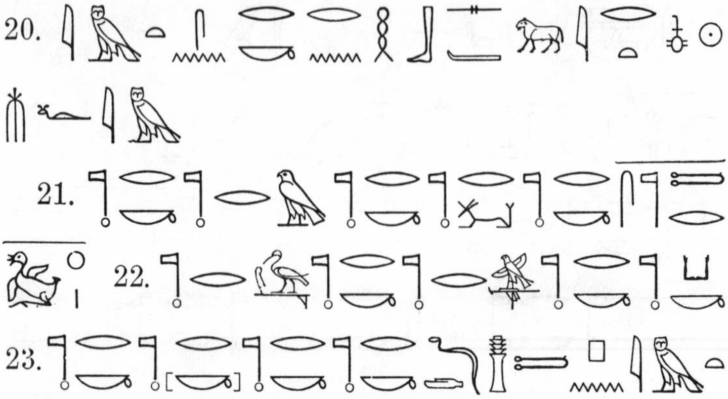

"20. among them.

"Thy mouth is the mouth of a sucking calf on the "day of his birth.

"21. Thou art purified with natron, and Horus is "purified with natron.

"Thou art purified with natron, and Set is purified "with natron.

"Thou art purified with natron,

Here offer one grain of natron.

"22. and Thoth is purified with natron.

"Thou art purified with natron, and Sep is purified "with natron.

"Thou art purified with natron, and thy KA is puri-"fied with natron.

"23. Thou art purified with natron.

"Thou art purified with natron.

"Thou art purified with natron.

"Thou art purified with natron,

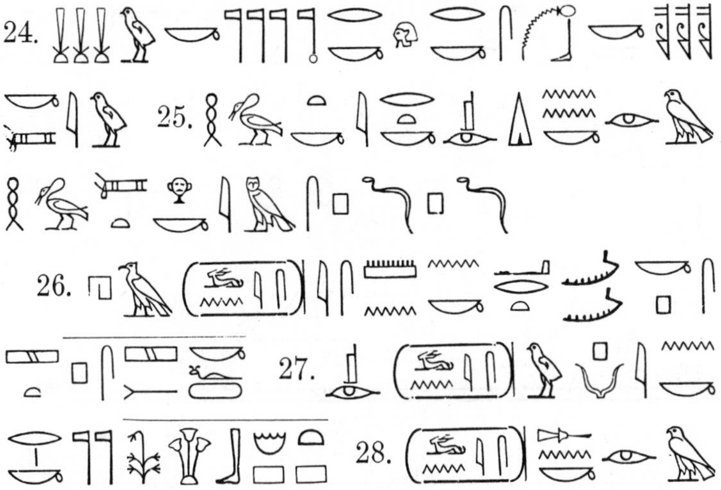

"O thou who art stablished among 24. thy brethren "the gods.

"Thy head is purified for thee with natron, and thy "bones have been thoroughly cleansed for thee, 25. and "thou art filled with that which belongeth to thee. "Osiris, I have given unto thee the Eye of Horus, and "thy face is filled therewith, and [it spreadeth abroad] "its odour.

"26. O Unȧs, thy two jaw-bones which were sepa-"rated have been established.

[*Here present*] *the Pesesh-kef.*

"27. O Unȧs, the two gods have opened for thee thy "mouth.

[*Here present*] *two instruments of iron, one of the North and one of the South.*

"28. [O] Unȧs, the Eye of Horus hath been presented

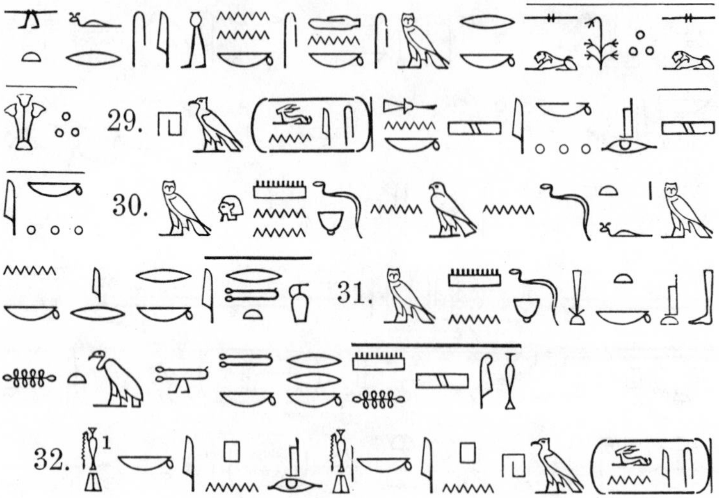

"unto thee, and with it the god passeth; I have brought "it unto thee, place thou it in thy mouth.

[*Here offer*] *cheese* (?) *of the South, and cheese* (?) *of the North.*

"29. O Unȧs, the *shȧku* cakes (?) of Osiris have been "presented unto thee, the *shȧku* 30. from the top of "the breast of Horus, of his body, hast thou taken to "thy mouth, [and that which is] 31.

[*Here offer*] *a vessel of milk.*

"from the breast of thy sister Isis, the emission of [thy] "mother, hast thou taken possession of for thy mouth.

[*Here offer*] *a jug of whey* (?).

"32. This libation is for thee, Osiris, this libation is "for thee, O Unȧs,

[1] Sethe omits this paragraph (*Die aegyptischen Pyramidentexte*, i., p. 30), and passes on to  (l. 37).

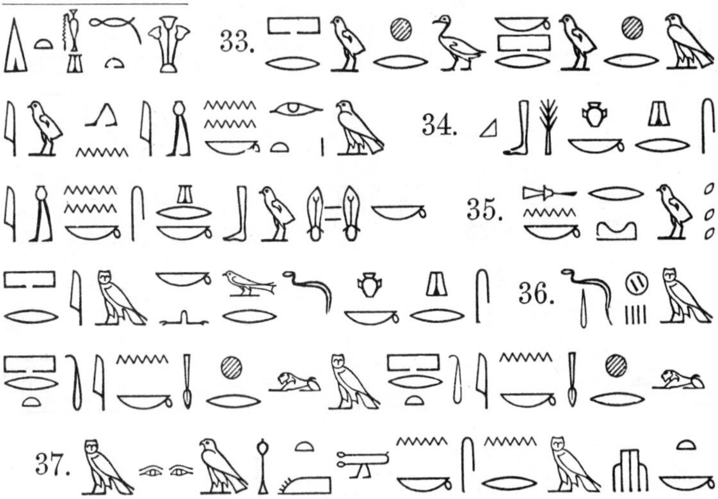

33. *Offer clean cold water of the North.*

"coming forth before thy son, coming forth before "Horus. I have come and I have brought unto thee the "Eye of Horus, 34. that thy heart may be refreshed "therewith. I have brought it under thee, [under] "thy sandals, 35. and I have presented unto thee that "which hath flowed forth from thee. There shall be no "stoppage to thy heart with it (i.e., whilst it is with thee),

36. *Recite four times.*

"and there shall be a coming forth to thee [of things "(or, persons)] through the word which is spoken (or, "through the voice), and there shall be a coming forth "to thee [of things (or, persons)] through the word "which is spoken (or, through the voice).

"37. [That which cometh forth] from the two Eyes "of Horus, the white and the black, thou hast taken

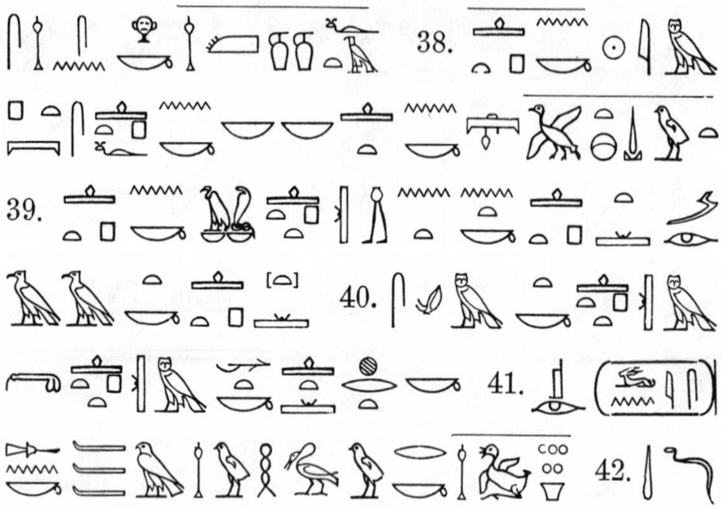

"possession of, and when they are in front of thee they "illumine thy face.

[*Here offer*] *two jugs, one white and one black.*

"38. Rā (i.e., Day) hath made an offering unto thee "in the sky. The South and the North have caused "an offering to be made unto thee. Ḳerḥ (i.e., Night) "hath made an offering unto thee. 39. The South and "the North have made an offering unto thee. An "offering is brought unto thee, an offering thou seest, "of an offering 40. thou hearest. There is an offering "in front of thee, there is an offering behind thee, there "is an offering with thee.

[*Here offer*] *a cake for the journey.*

"41. Osiris Unȧs, the white teeth of Horus are pre-"sented unto thee so that they may fill thy mouth.

[*Here offer*] *five bunches of onions.*

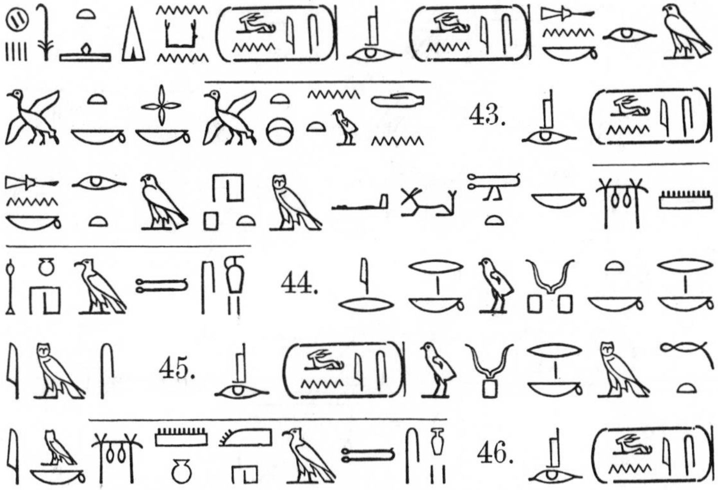

Recite four times [the words]

"42. Give a royal offering to the KA of Unȧs.

"Osiris Unȧs, the Eye of Horus hath been presented "unto thee, the bread which thou eatest.

[Here offer] the Uṭen cake.

"43. Osiris Unȧs, the Eye of Horus hath been pre-"sented unto thee; it hath been snatched from the "hand of Set, and thou hast taken possession of it

[Here offer] a white jug of wine [containing] two hathes measures.

"44. for thy mouth, and thou hast opened thy mouth "therewith.

"45. Osiris Unȧs, thy mouth is opened by that which "floweth from thee.

[Here offer] a black jug of wine [containing] two hathes measures.

"46. Osiris Unȧs, there hath been presented unto

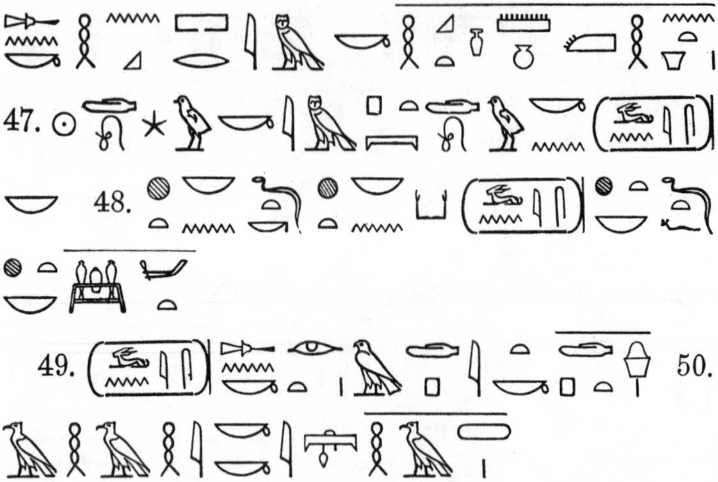

"thee that which hath been pressed out of thee, which "hath come forth from thee.

[Here offer] a black vessel [containing] one ḥent measure of beer.

"47. O Rā, may the worship which thou hast in "heaven, and the worship which is to thee of every "kind, [be] to Unȧs; 48. and may everything which "is [offered] to thy body be [offered] to the KA of "Unȧs, and may everything which is [offered] to his "body be thine.

[Here offer] the holy table of offerings.

"49. Unȧs, the Eye of Horus hath been presented "unto thee for thy tasting.

[Here offer] a Tept cake.

"50. The darkness (or, the night) becometh denser "and denser.

[Here offer] an Aḥ cake.

51. 

52. 

53. 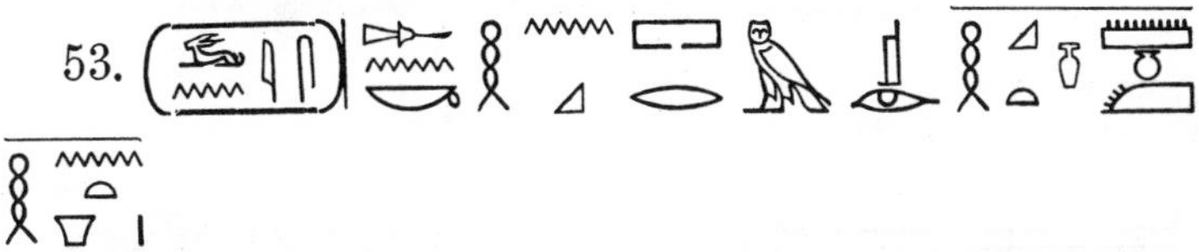

54. 

"51. Unås, the Eye of Horus hath been presented "unto thee that it may embrace thee.

[*Here offer*] *a breast.*

"52. Unås, the Eye of Horus hath been presented "unto thee, which was snatched from the hand of Set, "and was rescued for thee, and thou dost open thy "mouth with it.

[*Here offer*] *a white vessel* [*containing*] *one ḥent measure of wine.*

"53. Unås, there hath been presented unto thee "what hath been pressed out and cometh forth from "Osiris.

[*Here offer*] *a black vessel* [*containing*] *one ḥent measure of beer.*

"54. Unås, the Eye of Horus hath been presented

55. 

56. 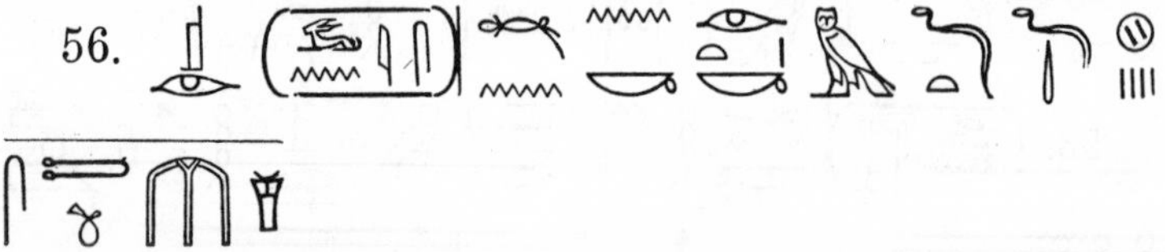

57. 

"unto thee, which was rescued for thee; there is no "iron therein, and it belongeth to thee.

[*Here offer*] *an iron vessel* [*containing*] *one ḥent measure of beer.*

"55. Unȧs, the Eye of Horus hath been presented "unto thee that thou mayest be filled therewith.

[*Here offer*] *a ḥetem vessel* [*containing*] *one measure of beer.*

"56. Osiris Unȧs, I have filled thine eye for thee "with *metchet* oil.

Recite four times [*and offer*] *Seth ḥeb unguent.*

"57. Osiris Unȧs, there hath been presented unto "thee that which hath been pressed out from thy face.

[*Here offer*] *Ḥeken ointment.*

[1] After line 55 there follow in the text of Pepi II. seventeen lines containing the names of articles of apparel and the formulae referring to them (see Maspero's text and Sethe, *op. cit.*, pp. 26, 27).

58. 

59. 

60. 

61. 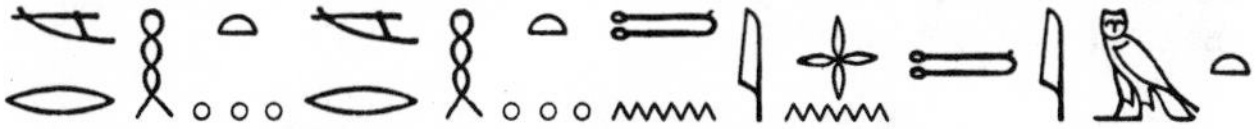

" 58. Osiris Unȧs, the Eye of Horus hath been presented unto thee, and [Set] hath been made weak for " thee thereby.

[Here offer] a jar of bitumen (or, pitch).

" 59. Osiris Unȧs, the eye of Horus hath been presented unto thee that it may unite itself unto thee.

[Here offer] a jar of Neshnem unguent.

" 60. Osiris Unȧs, the Eye of Horus hath been presented unto thee that the gods may be brought unto " thee thereby.

[Here offer] a jar of Tuatu unguent.

" 61. O ye Oils, ye Oils, which are on the forehead

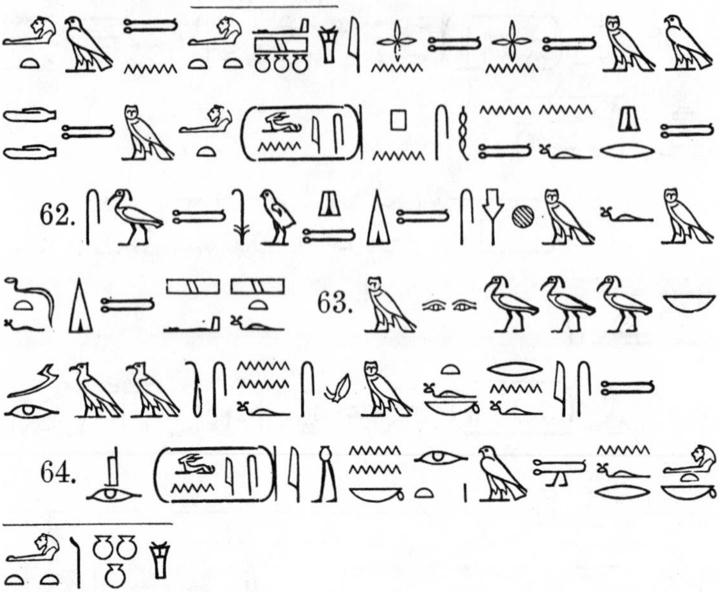

"of Horus, which are on the forehead of Horus, which "are on the forehead of Horus, place ye yourselves on "the forehead of this Unȧs, and make him to smell "sweet by means of you.

[*Here offer*] *oil of cedar of the finest quality.*

"62. Make ye him to be a *khu* (or, glorious) through "possessing you, and grant ye him to have the mastery "over his body [again], and grant ye him openings "63. before his eyes, and let all the KHU (or, Spirits) "see him, and let them all hear his name. Behold, "64. Osiris Unȧs, the Eye of Horus hath been brought "unto thee, for it hath been seized for thee that it may "be before thee.

[*Here offer*] *the finest Theḥennu oil.*

"65. Osiris Unȧs, I have painted for thee the Eye of "Horus with *mesṭem* so that there may be health over "thy face. *Recite four times.*

[*Here offer*] *one bag of uatch eye-paint, and one bag of mesṭemet.*

"66. Mayest thou watch in peace. The goddess Tȧat "watcheth in peace. The goddess Tatet watcheth

[*Here offer*] *two swathings.*

"67. in peace. The Eye of Horus which is in the "city of Ṭep-[Pe] is in peace. The Eye of Horus "which is in the temple-houses of the goddess Net "is in peace. 68. Receive thou the milk-[white] and "bleached swathings of the goddess Ur-ā. Cause "ye, O swathings, that the Two Lands may submit

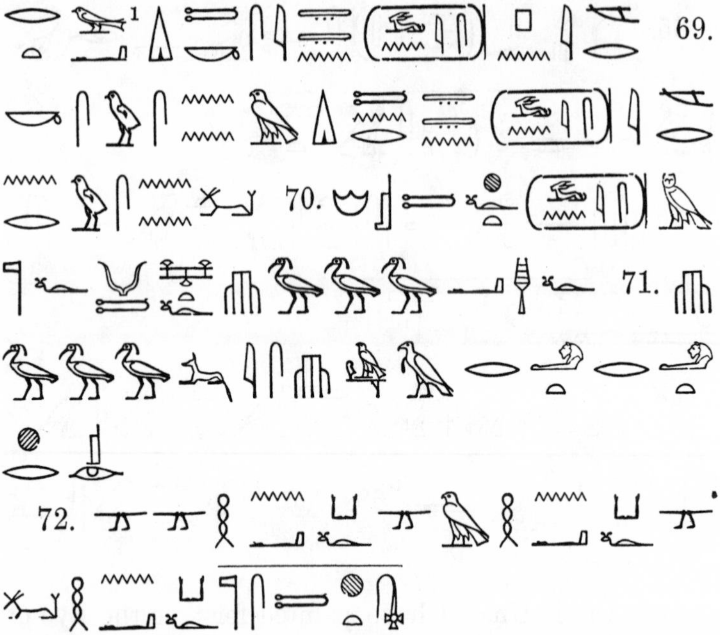

"to this Unås, even as they 69. bow down before "Horus, and make ye the Two Lands to be in awe of "Unås even as they are terrified before Set. 70. Tarry "ye (or, sit ye) before Unås in his divinity. Open ye "his way at the head of the KHU (i.e., Spirits), and let "him stand 71. at the head of the KHU. O Ånpu-"Khenti-Åmenti, forwards, forwards, to the Osiris [Unås].

"72. Let him advance! Let him advance with his "KA! [as] Horus advanceth with his KA, [as] Set "advanceth with his KA,

[*Here*] *burn incense.*

[1] Var. 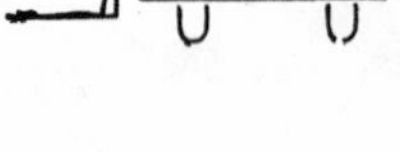 Pepi II., line 328.

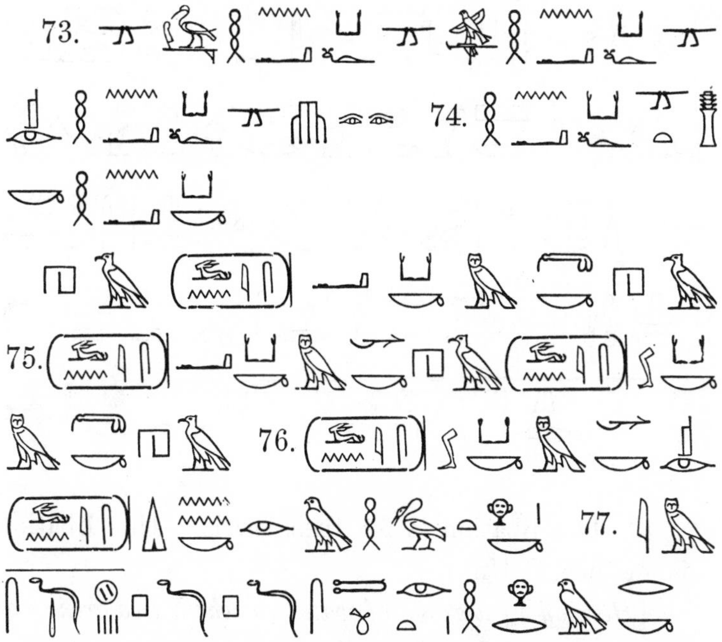

"73. [as] Thoth advanceth with his KA, [as] Sep "advanceth with his KA, [as] Osiris advanceth with his "KA, [as] Khenti-Maati advanceth 74. with his KA, "so shall thy backbone advance with thy KA.

"Hail, Unȧs, the arm of thy KA is before thee.

"75. Hail, Unȧs, the arm of thy KA is behind thee.

"Hail, Unȧs, the leg of thy KA is before thee.

"Hail, 76. Unȧs, the leg of thy KA is behind thee.

"Osiris Unȧs, I have given unto thee the Eye of "Horus, and thy face is filled therewith, 77.

Recite four times.

"and the perfume of the Eye of Horus spreadeth itself "over thee.

78. [hieroglyphs]

[hieroglyphs]   79. [hieroglyphs]

[hieroglyphs]   80. [hieroglyphs]

[hieroglyphs]

[hieroglyphs]   81. [hieroglyphs]

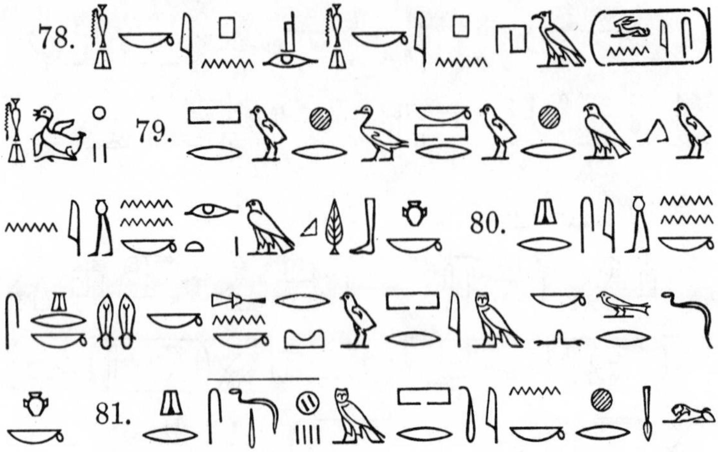

" 78. This libation is for thee, Osiris.   This libation
" is for thee, O Unás,

> [*Here offer*] *a vessel of water in which two grains of*
> *incense have been dissolved.*

" 79. coming forth before thy son, coming forth before
" Horus.   I have come and I have brought ụnto thee
" the Eye of Horus, that thy heart may be refreshed
" 80. therewith.   I have brought it under thee, [under]
" thy sandals, and I have presented unto thee that
" which hath flowed forth from thee.   There shall be
" no stoppage to thy heart   81. with it (i.e., whilst it
" is with thee),

> *Recite four times.*

" and there shall be a coming forth of things (or persons)
" to thee at the [sound of] the voice (or, through the
" voice).

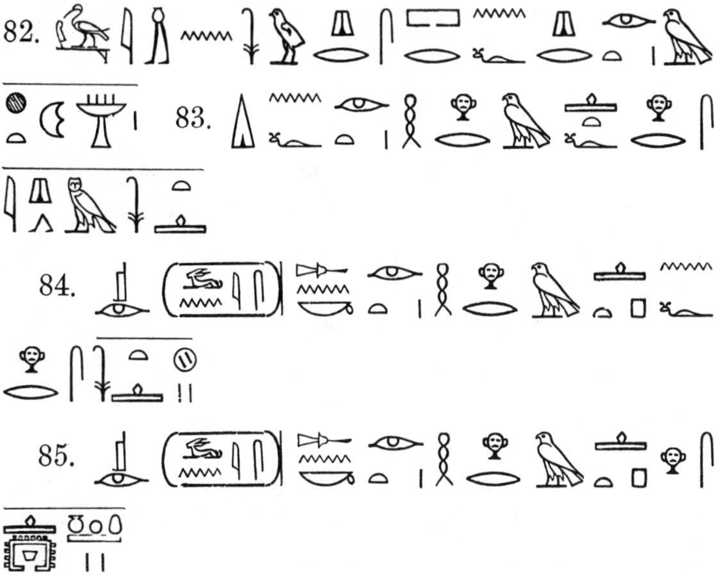

"82. Thoth returning bringeth it, and he hath come "forth with the Eye of Horus,

---

[*Here offer*] *a table of offerings.*

"83. he hath given the Eye of Horus, and he is con- "tent therewith.

[*Here*] *one shall enter with the suten ḥetep.*

"84. Osiris Unȧs, the Eye of Horus hath been pre- "sented unto thee, and he is content therewith.

[*Here present*] *suten ḥetep twice.*

"85. Osiris Unȧs, the Eye of Horus hath been pre- "sented unto thee, and he is content therewith.

[*Here present*] *two tables of offerings in the usekh hall.*

86. 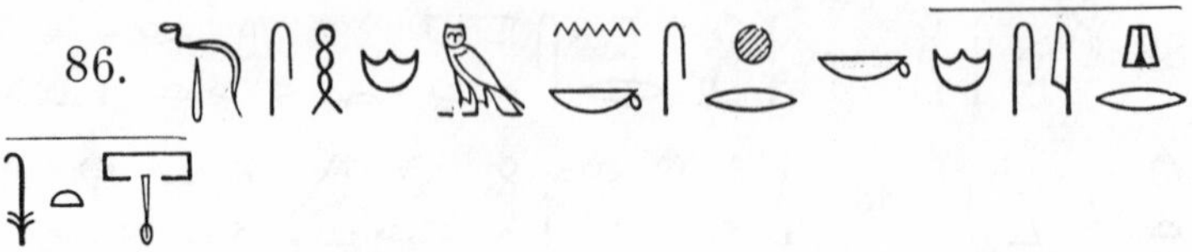

87. 

88. 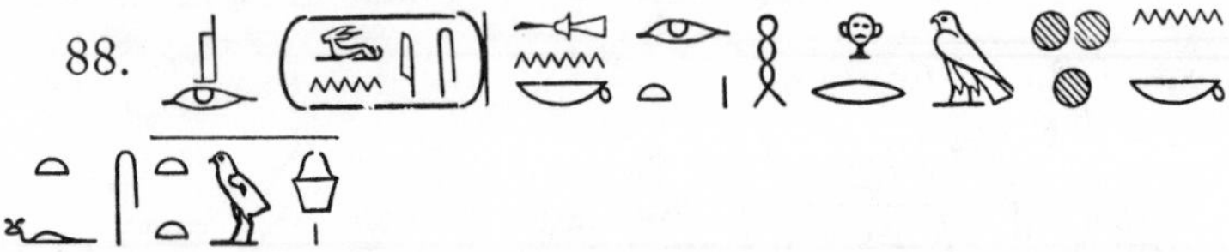

89. 

"86. [*Here*] *say:* 'Thou hast made it (i.e., the Eye "of Horus) under thee.'"

Here shall he (or, they, i.e., the assistants) sit down at the suten pert kheru.

"87. Osiris Unȧs, the Eye of Horus hath been pre- "sented unto thee, and it hath been made to approach "thy mouth for thee.

[*Here present*] *a cake and a bread-cake.*

"88. Osiris Unȧs, the Eye of Horus hath been pre- "sented unto thee, protecting . . . . . .

[*Here offer*] *one Tut cake.*

"89. Osiris Unȧs, the Eye of Horus hath been pre- "sented unto thee, which was chained up by him [Set].

[*Here offer*] *a Reṭhu cake.*

90.

91.

92.

93.

"90. Osiris Unȧs, the Eye of Horus hath been pre-"sented unto thee, the little one which Set hath eaten.

[*Here offer*] *a vessel of Tchesert drink.*

"91. Osiris Unȧs, the Eye of Horus hath been pre-"sented unto thee, which hath been smitten, for thy "mouth.

[*Here offer*] *a vessel of Khenem beer.*

"92. Osiris Unȧs, the Eye of Horus hath been pre-"sented unto thee, it hath been lifted up for thee to "thy face,

[*Here*] *lift up a cake and a vessel of drink.*

"93. Osiris lifting up thy face. Lift up thy face, O "thou Unȧs, may thy soul advance!

94. [hieroglyphs]

[hieroglyphs]   95. [hieroglyphs]

[hieroglyphs]   96. [hieroglyphs]

[hieroglyphs]

97. [hieroglyphs]

[hieroglyphs]

98. [hieroglyphs]

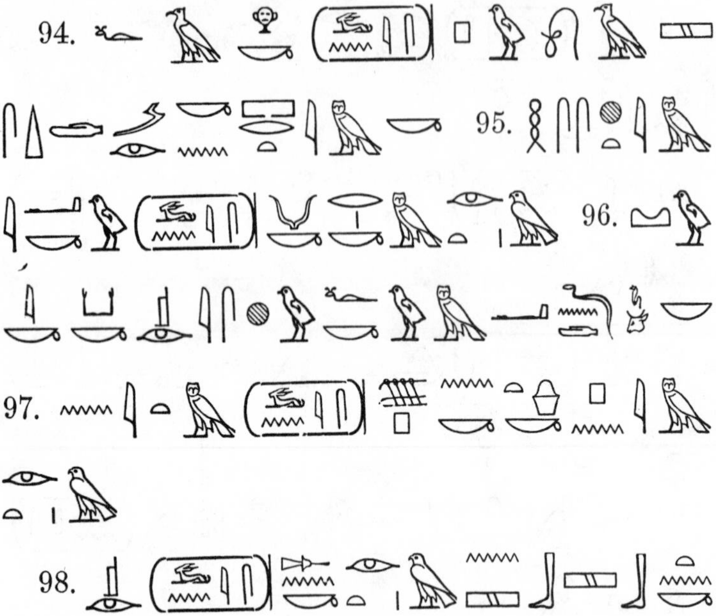

"94. Lift up thy face, Unás, [and look] afar off, and
"fix thy gaze intently on that which cometh forth from
"thee.   95. That which is corrupt in thee hath been
"washed away, Unás, and is opened for thee thy
"mouth by the Eye of Horus.   96. Let there be praise
"to thee and to thy KA, Osiris, which hath been cut
"away for thee from the hand of him that doeth
"violence   97. to the dead.   Unas, thou hast received
"these thy bread-cakes which are from the Eye of
"Horus.

"98. Osiris Unás, the Eye of Horus hath been pre-
"sented unto thee, [that is to say,] that which hath

99.

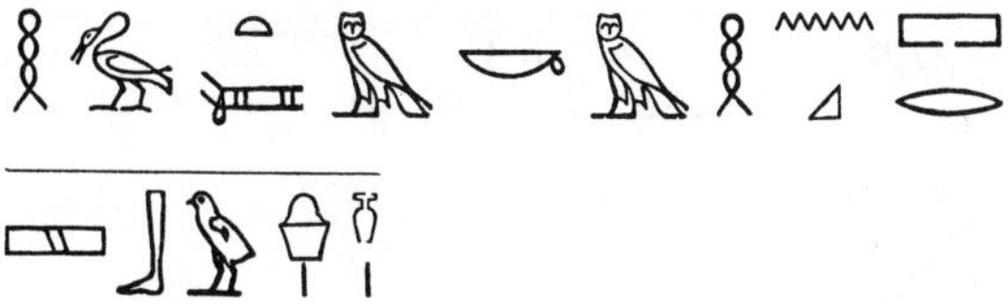

100.

101.

"been mixed for thee by it, 99. so that thou mayest "be filled with that which hath been pressed out and "hath come forth from thee.

Recite four times.

Here offer a Shebu cake and one vessel of drink.

"100. Osiris Unȧs, the *sut* joint of meat hath been "presented to thee [as] the Eye of Horus.

[*Here offer*] *one sut joint.*[1]

"101. Osiris Unȧs, the water which is in them hath "been offered unto thee.

[*Here offer*] *two vases of water.*

[1] From the text of Pepi II. we see that at this place several offerings were laid, some on the palm of the left hand of the statue and some on the right, but what they were cannot be said, for the text is mutilated.

102. 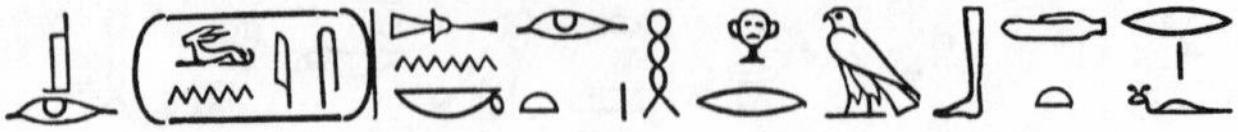

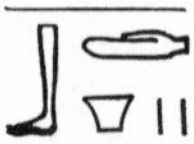

103. 

104. 

105. 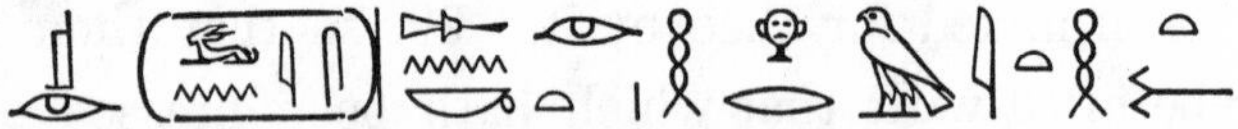

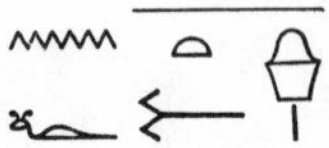

"102. Osiris Unȧs, the Eye of Horus hath been "offered unto thee that it may purify thy mouth.

[*Here offer*] *two vessels of cakes of Beṭ incense.*

"103. Osiris Unȧs, the Eye of Horus hath been pre- "sented unto thee, and it hath been offered unto thee "for thy mouth.

[*Here offer*] *a Ṭua cake and a Shens cake.*

"104. Osiris Unȧs, the Eye of Horus hath been pre- "sented unto thee which struck down Set.

[*Here offer*] *two Tut cakes.*

"105. Osiris Unȧs, the Eye of Horus hath been pre-

106. 

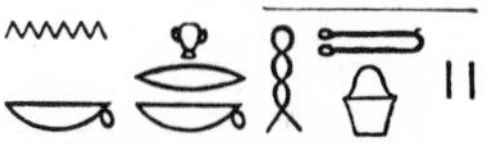

107. 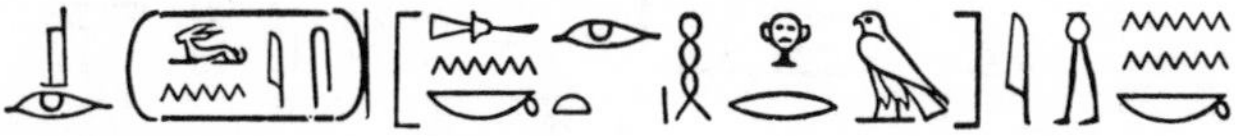

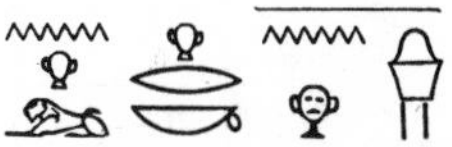

108. 

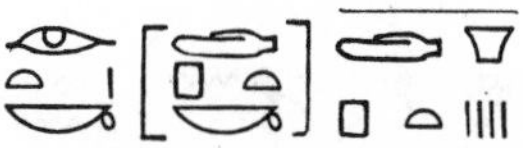

"sented unto thee, which was put under restraint by "him [i.e., Set].

[Here offer] a Reṭhu cake.

"106. Osiris Unȧs, [the Eye of Horus hath been pre-"sented unto thee] that thou mayest seize it for thy "face.

[Here offer] two Ḥeth cakes.

"107. Osiris Unȧs, [the Eye of Horus hath been pre-"sented unto thee], and there hath been brought unto "thee . . . that which is for thy face.

[Here offer] two Neḥrȧ cakes.

"108. Osiris Unȧs, [the Eye of Horus hath been pre-"sented unto thee], and hath been given to thine eye "for thee to taste.

[Here offer] four Tept cakes.

109. 

110. 

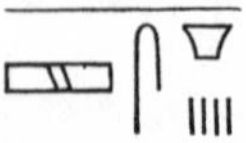

111. 

112. 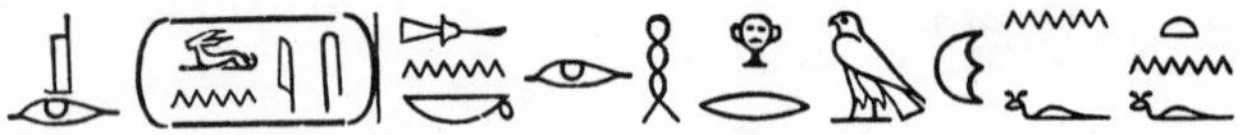

"109. Osiris Unȧs, the Eye of Horus hath been pre-
"sented unto thee, the glorious one; [these cakes] were
"baked thereby.

[*Here offer*] *four Peṭen cakes.*

"110. Osiris Unȧs, thou hast received thy head.

Recite four times, [*and offer*] *four Shes cakes.*

"111. Osiris Unȧs, thine Eye hath been presented (?)
"that thou mayest take possession of it.

Recite four times, [*and offer*] *four Ȧm-ta cakes.*

"112. Osiris Unȧs, the Eye of Horus hath been pre-
"sented unto thee, which hath been made in the form
"of fish-scales for thee.

[*Here offer*] *four Khenfu cakes.*

113. 

114. 

115. 

116. 

"113. Osiris Unås, the Eye of Horus hath been pre-"sented unto thee that it may well up [before thee].

[*Here offer*] *four vessels full of Ḥebennet cakes.*

"114. Osiris Unås, the Eye of Horus hath been pre-"sented unto thee, which was put in restraint by him "[i.e., by Set].

[*Here offer*] *four cakes of fine white flour.*

"115. Osiris Unås, the Eye of Horus hath been "seized and placed for thee in thy mouth.

[*Here offer*] *four Ȧtet cakes.*

"116. Osiris Unås, the Eye of Horus hath been pre-"sented unto thee; [it is] thy cake which thou eatest.

[*Here offer*] *four Pat cakes.*

117. 

118. 

119. 

120. 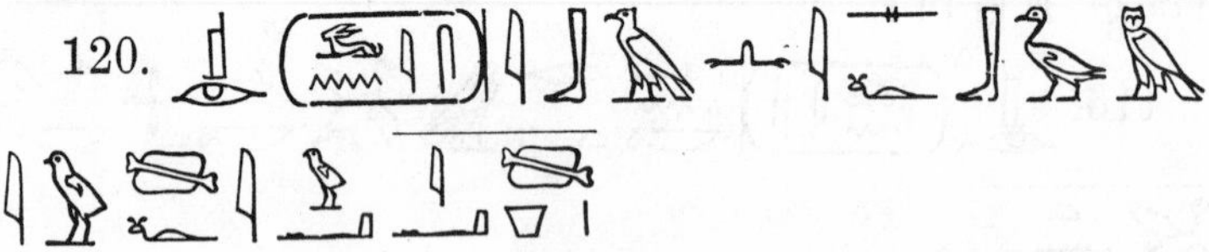

"117. Osiris Unȧs, the Eye of Horus hath been pre-"sented unto thee, which was put under restraint by "him [i.e., by Set].

[*Here offer*] *four Asht cakes* [i.e., *baked cakes*].

"118. Osiris Unȧs, his teeth (i.e., the teeth of Horus), "which are white and health-giving, have been brought "unto thee.

[*Here offer*] *four bunches of onions.*

"119. Osiris Unȧs, accept (?) the haunch [as] the "Eye of Horus.

[*Here offer*] *one haunch of beef.*

"120. Osiris Unȧs, the marked piece of the flesh and "bone from which Seb cuts not off the *ȧāu* joint.

[*Here offer*] *an ȧā joint.*

121. 

122. 

123. 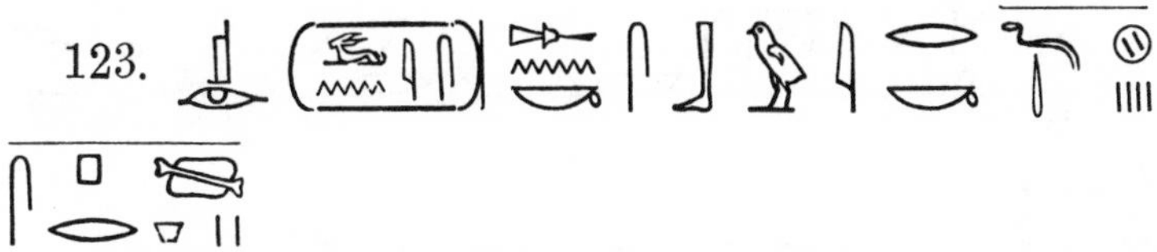

124. 

"121. Osiris Unȧs, the Eye of Horus hath been pre-"sented unto thee that it may embrace thee.

[*Here offer*] *the breast of the animal.*

"122. Osiris Unȧs, the *Sut* joint hath been presented "unto thee as the Eye of Horus.

[*Here offer*] *the Sut joint.*

"123. Osiris Unȧs, the enemies have been presented "unto thee.

Recite four times, [*and offer*] *two ribs of beef.*

"124. Osiris Unȧs, the things which are thine have "been offered to thee.

Recite four times, [*and offer*] *roasted flesh.*

125. 

126. 

127. 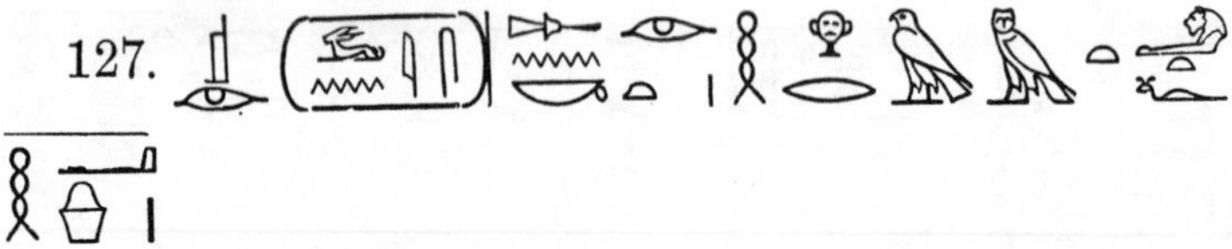

128. 

"125. Osiris Unȧs, the Eye of Horus hath been pre-
"sented unto thee that thou mayest journey with it.

[*Here offer*] *a liver.*

"126. Osiris Unȧs, the Eye of Horus hath been pre-
"sented unto thee that thou mayest go with it.

[*Here offer*] *a Nenshem joint.*

"127. Osiris Unȧs, the Eye of Horus hath been pre-
"sented unto thee in the form of his fore-quarter [i.e.,
"the fore-quarter of Set].

[*Here offer*] *a Ḥā joint.*

"128. Osiris Unȧs, accept (?) the Eye of Horus which
"is in the form of the fore-quarter of Set.

[*Here offer*] *a vessel filled with cuttings of meat from the fore-quarter.*

129. 

130. 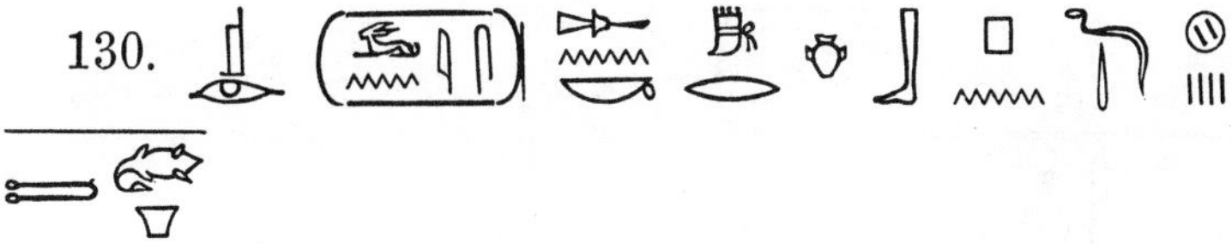

131. 

132. 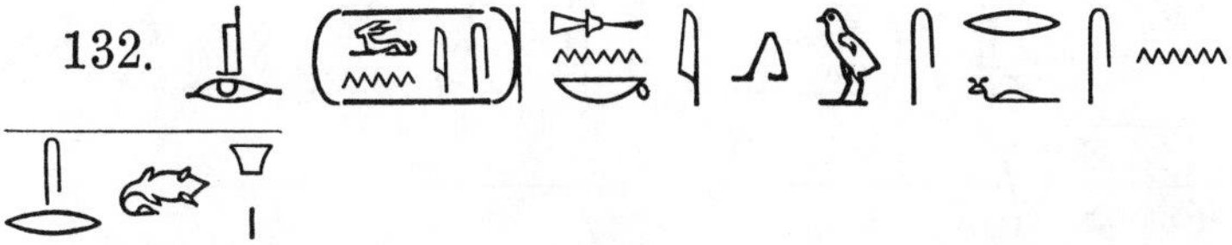

"129. Osiris Unȧs, the heads of the followers of Set "have been presented unto thee [in the form of this] "goose (*serȧ*).

[*Here offer*] *a Re goose.*

"130. Osiris Unȧs, hath been presented unto thee "this [goose] according to thy heart's desire.

Recite four times, [*and offer*] *a Therp goose.*

"131. Osiris Unȧs, the Eye of Horus hath been pre- "sented unto thee, and it is carried unto thee.

[*Here offer*] *a Set goose.*

"132. Osiris Unȧs, the Eye of Horus hath been pre- "sented unto thee [in the form of] the things which "come for thee.

[*Here offer*] *a Ser goose.*

133. 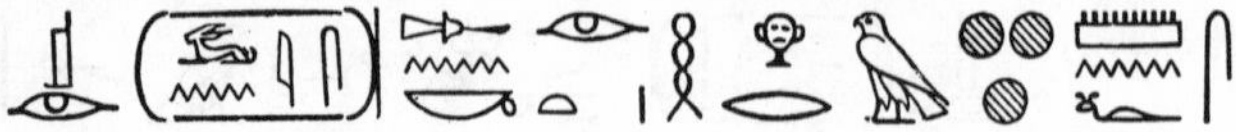

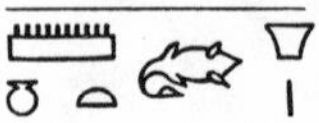

134. 

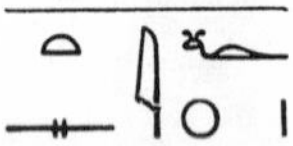

135. 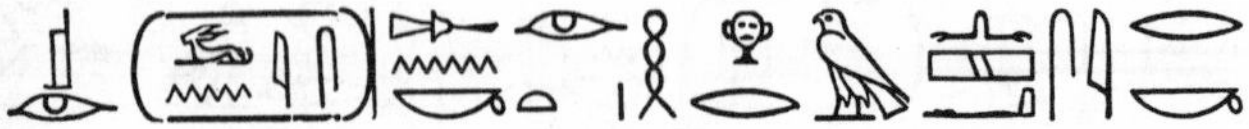

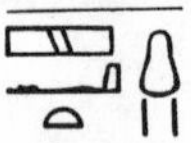

136. 

"133. Osiris Unȧs, the Eye of Horus hath been pre-"sented unto thee, the glorious one, the dove which is "thine.

[*Here offer*] *a Ment bird.*

"134. Osiris Unȧs, the Eye of Horus hath been pre-"sented unto thee, which was put under restraint by "him [i.e., by Set].

[*Here offer*] *one Sȧf cake.*

"135. Osiris Unȧs, the Eye of Horus hath been pre-"sented unto thee, and it shall not be cut off from thee.

[*Here offer*] *two Shāt cakes.*

"136. Osiris Unȧs, the Eye of Horus hath been "reckoned up [and presented] unto thee.

[*Here offer*] *two baskets of Nepat grain.*

137. 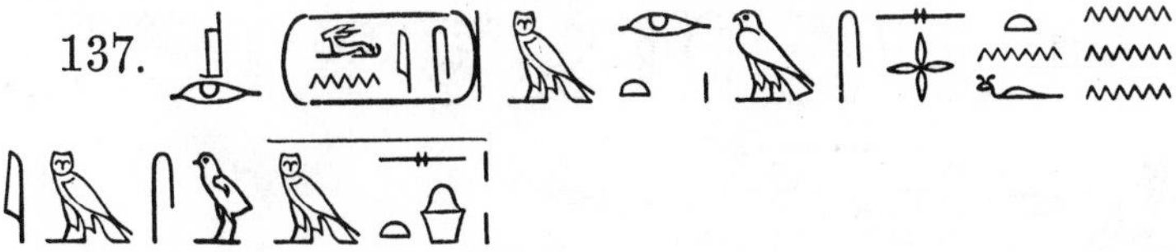

138. 

139. 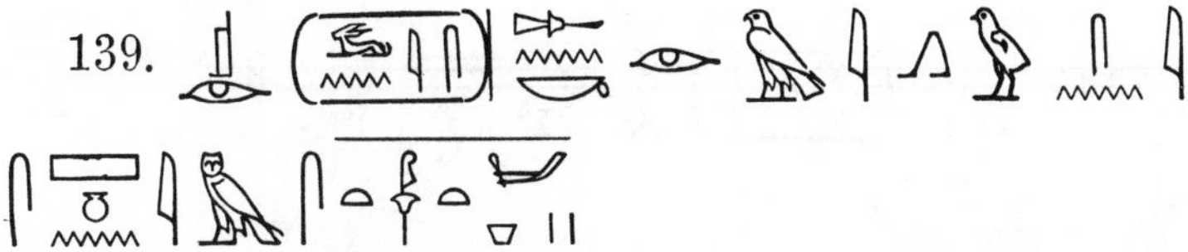

140. 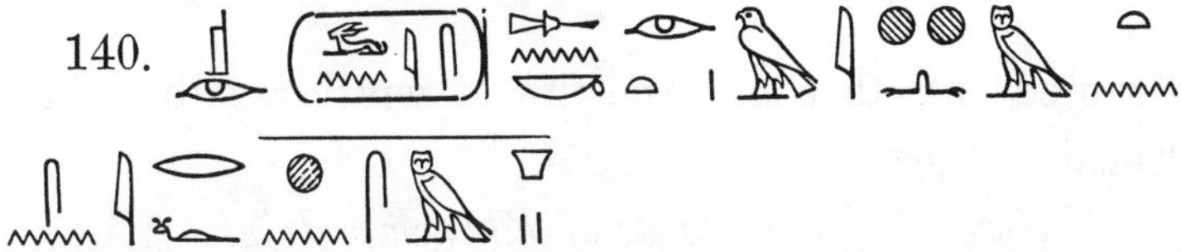

"137. Osiris Unȧs, the Eye of Horus hath been "seized (?), and the water which is in it hath been "made to be with thee.

[Here offer] two vessels of Mest grain.

"138. Osiris Unȧs, the Eye of Horus hath been pre-"sented unto thee, the little one which Set hath eaten.

[Here offer] two vessels of Tchesert drink.

"139. Osiris Unȧs, the Eye of Horus hath been pre-"sented unto thee, to which one cometh to . . . what "is in it.

[Here offer] two vessels of Tchesert drink.

"140. Osiris Unȧs, the Eye of Horus hath been pre-

141. 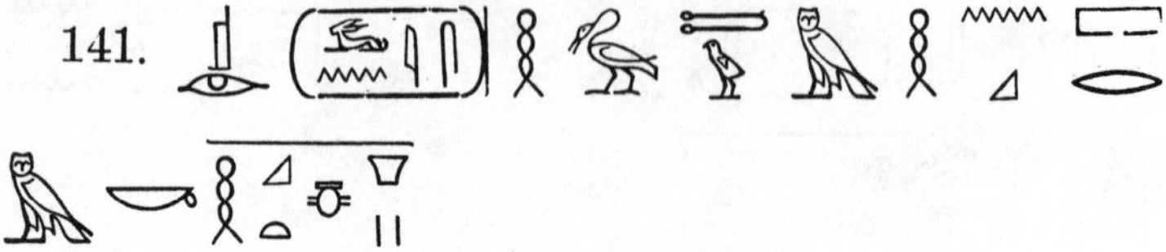

142. 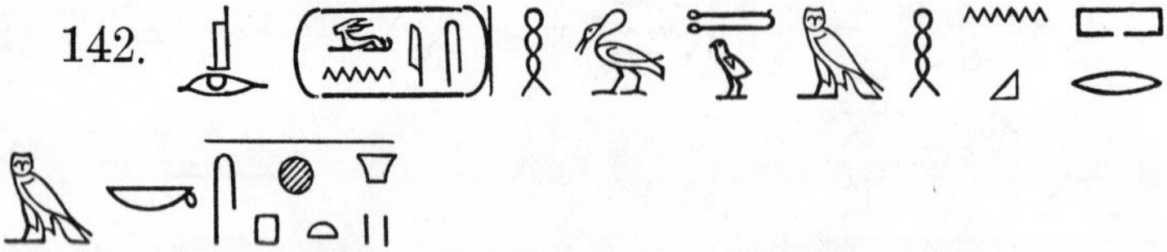

143. 

" sented unto thee, and the fire of wrath rageth in him " against thee.

[*Here offer*] *two vessels of Khenemes drink.*

" 141. Osiris Unȧs, thou art filled with that which " hath been pressed out and hath come forth from " thee.

[*Here offer*] *two vessels of Ḥeqt beer.*

" 142. Osiris Unȧs, thou art filled with that which " hath been pressed out and hath come forth from " thee.

[*Here offer*] *two vessels of Sekhpet grain.*

" 143. Osiris Unȧs, thou art filled with that which " hath been pressed out and hath come forth from " thee.

[*Here offer*] *two vessels of Pekh grain.*

144. 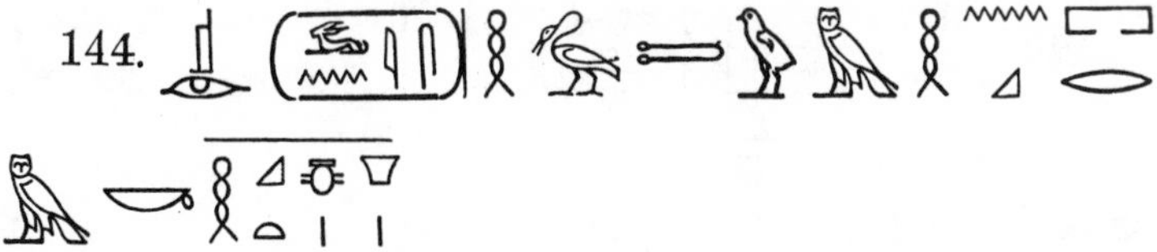

145. 

146. 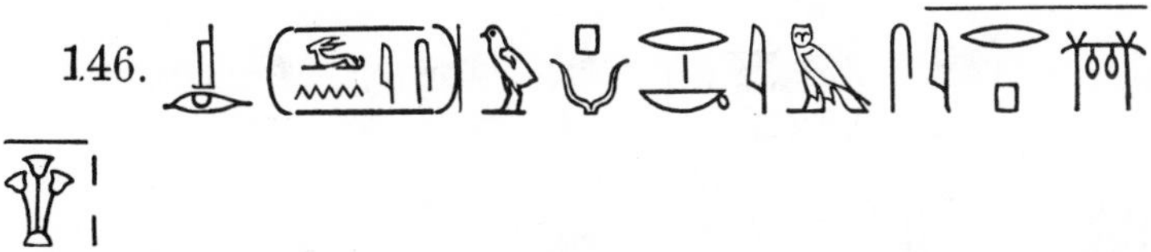

147. 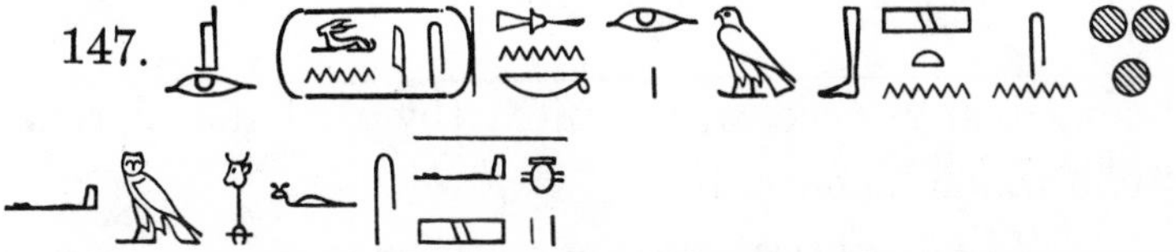

"144. Osiris Unȧs, thou art filled with that which "hath been pressed out and hath come forth from thee.

[*Here offer*] *two vessels of Ḥeqt beer.*

"145. Osiris Unȧs, the breast of Horus hath been "presented unto thee, and they [the gods] partake [of "it with thee].

[*Here offer*] *two baskets of figs.*

"146. Osiris Unȧs, thy mouth hath been opened "with it.

[*Here offer*] *two vessels of wine of the North.*

"147. Osiris Unȧs, the Eye of Horus hath been pre-

148. 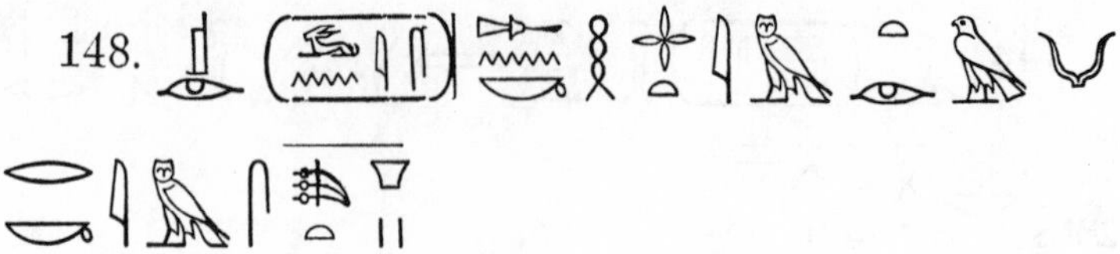

149. 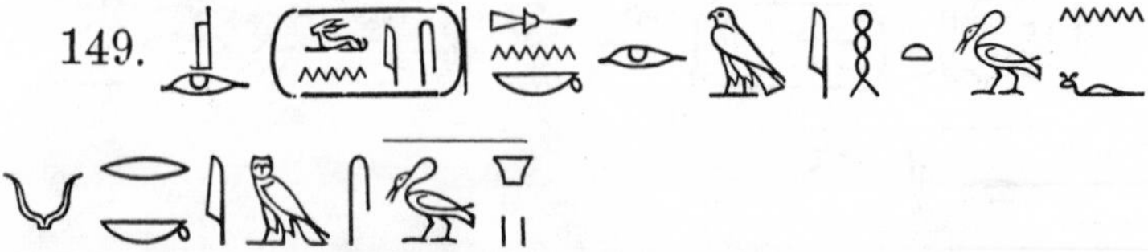

150. 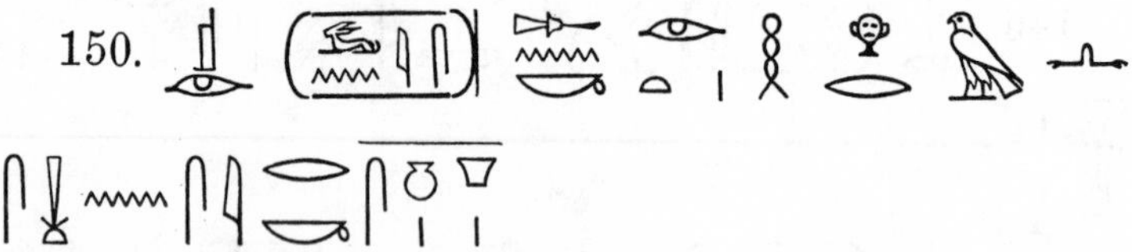

"sented unto thee, was vomited [by Set] the glorious "one which he devoured.

[*Here offer*] *two vessels of white wine.*

"148. Osiris Unȧs, the pupil of the eye of Horus "hath been presented unto thee, and thy mouth hath "been opened thereby.

[*Here offer*] *two vessels of Amt* (?) *wine.*

"149. Osiris Unȧs, the Eye of Horus hath been pre- "sented unto thee, it was snared in a net, and thy "mouth hath been opened thereby.

[*Here offer*] *two vessels of Ḥetem wine.*

"150. Osiris Unȧs, the Eye of Horus hath been pre- "sented unto thee, it hath no fellow, and it is to thee.

[*Here offer*] *two vessels of Senu wine.*

151. 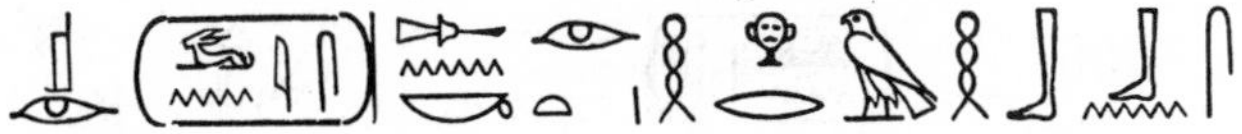

152. 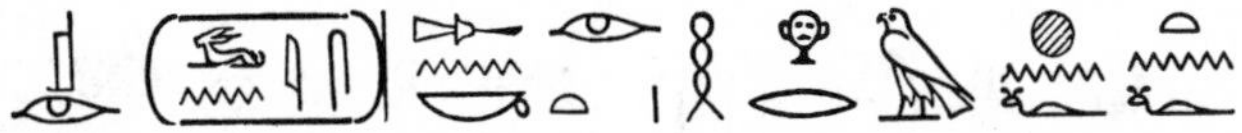

153. 

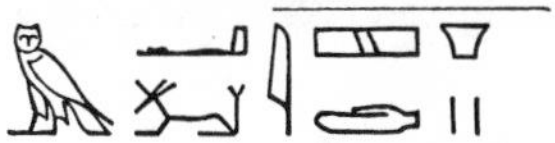

154. 

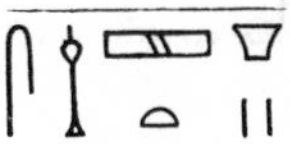

"151. Osiris Unås, the Eye of Horus hath been pre-"sented unto thee, and it hath overthrown [the com-"panions of Set].

[*Here offer*] *two vessels of Ḥebnent wine.*

"152. Osiris Unås, the Eye of Horus hath been pre-"sented unto thee, which hath been made in the form "of these scale-shaped cakes for thee.

[*Here offer*] *two vessels of Khenfu cakes.*

"153. Osiris Unås, the Eye of Horus hath been pre-"sented unto thee, which hath been snatched out of "the hand of Set.

[*Here offer*] *two vessels of Åsheṭ fruit.*

"154. Osiris Unås, the Eye of Horus hath been pre-

155. 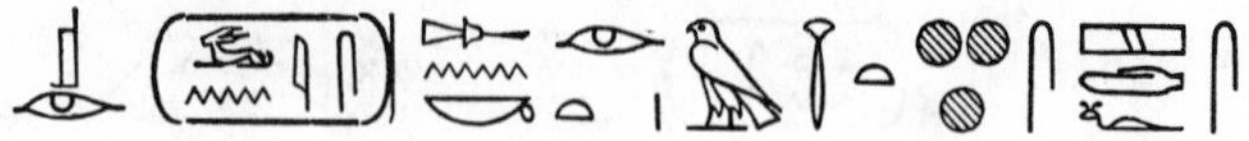

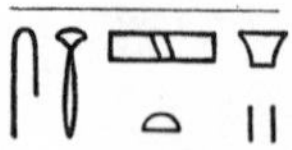

156. 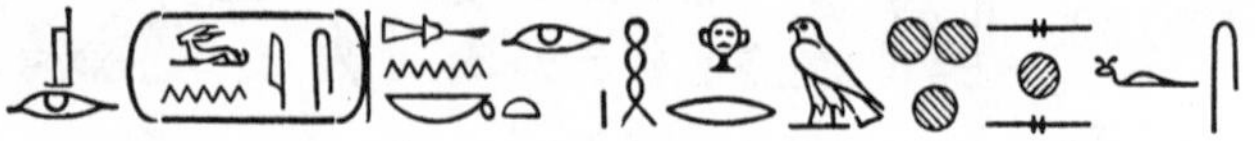

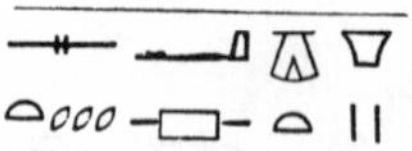

157. 

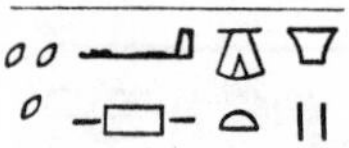

"sented unto thee, the White One, the glorious one, "and it shall serve for thy good.

[*Here offer*] *two vessels of White Seshet grain.*

"155. Osiris Unȧs, the Eye of Horus hath been pre-"sented unto thee, the Green One, the glorious one, "and it shall serve for thy food.

[*Here offer*] *two vessels of Green Seshet grain.*

"156. Osiris Unȧs, the Eye of Horus hath been pre-"sented unto thee, the glorious one, which shall turn "back [thy foes].

[*Here offer*] *two vessels of roasted grain.*

"157. Osiris Unȧs, the Eye of Horus hath been pre-"sented unto thee, the glorious one, which shall turn "back [thy foes].

[*Here offer*] *two vessels of roasted grain.*

158. 

159. 

160. 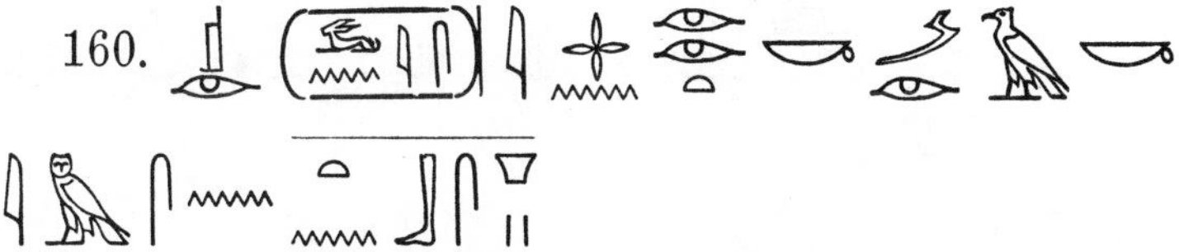

161. 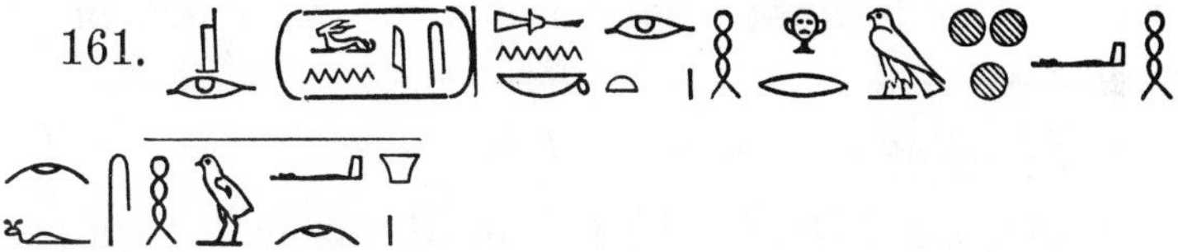

"158. Osiris Unȧs, the Eye of Horus hath been pre-
"sented unto thee, behold it is of Baba (?).

[*Here offer*] *two vessels of Babat fruit.*

"159. Osiris Unȧs, the Eye of Horus hath been pre-
"sented unto thee, which burned with fire against them (i.e., the fiends of Set).

[*Here offer*] *two vessels of Nebes fruit.*

"160. Osiris Unȧs, thine eyes have been made to
"open, and thou seest with them.

[*Here offer*] *two vessels of Tenbes cakes.*

"161. Osiris Unȧs, the Eye of Horus hath been pre-

162.

163.

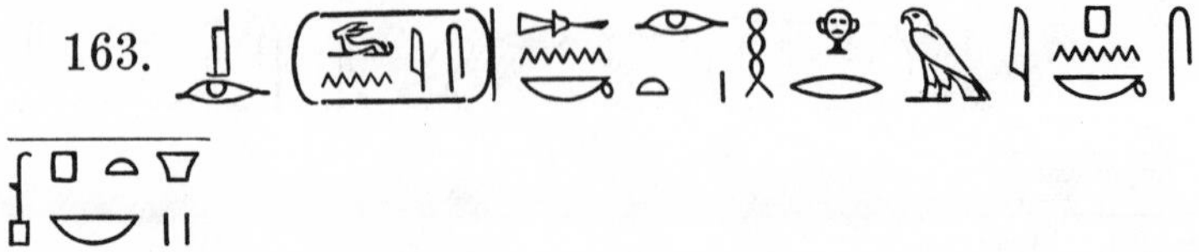

164.

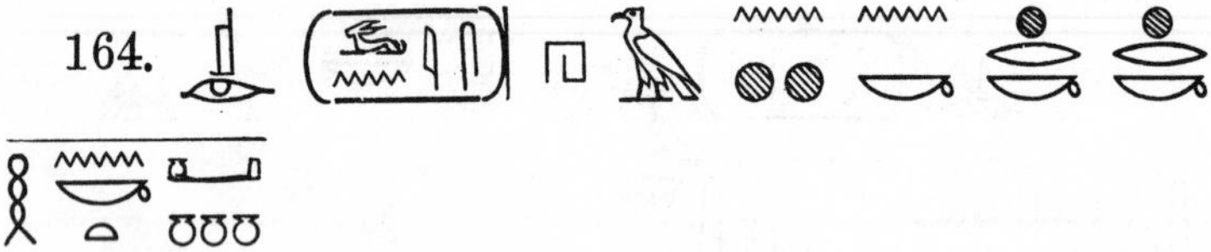

"sented unto thee, the glorious one who was in his "throat (?).

[*Here offer*] *two vessels of Ḥuā grain.*

"162. Osiris Unȧs, the Eye of Horus hath been pre- "sented unto thee, the sweetness of which followeth "thee (?).

[*Here offer*] *two vessels of things of sweetness of all kinds.*

"163. Osiris Unȧs, the Eye of Horus hath been pre- "sented unto thee, and thou hast had experience "thereof.

[*Here offer*] *two baskets of spring products* (i.e., *fruit, flowers, vegetables*).

"164. Osiris Unȧs, thou hast swallowed the things "which belong to thee."

[*Here offer*] *gifts of all kinds.*

The following section is taken from the text of Pepi II. Nefer-ka-Rā (Maspero, *Pyramides*, pl. v.).

501. 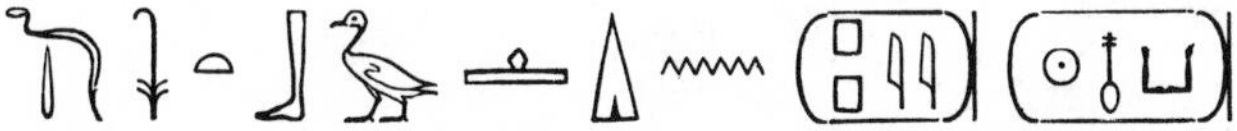

502. 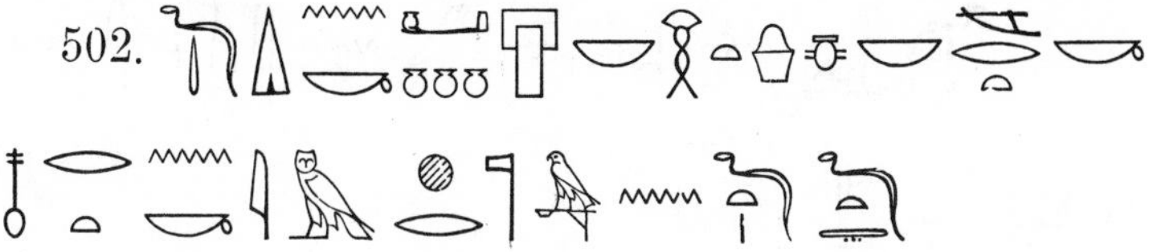

503. 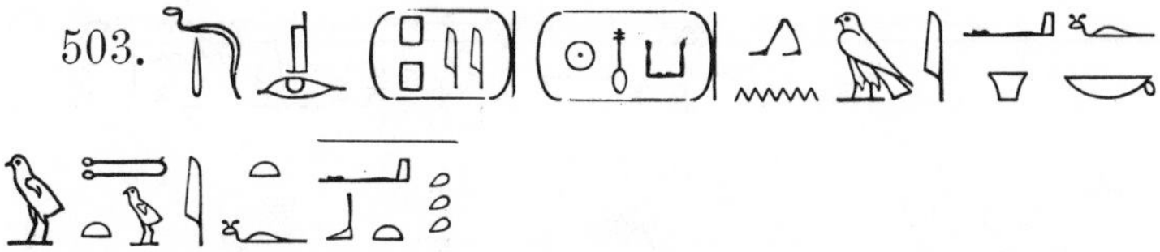

·504. 

505. 

506. 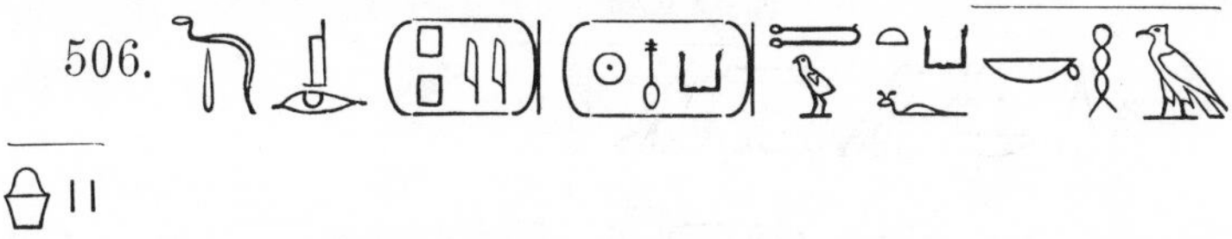

507. 

508. 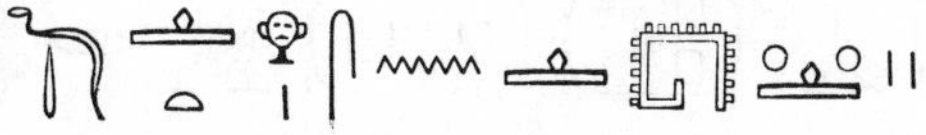

509. 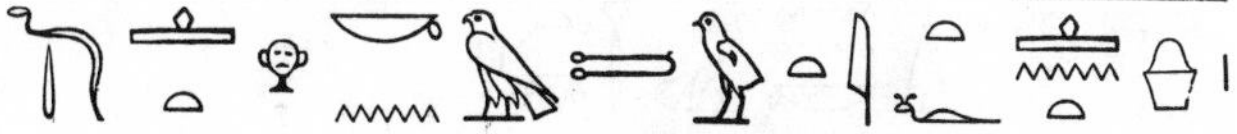

510. 

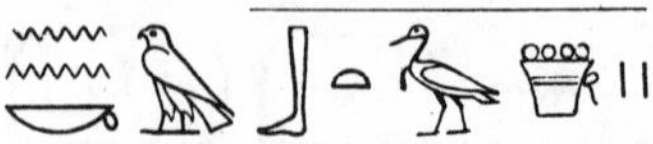

511. 

512. 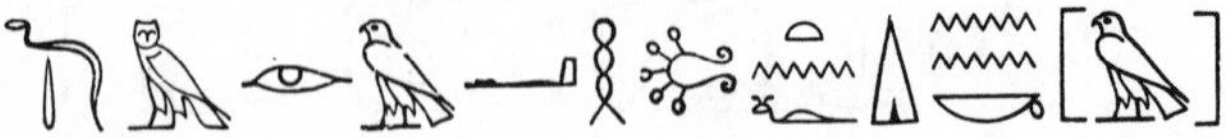

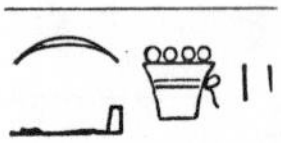

513. 

514. 

515. 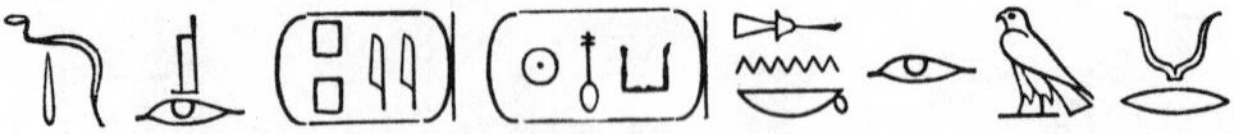

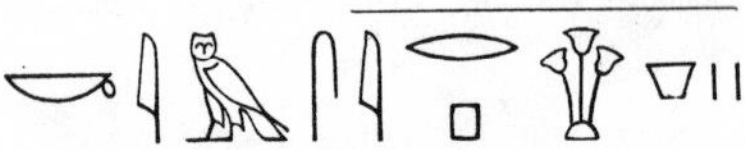

516. 

517. 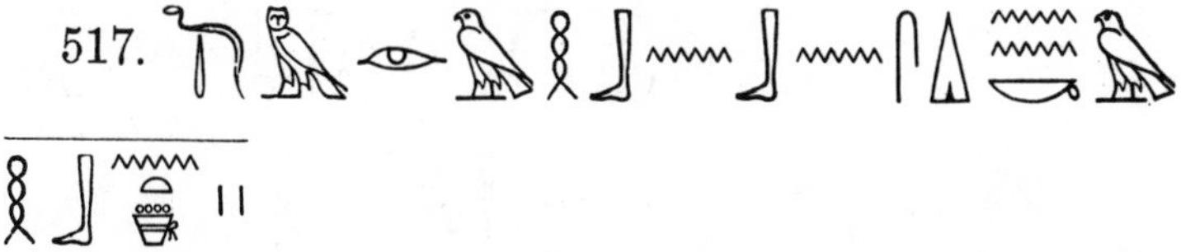

518. 

519. 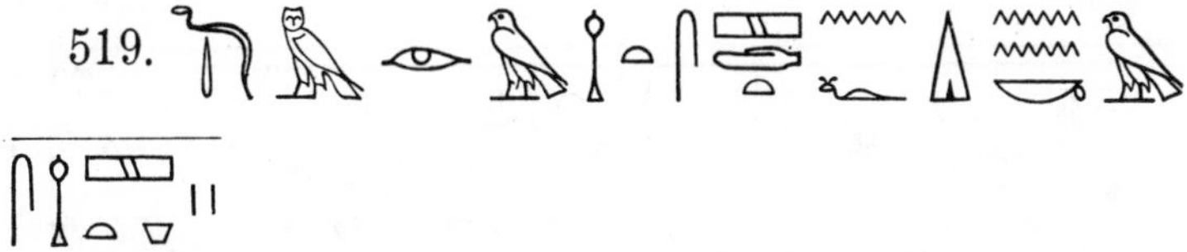

520. 

521. 

522. 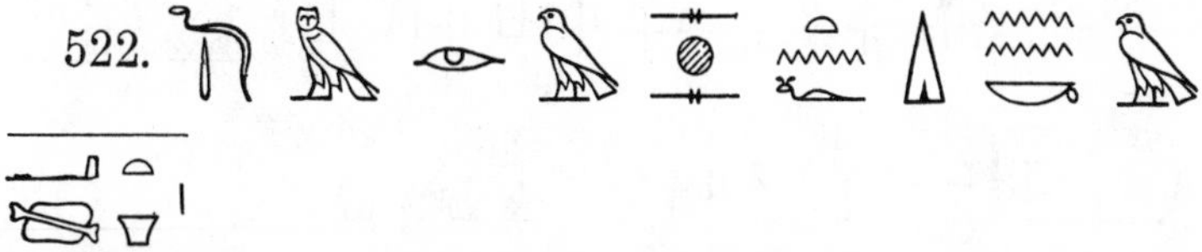

523. 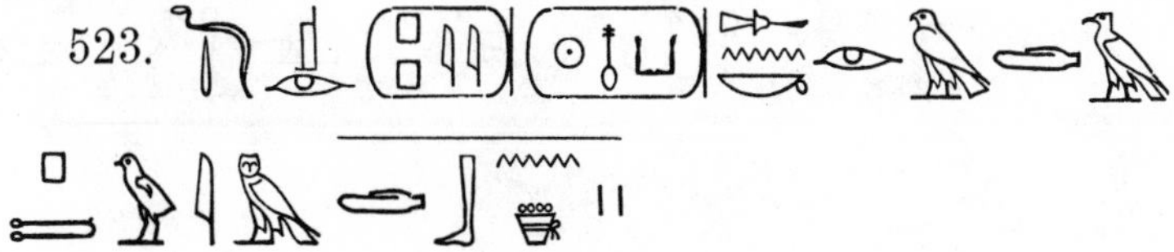

524. 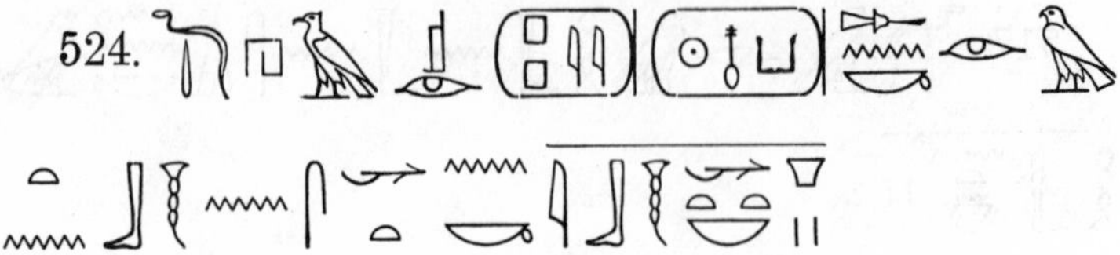

525. 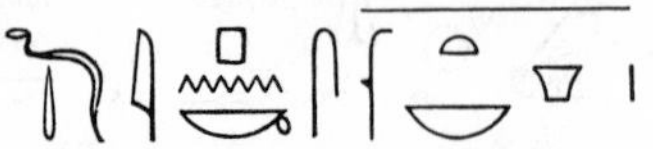

526. 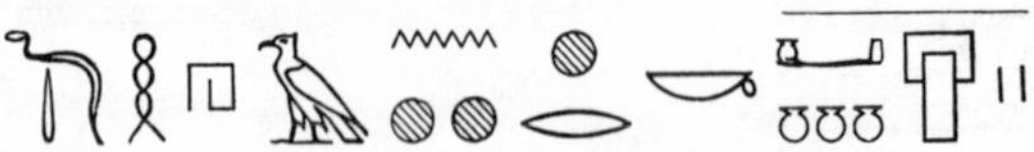

527. 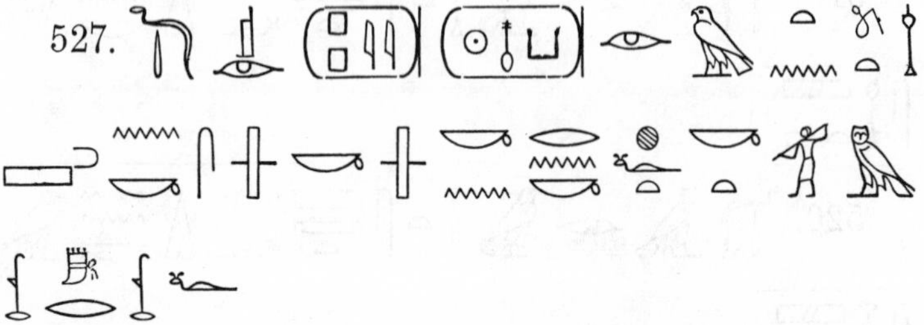

528. 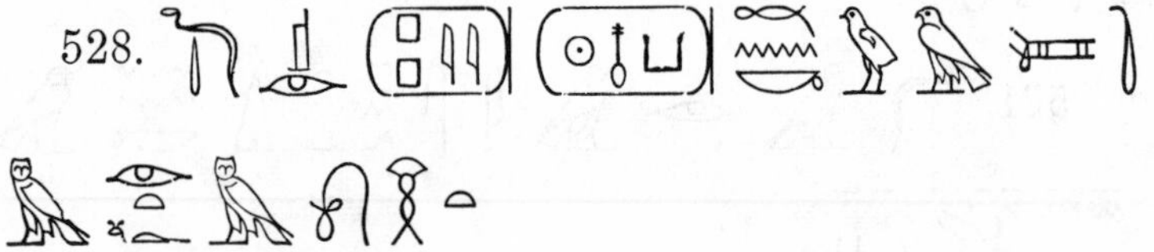

529. 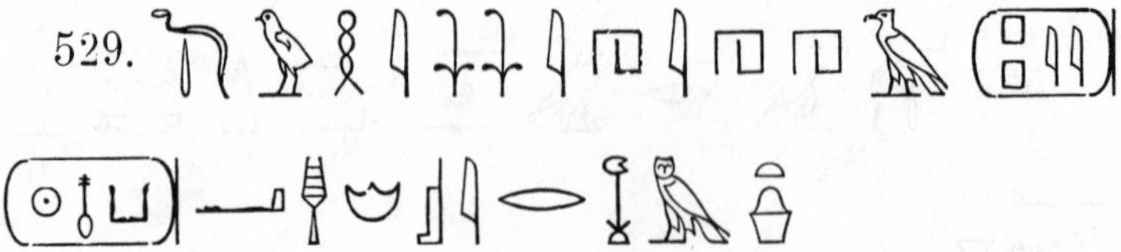

530. 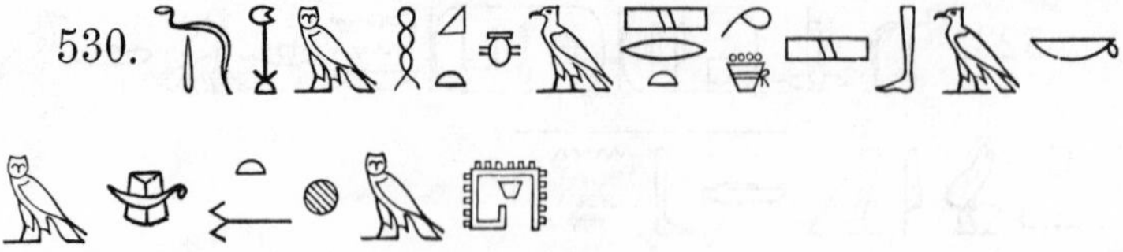

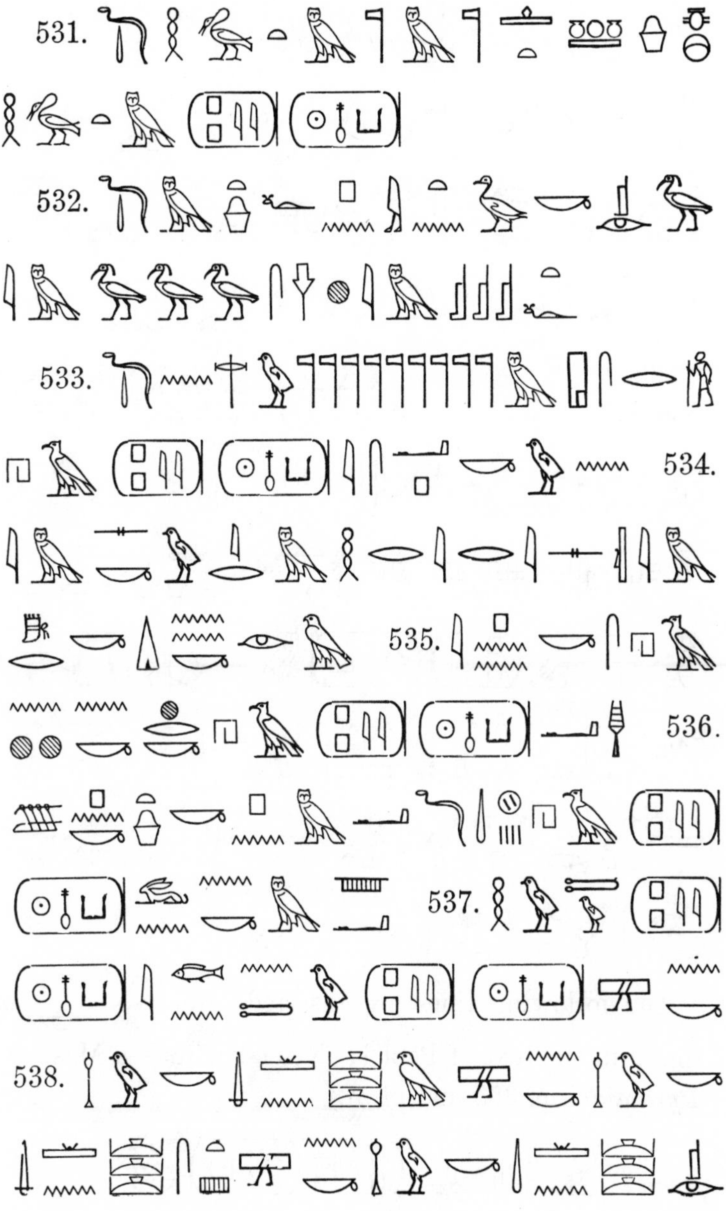
531.
532.
533.
534.
535.
536.
537.
538.

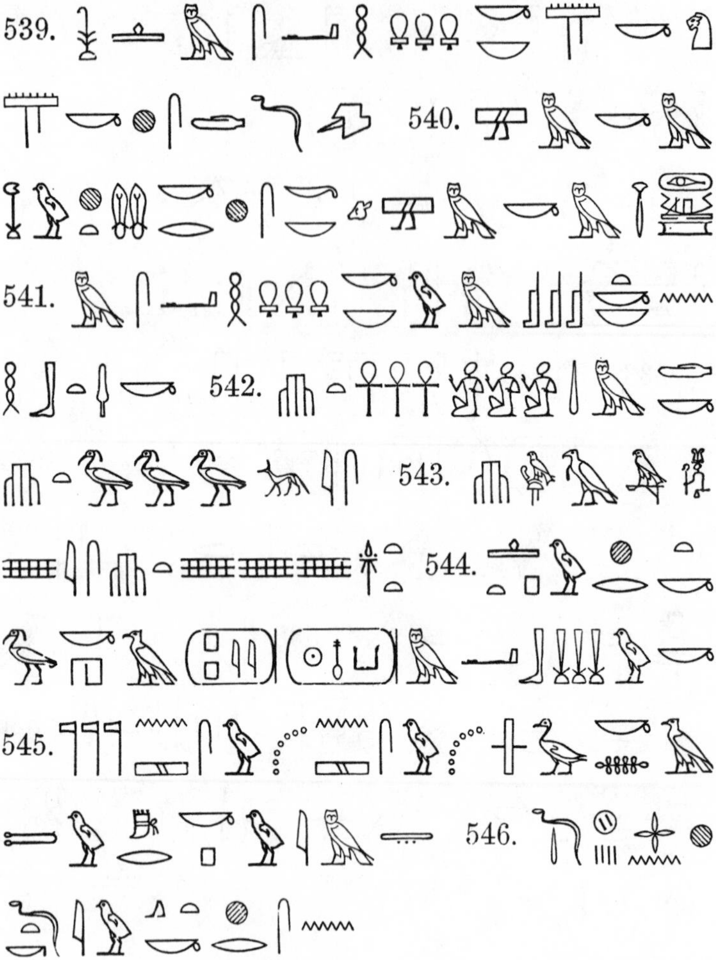

The following lines are inserted after  of line 9 in the text of Pepi II. Nefer-ka-Rā (see Maspero, *Pyramides*, p. 355 and pl. ii.).

339. 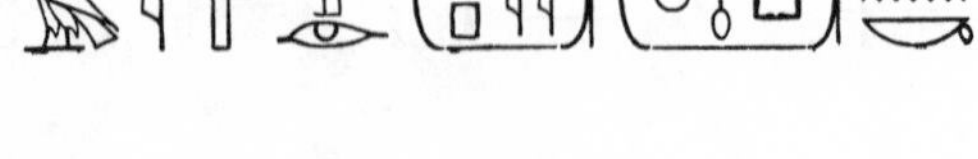

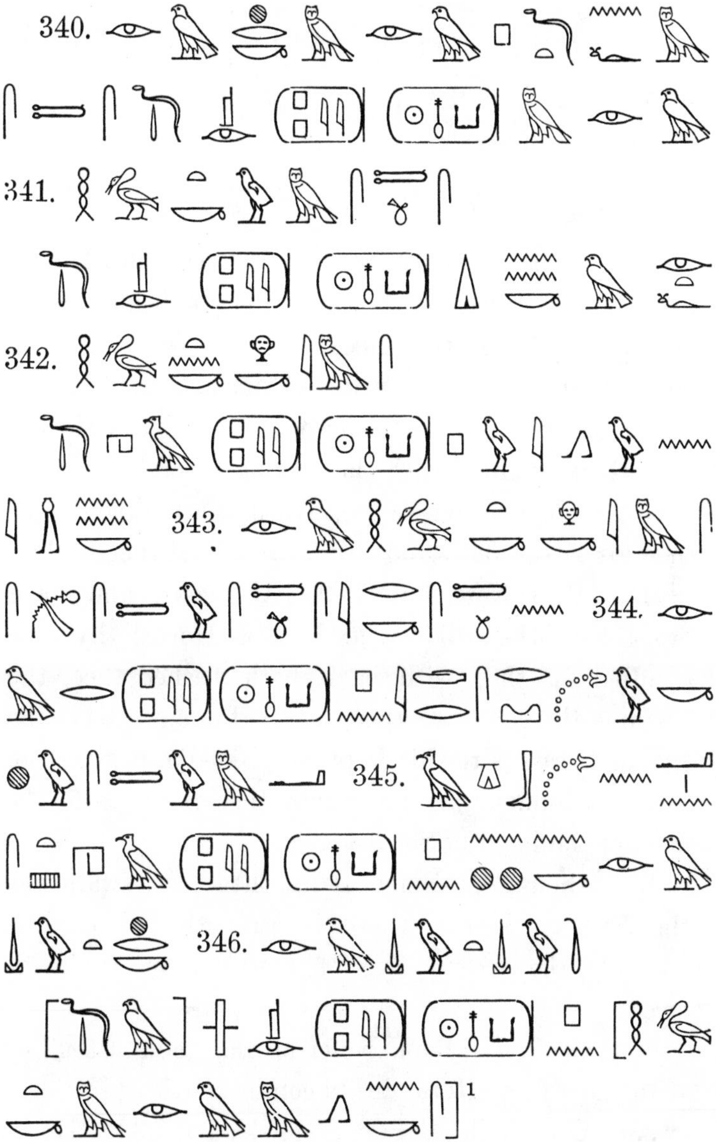

[1] Supplied from line 46.

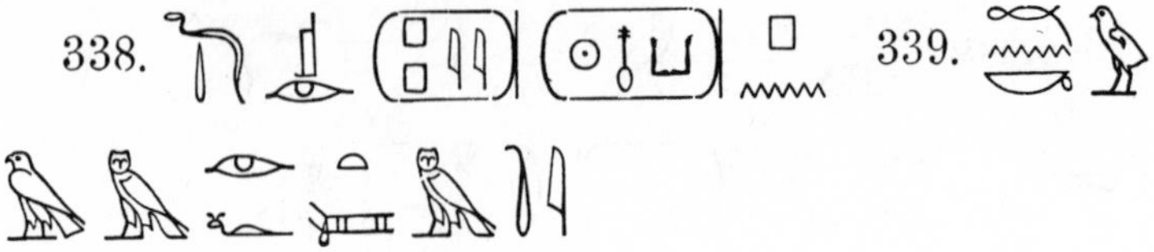

After line 9 the text of Pepi II. has :—

"339. Horus who is there. Osiris Pepi Nefer-ka-Rā, "the Eye of Horus hath been presented unto thee, "340. [it is] before thee, accept (?) the Eye of Horus, "which is spread abroad in its perfume.

"Osiris Pepi Nefer-ka-Rā, accept (?) the Eye of Horus; "341. thou art filled with the perfume thereof.

"Osiris Pepi Nefer-ka-Rā, Horus hath given unto "thee his Eye, 342. and thy face is filled therewith.

"Hail, Pepi Nefer-ka-Rā, I have come and have "brought to thee 343. the Eye of Horus, thy face "is filled for thee with it, it hath washed thee, the "perfume thereof is to thee, the perfume of 344. the "Eye of Horus is to this Pepi Nefer-ka-Rā, it giveth to "thee thy humours, it protecteth thee from 345. the "flood of the hand of Set.

"Hail, thou Pepi Nefer-ka-Rā, thou hast swallowed "the Eye of Horus, there is strength before thee. "346. By the strong Eye of Horus thou art made "strong.

"O thou Osiris Pepi Nefer-ka-Rā, thou art filled "with the Eye of Horus in its coming to thee.

"338. O thou Osiris Pepi Nefer-ka-Rā, 339. Horus "hath filled thee completely with his Eye."

After line 13 the text of Pepi II. has:—

351. [hieroglyphs]

[hieroglyphs]

352. [hieroglyphs]

[hieroglyphs]

353. [hieroglyphs]

[hieroglyphs] 354. [hieroglyphs]

[hieroglyphs]

355. [hieroglyphs]

[hieroglyphs]

After line 65 the text of Pepi II. has:—

321. [hieroglyphs]

[hieroglyphs]

322. [hieroglyphs]

[hieroglyphs]

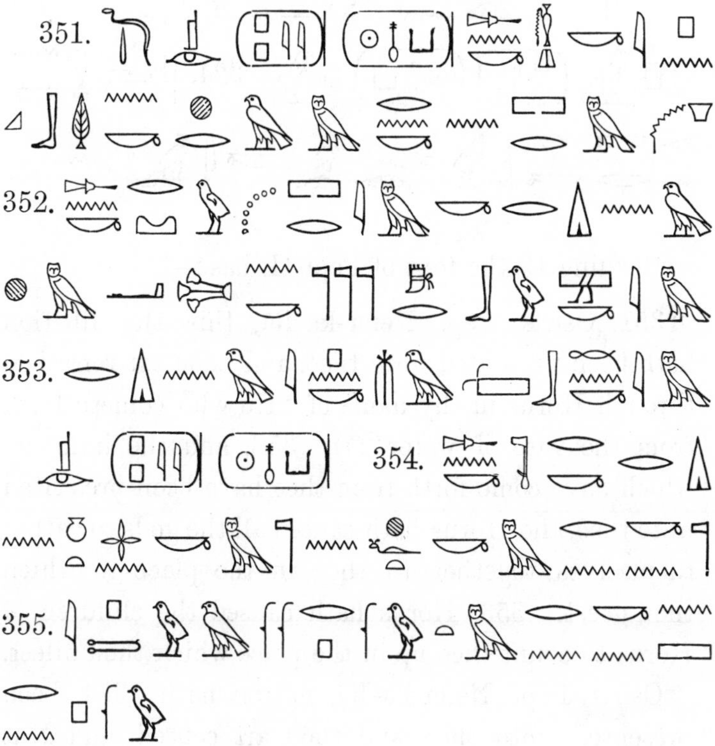

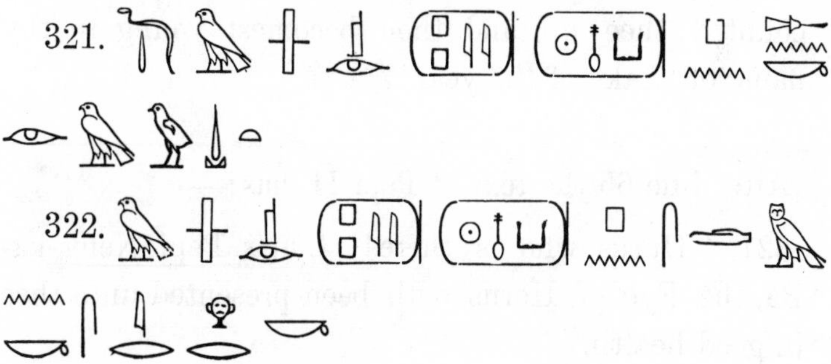

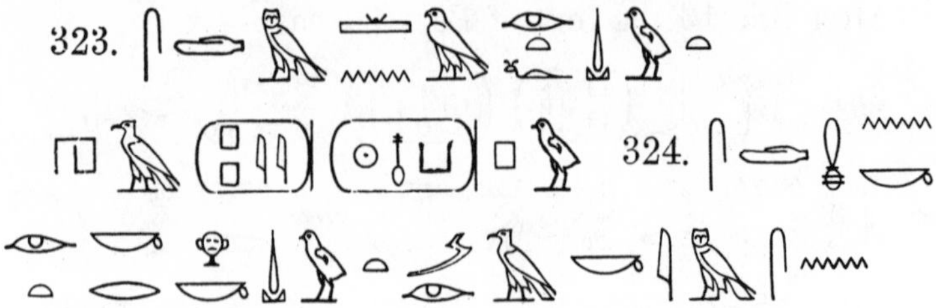

After line 13 the text of Pepi II. has :—

"351. Osiris Pepi Nefer-ka-Rā, this thy libation "hath been presented unto thee, and thou art refreshed "through Horus in thy name of 'He who cometh forth "from the vase of water' (?), 352. and the humours "which have come forth from thee have been presented "unto thee, and Horus hath caused all the gods to gather "themselves together to thee in the place to which "thou goest. 353. Horus hath caused the children of "Horus to count thee up in the place which thou fillest.

"Osiris Pepi Nefer-ka-Rā, natron hath 354. been "presented unto thee, and thou art censed, and Nut "hath given thee to be as a god to thine enemy in thy "name of 'God.' 355. Horus of the two years hath "counted thee up, and thou becomest young in thy "name of 'Lake of the year.'"

After line 65 the text of Pepi II. has :—

321. "Horus who is there! Osiris Pepi Nefer-ka-"Rā, the Eye of Horus hath been presented unto thee "in good health.

"322. Horus who is there! Osiris Pepi Nefer-ka-"Rā, I anoint for thee thy face with it, [and it is in "good health, even as] 323. when Horus anointed his "Eye it was in good health.

"Hail, thou Pepi Nefer-ka-Rā, 324. thou hast "anointed thine eyes in thy face and it is in good "health, and thou seest with them."

THE LITURGY OF FUNERARY OFFERINGS.

II. From the Tomb of Peṭā-Ȧmen-Ȧp.

1.

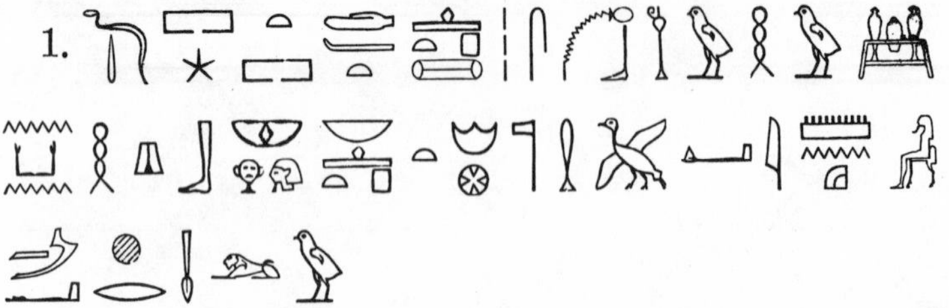

2.

1. The chamber wherein the ceremony Ṭuat shall be performed having been provided with offerings, the altar shall be purified for the Ka (or the Double) of the chief Kher ḥeb of Neb-ḥetepet, the priest Peṭā-Ȧmen-Ȧp.

The following shall be recited by the priest four times:—

"2. O Osiris, that which is hateful hath been seized "and carried off for thee. O chief Kher ḥeb Peṭā-"Ȧmen-Ȧp, that which is spoken in thy name Thoth

3. 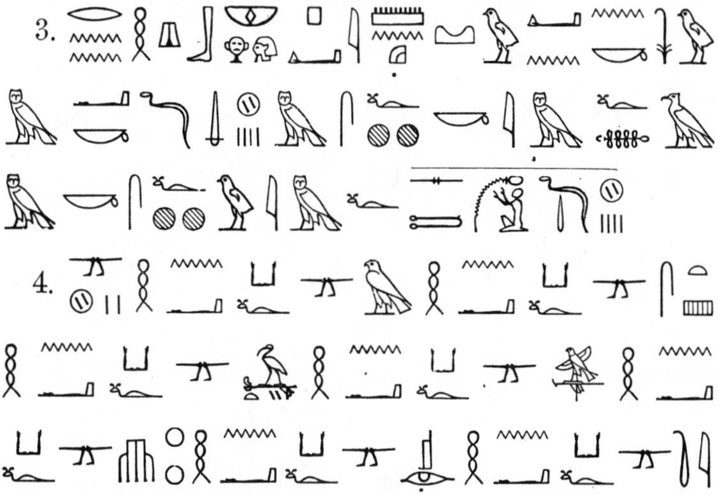

"goeth about with and carrieth it to Osiris. What "hath been spoken in

"3. the name of the chief KHER ḤEB PEṬĀ-ÅMEN-ÅP "[of] evil hath been brought, and I have placed it for "thee in thy hand."

Here water shall be sprinkled, and the following words shall be recited four times:—

"the fluid [of life] shall not be destroyed in thee, "and thou shalt not be destroyed in it."

During the recital of the following words incense shall be burned.

"4. Let him that advanceth advance with his KA. "Horus advanceth with his KA. Set advanceth with "his KA. Thoth advanceth with his KA. Sep ad-"vanceth with his KA. Khenti-maati advanceth with "his KA. Osiris advanceth with his KA. Let thy

5.
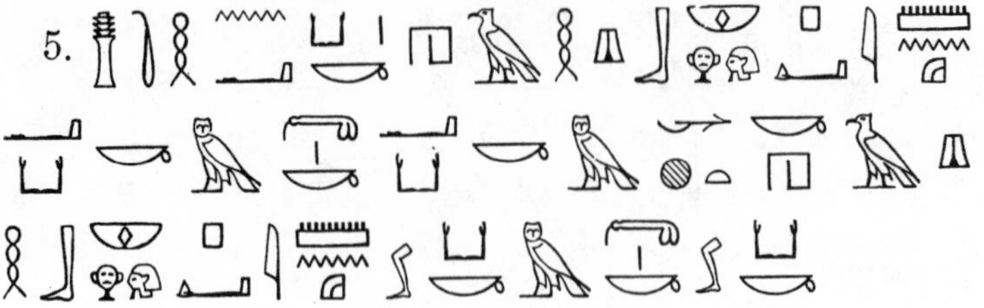

6.

7.
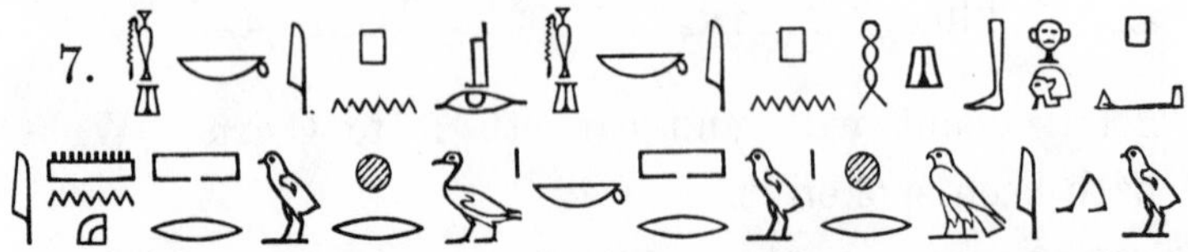

"5. Ṭeṭ advance with thy KA. Hail, chief KHER ḤEB "PEṬĀ-ÅMEN-ÅP! The arm of thy KA is before thee, "the arm of thy KA is behind thee. Hail, chief KHER "ḤEB PEṬĀ-ÅMEN-ÅP! The foot of thy KA is before "thee, the foot of thy Ka

"6. is behind thee. Hail, chief KHER ḤEB PEṬĀ-"ÅMEN-ÅP! I have given unto thee the Eye of Horus, "thy face is filled therewith, and the perfume of the "Eye of Horus is to thee."

The priest shall say the following words four times, and a libation, made with one grain of Shet-pet incense and one grain of incense of Nekheb, shall be poured out during their recital.

"7. This libation is for thee, O Osiris, this libation

8. 

9. 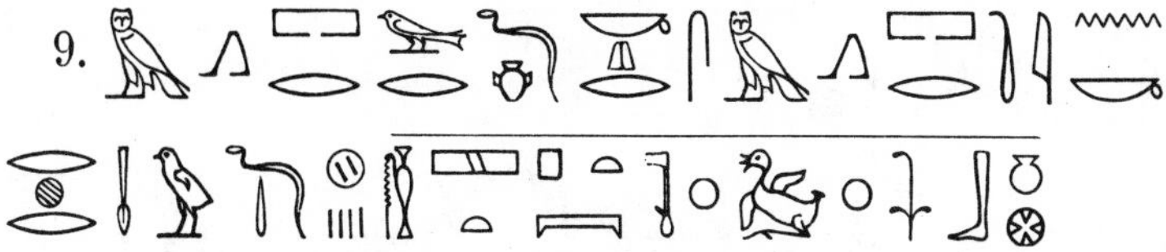

10. 

"is for thee, O chief KHER ḤEB PEṬĀ-ÀMEN-ÀP, coming "forth from thy son, coming forth from Horus.

"8. I have come, and I have brought unto thee the "Eye of Horus, that thy heart may be refreshed thereby. "I have brought it unto thee under thy feet, and have "presented unto thee the efflux which cometh forth "therefrom.

"9. No stoppage of thy heart shall arise therefrom, "and there shall be a coming forth to thee through "the word which is spoken (or the voice)."

Here pour out water in which a cake of incense of Nekhebet of the South hath been dissolved, and say:—

"10. [Cleansing by] *semmânu* (i.e., water of natron)! "[Cleansing by] *semmânu!* Open thy mouth, O chief

11.

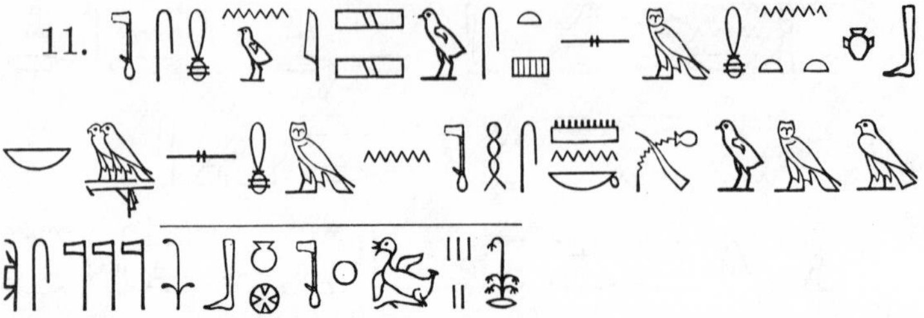

12.

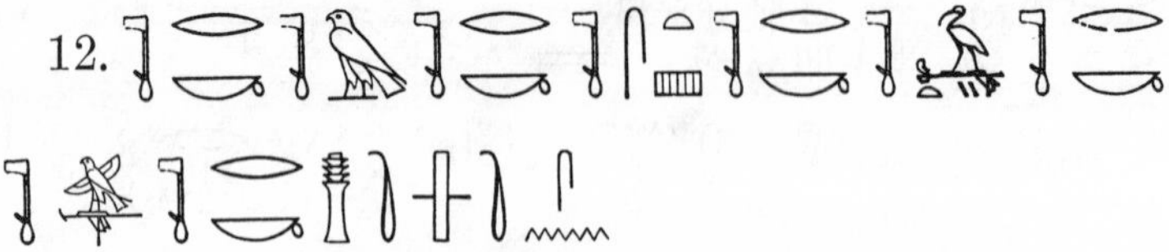

"KHER ḤEB PEṬĀ-ÅMEN-ÅP, and taste thou the taste "thereof in the divine hall. An emission of Horus

"11. is the cleansing water of natron, an emission of "Set is the cleansing water of natron, and the cleansing "water of natron stablisheth the heart of the Two "Divine Lords. Thou art cleansed with natron, and "thou art a pure being among the divine Followers of "Horus."

Here shall be poured out water in which a cake of incense of the North from Shet-pet hath been dissolved.

"12. Thou art purified with natron, and Horus is "purified with natron. Thou art purified with natron, "and Set is purified with natron. Thou art purified "with natron, and Thoth is purified with natron. Thou "art purified with natron, and Sep is purified with "natron. Thou art purified with natron, and thou art "stablished among them.

13. 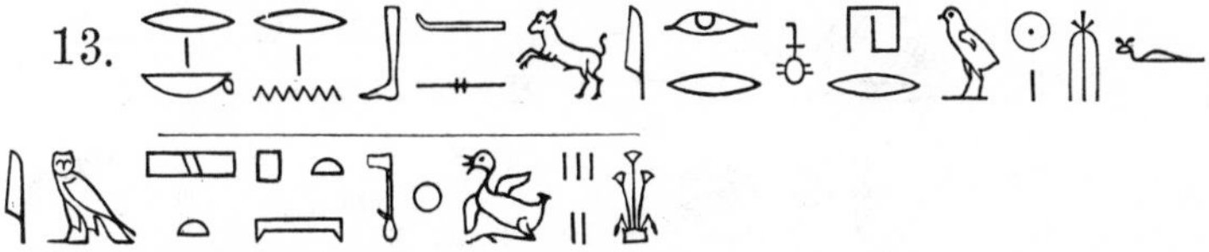

14. 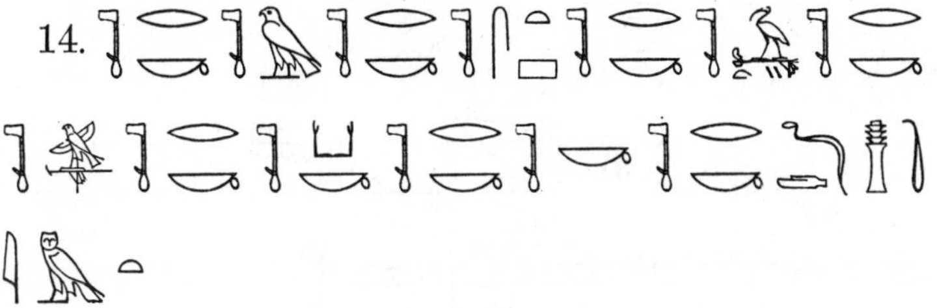

15. 

"13. Thy mouth is the mouth of a sucking calf on "the day of his birth."

Here take a cake of incense, and lift it up to the face, and say:—

"14. Thou art purified with natron, and Horus is "purified with natron. Thou art purified with natron, "and Set is purified with natron. Thou art purified "with natron, and Thoth is purified with natron. Thou "art purified with natron, and Sep is purified with "natron. Thou art purified with natron, and thy KA is "purified with natron. Thou art purified with natron. "Thou art purified with natron. Thou art purified "with natron, O thou who art stablished among

"15. the gods thy brethren. Thou art purified in "respect of thy head. Thou art purified in respect of "thy mouth. Thy bones have been made pure wholly.

16. 

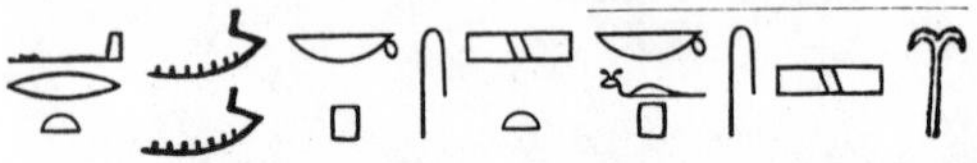

17. 

"Thou art filled by that which cometh to thee, O PEṬĀ-"ÅMEN-ÅP. I have given unto thee the Eye of Horus, "and thy face is filled therewith, and it spreadeth "abroad its odour."

Here the priest shall take the instrument Kef-pesesh (i.e., "*Overcomer of the division*"), *and shall say:*—

"16. Hail, chief KHER ḤEB PEṬĀ-ÅMEN-ÅP, thy two "jaw-bones which were separated have been established "(i.e., restored to their former state).

Here the priest shall take the ⌝ *of iron of the South and the* ⌝ *of iron of the North, and shall say:*—

"17. Hail, chief KHER ḤEB PEṬĀ-ÅMEN-ÅP! Thy

18.

19.

20.

"mouth hath been opened for thee, O Erpā, Ḥā Prince, "chief KHER ḤEB PEṬĀ-ÅMEN-ÅP.

"18. Hail, chief KHER ḤEB PEṬĀ-ÅMEN-ÅP! Thy "mouth hath been opened for thee, O Erpā, Ḥā Prince, "chief KHER ḤEB PEṬĀ-ÅMEN-ÅP."

Here shall the priest take cakes of cheese (?) of the South and of the North, and say:—

"19. Hail, chief KHER ḤEB PEṬĀ-ÅMEN-ÅP, the Eye "of Horus hath been presented unto thee, and he "cometh with it. I have brought it unto thee, place "thou it in thy mouth."

Here shall the priest take Sheku cakes, and say:—

"20. Hail, chief KHER ḤEB PEṬĀ-ÅMEN-ÅP! *Sheku* "cakes have been presented unto thee, O Osiris, chief "KHER ḤEB PEṬĀ-ÅMEN-ÅP."

21.

22.

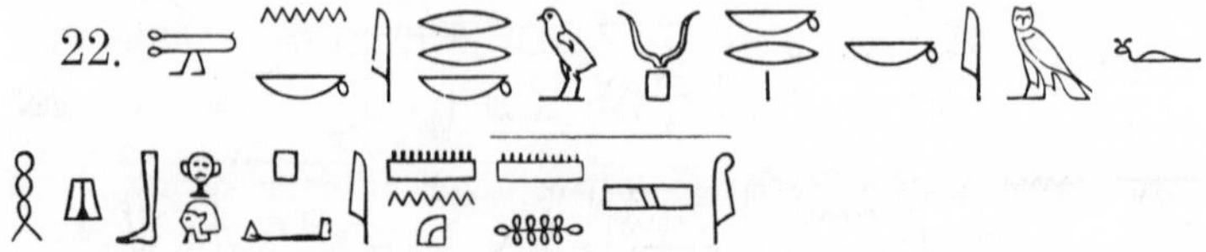

23.

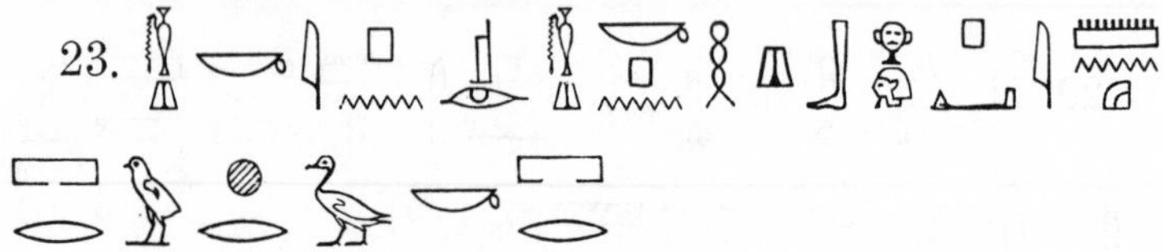

Here shall the priest take a vessel of milk and a vessel of water, and say:—

"21. [That which floweth] from the breast of Horus, "and is of his body, hath been presented unto thee for "thy mouth. That which cometh from the breast of "thy sister Isis, the emission of the mother, 22. hath "been seized by thee for thy mouth, and thou openest "thy mouth by means of it, O chief KHER ḤEB PEṬĀ-"ÅMEN-ÅP."

Here shall the priest pour out fresh water of the North and of the South, and say:—

"23. This [is] a libation unto thee, Osiris, a libation "unto thee, O chief KHER ḤEB PEṬĀ-ÅMEN-ÅP, which "cometh forth from thy son. 24. I have come and I "have brought unto thee the Eye of Horus whereby "thy heart shall be refreshed. I have brought it to

24. 

25. 

26. 

"thy feet, and have presented unto thee that which "hath flowed forth from thee. No stoppage of thy "heart [shall there be] to thee. Having it, 25. a "going forth [of things (or, persons)] shall there be to "thee through the word."

The above shall be said four times.

Here shall the priest take a black vessel and a white vessel, each containing one hathes measure, on the right and left, and say:—

"26. That which cometh forth from the two Eyes of "Horus, the White and the Black, thou hast taken "possession of, and when they are [set] before thee "they illumine for thee thy face."

27. 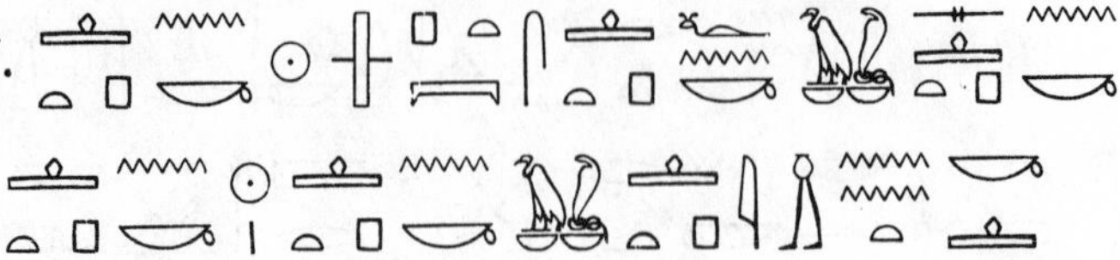

28. 

29. 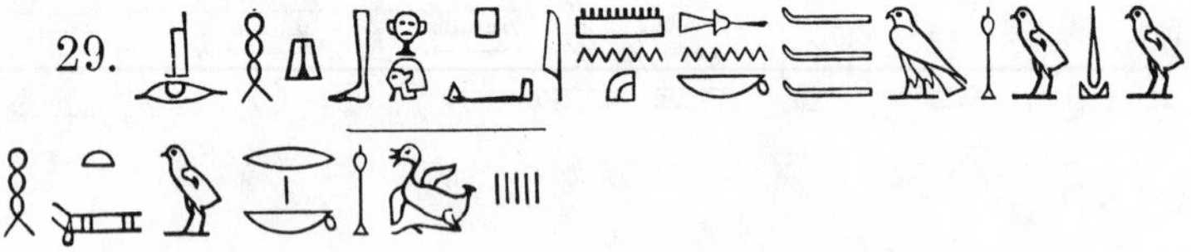

Here shall the priest take a cake of Ḥem bread of the journey for the lifting up of the face, and say:—

"27. Rā (i.e., Day) maketh an offering unto thee in "the sky. The South and the North make an offering "unto thee. Ḳerḥ (i.e., the Night) maketh an offering "unto thee, and the Day maketh an offering unto thee. "The South and the North make an offering unto thee. "An offering is brought unto thee. An offering 28. "thou seest, of an offering thou hearest. There is an "offering before thee, an offering behind thee, an offer- "ing with thee."

Here shall the priest present five bunches of onions, and say:—

"29. O Osiris, the chief KHER ḤEB PEṬĀ-ÅMEN-ÅP,

30. 

31. 

"are presented unto thee the white teeth of Horus for "the journey, so that they may fill thy mouth."

Here shall the priest offer one Uṭen cake [as an offering] for the lifting up of the face, and shall say four times:—

"30, 31. 'SUTEN ṬĀ ḤETEP' for the KA of the chief "KHER ḤEB PEṬĀ-ȦMEN-ȦP."

And he shall say four times:—

"'SUTEN ṬĀ ḤETEP' for the KA of the chief KHER "ḤEB PEṬĀ-ȦMEN-ȦP."

And the KHER ḤEB *shall say, whilst the* SMER *priest bringeth the two halves of the Uṭen cake for the opening of the mouth, four times:—*

"O Osiris, the chief KHER ḤEB PEṬĀ-ȦMEN-ȦP, the "Eye of Horus hath been presented unto thee, thy "bread which thou eatest, and thy mouth hath been "opened thereby."

32.
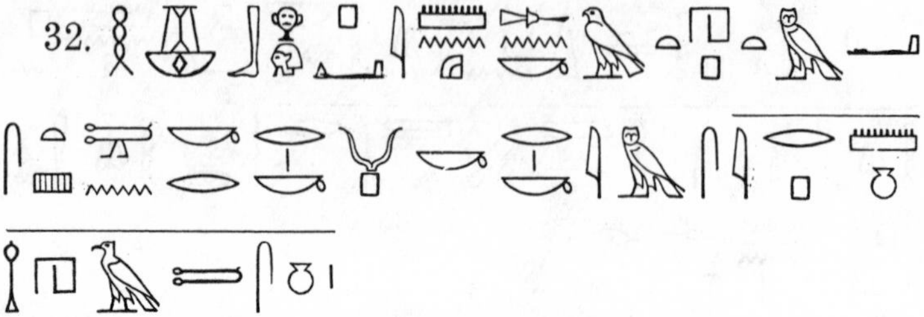

33.
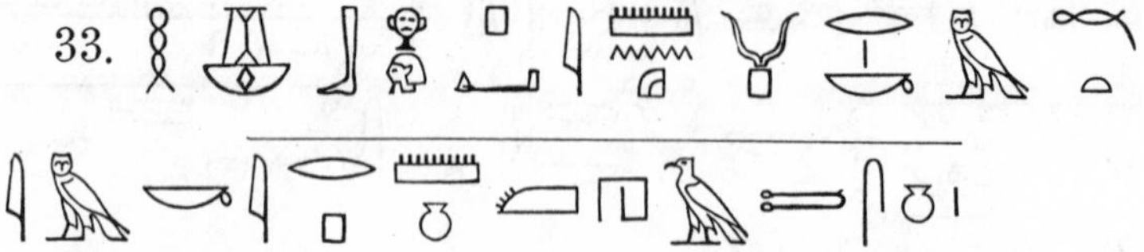

34.
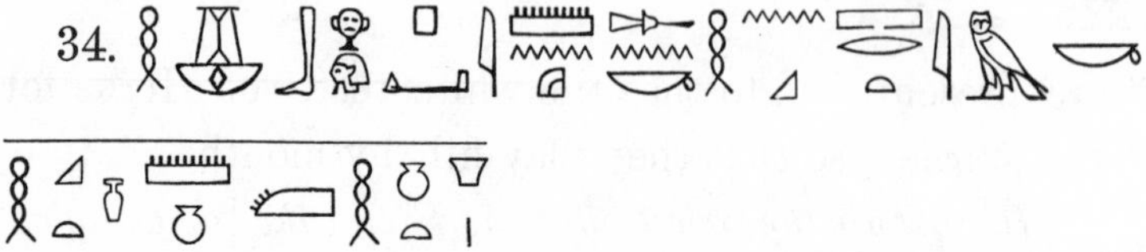

Here shall the priest offer a white vessel containing a hathes of wine, and say:—

"32. O chief KHER ḤEB PEṬĀ-ÅMEN-ÅP, the Eye of "Horus hath been presented unto thee, snatched from "the hand of Set. Thou hast seized it for thy mouth, "and thou hast opened thy mouth therewith."

Here shall the priest offer a black vessel containing a hathes of wine, and say:—

"33. O chief KHER ḤEB PEṬĀ-ÅMEN-ÅP, thy mouth "is opened through that which floweth from thee."

Here shall the priest offer a black vessel containing a ḥent of beer, and say:—

"34. O chief KHER ḤEB PEṬĀ-ÅMEN-ÅP, there is pre-

35. 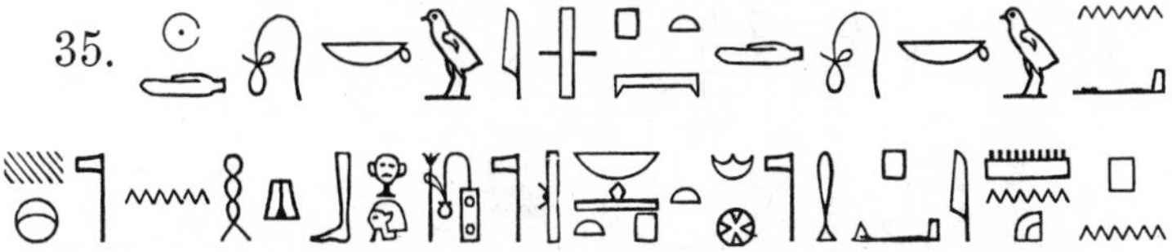

36. 

37. 

"sented unto thee that which hath been pressed [out "of thee] and cometh forth from thee."

Here shall the priest offer the equipment of the table of offerings, the great one, for the lifting up of the face,[1] and shall say:—

"35, 36. O Rā, may the worship which thou hast in "heaven, may the worship which thou hast from the "Company of the Gods, be to the chief KHER ḤEB, "the divine scribe and prophet of the Lady of Ḥetep, "PEṬĀ-ÅMEN-ÅP, and may everything be for the KA of "the chief KHER ḤEB PEṬĀ-ÅMEN-ÅP, and everything "for his body, and everything every day."

Then shall the priest offer a Ṭept loaf, and say:—

"37. O chief KHER ḤEB PEṬĀ-ÅMEN-ÅP, the Eye of

[1] Perhaps, "to be lifted up before the face."

38. 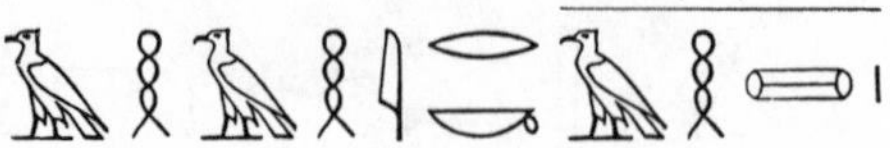

39. 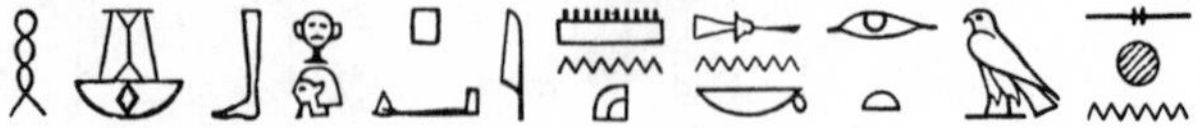

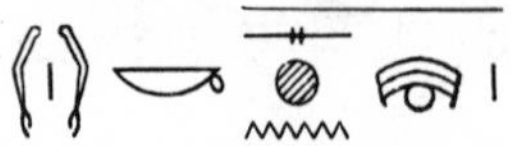

40. 

"Horus hath been presented unto thee [as] thy food "(for thy tasting)."

Then shall the priest offer an Aḥ cake, and say:—

"38. The *Aḥ* food is spread out before thee like a "field."

Then shall the priest offer a breast-joint, and say:—

"39. O chief KHER ḤEB PEṬĀ-ÅMEN-ÅP, the Eye of "Horus hath been presented unto thee that it may be "united unto thee."

Then shall the priest offer a white vessel containing a ḥent of wine, and say:—

"40. O chief KHER ḤEB PEṬĀ-ÅMEN-ÅP, the Eye of "Horus hath been presented unto thee, which was won "from the hand of Set, and was rescued for thee, and "thou dost open thy mouth with it."

41. 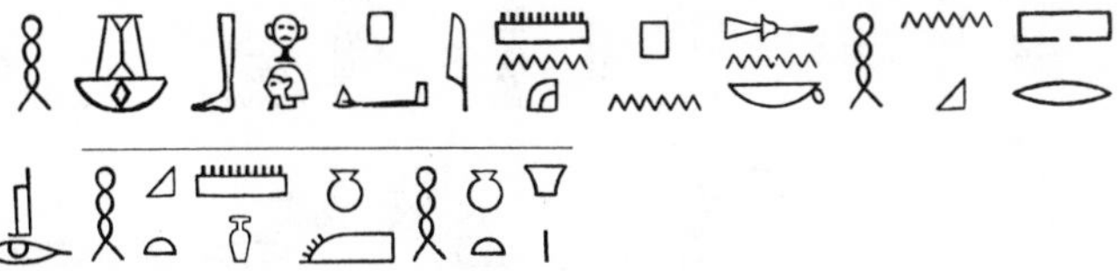

42. 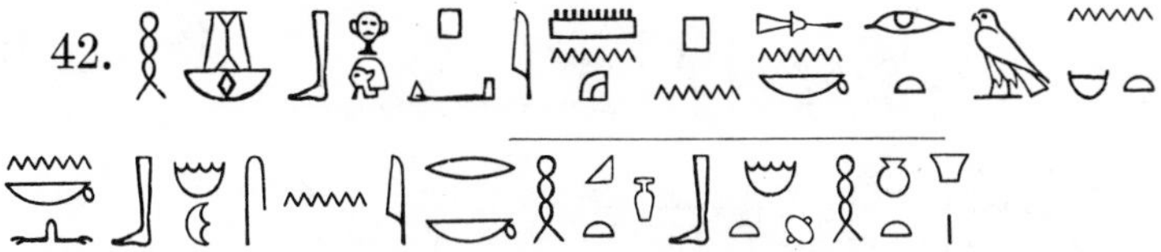

43. 

Then shall the priest offer a black vessel containing a ḥent of beer, and say:—

"41. O chief KHER ḤEB PEṬĀ-ÅMEN-ÅP, there hath "been presented unto thee that which hath been pressed "out, and cometh forth from Osiris."

Then shall the priest offer an iron vessel containing a ḥent of beer, and say:—

"42. O chief KHER ḤEB PEṬĀ-ÅMEN-ÅP, the Eye of "Horus hath been presented unto thee in the iron "[vessel] which is [ordained] for thee, wherein no iron cometh, it belongeth to thee."

Then shall the priest offer a ḥetemet vessel containing one ḥent of beer, and say:—

"43. O chief KHER ḤEB PEṬĀ-ÅMEN-ÅP, the Eye of "Horus hath been presented unto thee, so that thou "mayest be filled thereby."

44. 

45. 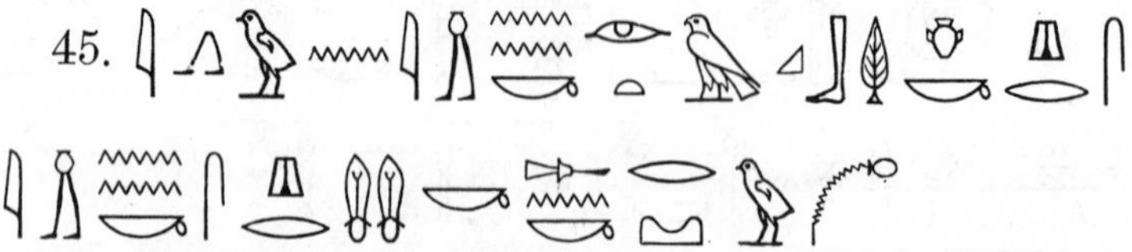

46. 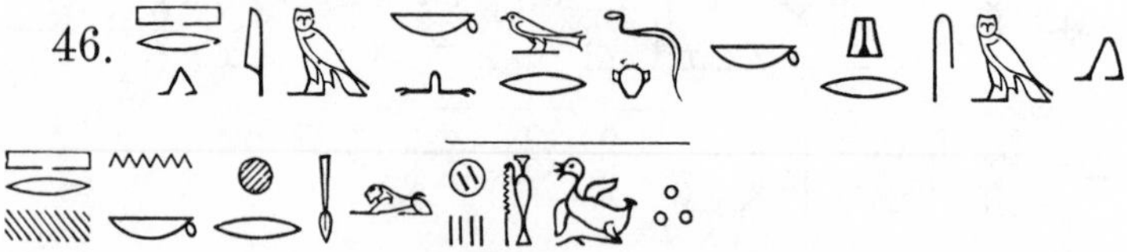

Then shall the priest pour out a vessel of water in which three cakes of natron have been dissolved, and say:—

"44. This [is] a libation unto thee, O Osiris, a libation "unto thee, O chief KHER ḤEB PEṬĀ-ÅMEN-ÅP, which "hath come forth from thy son, which hath come forth "from Horus. 45. I have come, and I have brought "unto thee the Eye of Horus, whereby thy heart shall "be refreshed. I have brought it to thy feet, and pre-"sented unto thee that which hath flowed 46. and "come forth from thee. No stoppage of thy heart "[shall there be] to thee with the things which come "forth at the word."

The above (lines 44—46) *shall be said four times.*

47. 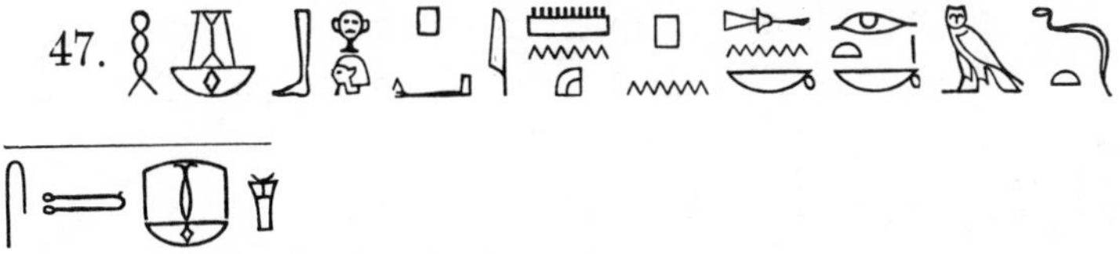

48. 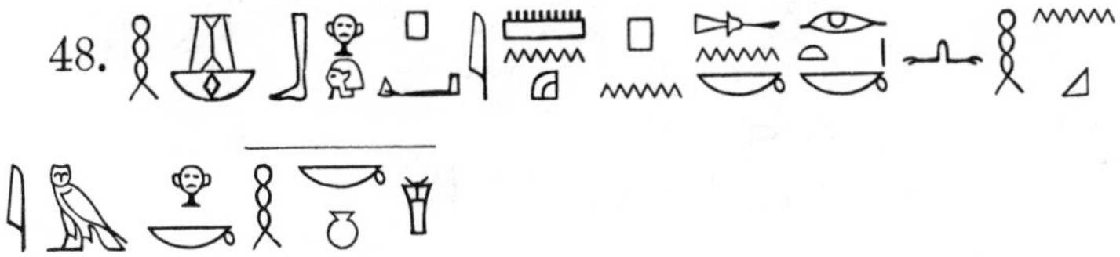

49. 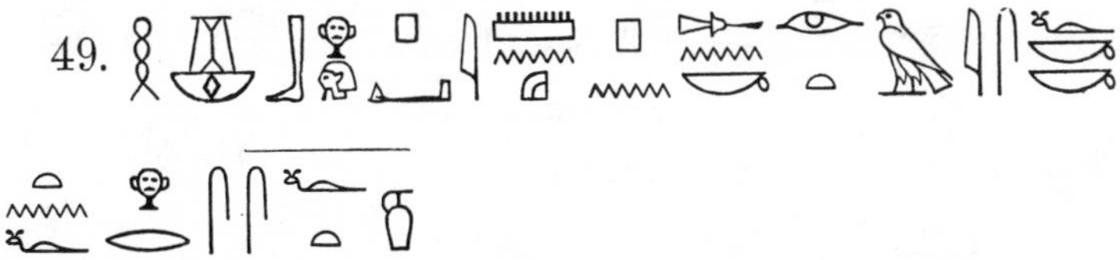

Here shall the priest offer Seth ḥeb ointment, and say:—

"47. O chief KHER ḤEB PEṬĀ-ÅMEN-ÅP, thine eye "hath been filled (i.e., smeared) with *metchet* oint- "ment."

Here shall the priest offer Ḥeken ointment, and say:—

"48. O chief KHER ḤEB PEṬĀ-ÅMEN-ÅP, thine eye hath "been filled (i.e., smeared) and no injury shall [come] to "thy face."

Here shall the priest offer Seft ointment, and say:—

"49. O chief KHER ḤEB PEṬĀ-ÅMEN-ÅP, the Eye of "Horus hath been presented unto thee, and [Set] hath "been made weak for thee thereby."

50. 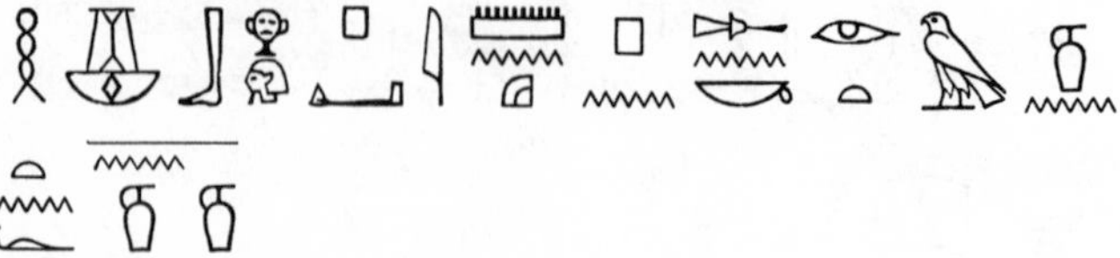

51. 

52. 

Here shall the priest offer Nem ointment, and say:—

"50. O chief KHER ḤEB PEṬĀ-ÅMEN-ÅP, the Eye of "Horus hath been presented unto thee that it may "unite itself unto thee."

Here shall the priest offer Ṭua ointment, and say:—

"51. O chief KHER ḤEB PEṬĀ-ÅMEN-ÅP, the Eye of "Horus hath been presented unto thee. It hath been "been brought [unto thee] that thou mayest worship "(or, give thanks to) the gods by means of it."

Here shall the priest offer the finest cedar oil and the finest oil of the Theḥennu, and say:—

"52. O ye oils which are on the forehead of Horus, "O ye oils which are on the forehead of Horus, place "ye yourselves on the forehead of the chief KHER ḤEB

53. 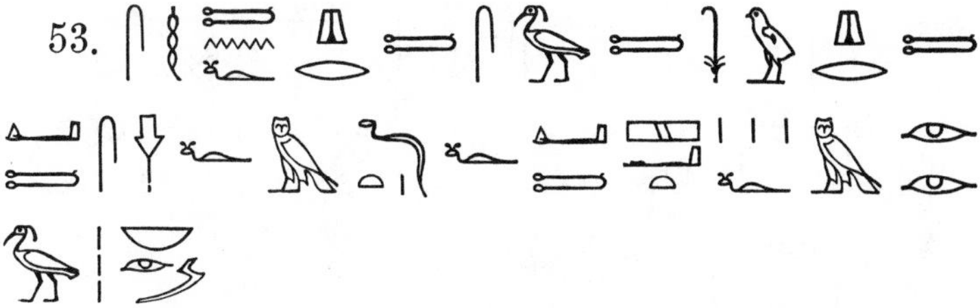

54. 

55. 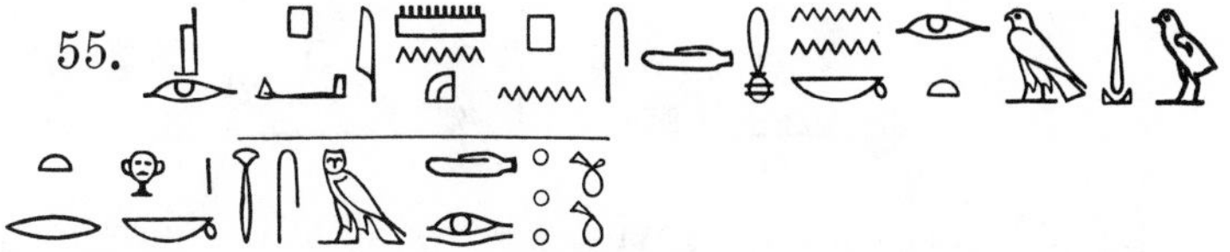

"PEṬĀ-ÅMEN-ÅP! 53. Make ye him to [smell] sweet "in possessing you, make ye him to be a KHU (or, "glorious) possessing you, make ye him to have the "mastery over his body [again], and make ye him to "have openings [before] his eyes. And let all the "Spirits (KHU) see 54. him, and let them hear his "name. Behold, O Osiris, chief KHER ḤEB PEṬĀ-"ÅMEN-ÅP, the Eye of Horus hath been brought unto "thee, and it hath been seized for thee that it may be "before thee."

Here shall the priest offer one bag of uatch eye-paint and one bag of mesṭem eye-paint, and say:—

"55. O Osiris PEṬĀ-ÅMEN-ÅP, I have painted the

56.

57.

58.
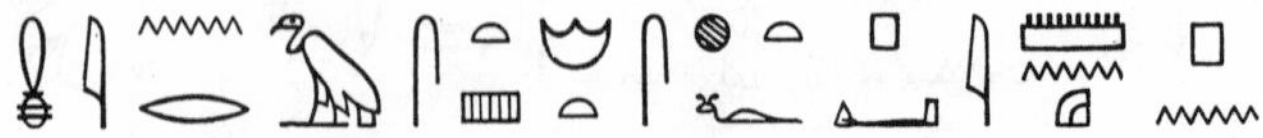

"Eye of Horus for thee with *mesṭem* so that there may "be health to thy face."

Here shall the priest offer swathings, and say :

"56. Mayest thou watch in peace. The goddess "Taȧtet watcheth in peace. The goddess Taȧtet "watcheth in peace. The Eye of Horus which is in "the city of Ṭep-Pe watcheth in peace. The Eye of "Horus which is in the temple houses 57. of Net "(Neith) watcheth in peace. Receive the milk-[white] "and bleached swathings of the goddess UR-Ā. Cause "ye, O swathings, that the lands may bow themselves "before PEṬĀ-ȦMEN-ȦP even as they bow themselves "before Horus, and make the lands to be in awe of the "Osiris PEṬĀ-ȦMEN-ȦP, 58. as they are in awe of Set.

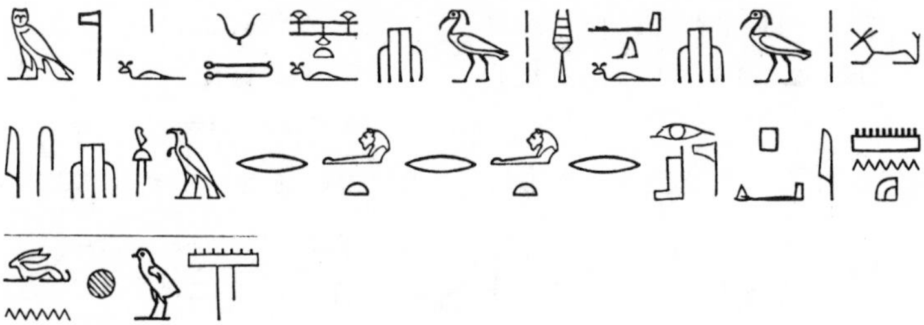

59. 

60. 

"Let them tarry with PEṬĀ-ÅMEN-ÅP in his divinity. "Open ye his way so that he may be at the head of the "Spirits (KHU), and let him stand at the head of the "Spirits, O Ånpu (Anubis)-Khent-Åmenti, to the front, "to the front—to the Osiris PEṬĀ-ÅMEN-ÅP."

Here shall the priest set fire to the incense, and say:—

"59. Let him advance! Let him advance with his "KA! [As] Horus advanceth with his KA, [as] Set "advanceth with his KA, [as] Thoth advanceth with his "KA, [as] Sep advanceth with his Ka, [as] Khenti-maati "advanceth 60. with his KA, [so] may advance thy "backbone with thy KA.

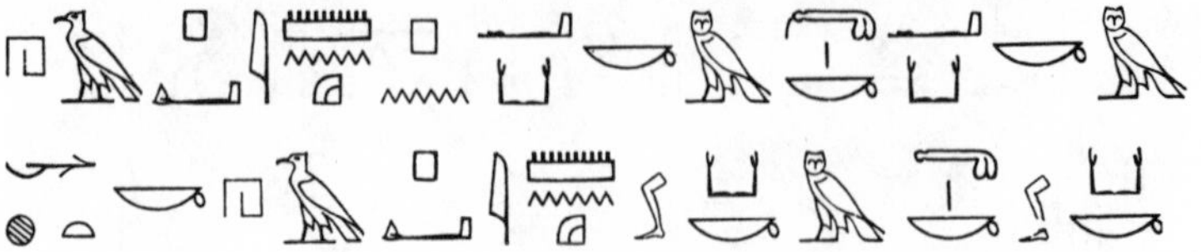

61.

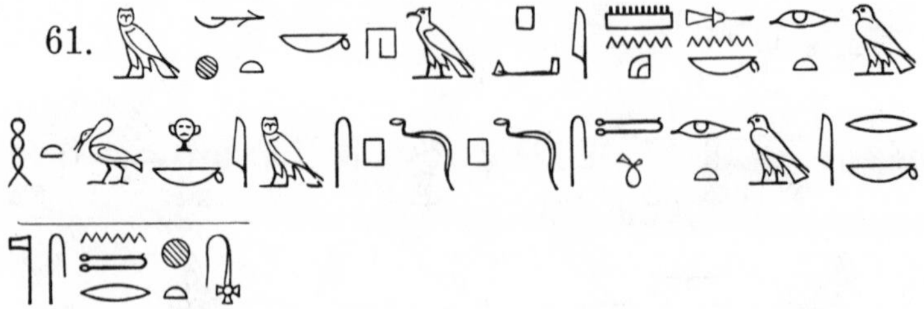

62.

"Hail, PEṬĀ-ÅMEN-ÅP! The arm of thy KA is before "thee, the arm of thy KA is behind thee.

"Hail, PEṬĀ-ÅMEN-ÅP! The foot of thy KA is before "thee, the foot of thy KA 61. is behind thee.

"Hail, PEṬĀ-ÅMEN-ÅP! The eye of Horus hath been "presented unto thee, and thy face is filled therewith, "and the perfume of the Eye of Horus spreadeth itself "over thee."

Here shall the priest pour out a vase of water wherein two cakes of natron have been dissolved, and say:—

"62. This [is] a libation unto thee, O Osiris, a liba-

63. 

64. 

"tion unto thee, O chief KHER ḤEB PEṬĀ-ÀMEN-ÀP,
"which hath come forth from thy son, which hath come
"forth from Horus. I have come and I have brought
"unto thee 63. the Eye of Horus, whereby thy heart
"shall be refreshed. I have brought it to thy feet, and
"have presented unto thee that which hath flowed
"forth and come out from thee. No stoppage of thy
"heart [shall there be] to thee. [Possessing it] a going
"forth of things (or, persons) shall be to thee at the
"[sound of] the voice."

The above (lines 62, 63) *shall be recited four times.*

PART II.

Here shall be set forth the food and drink and the things which are to be placed on the altar, and one shall enter with the offerings of food. And the priest shall say:—

"64. It is Thoth who returneth bringing it (i.e.,

65. 

66. 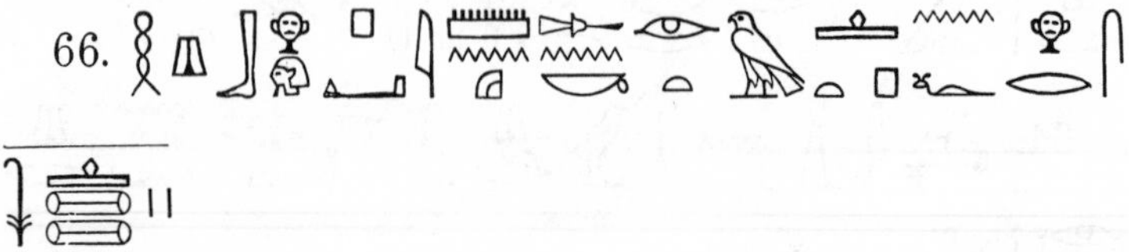

67. 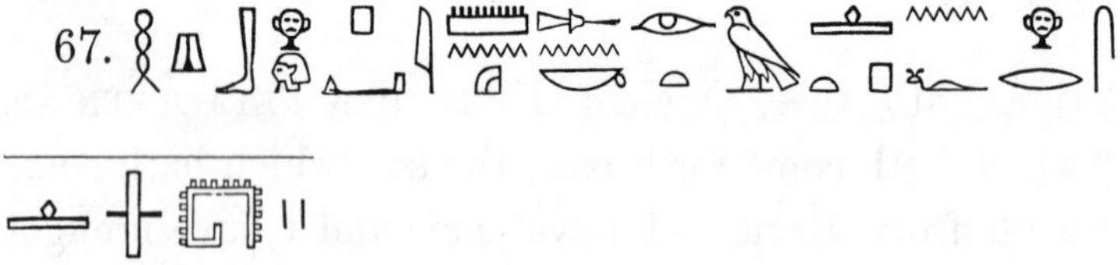

"the Eye of Horus)." *And then shall be said:* "He "cometh forth with the Eye of Horus. 65. He "hath given the Eye of Horus, and he is content "therewith."

Here shall the priest present two cakes, and say:—

"66. O chief KHER ḤEB PEṬĀ-ÅMEN-ÅP, the Eye of "Horus hath been presented unto thee, and he is con- "tent therewith."

Here shall the priest present two vessels [of beer] in the usekh chamber, and say:—

"67. O chief KHER ḤEB PEṬĀ-ÅMEN-ÅP, the Eye of "Horus hath been presented unto thee, and he is con- "tent therewith."

68. 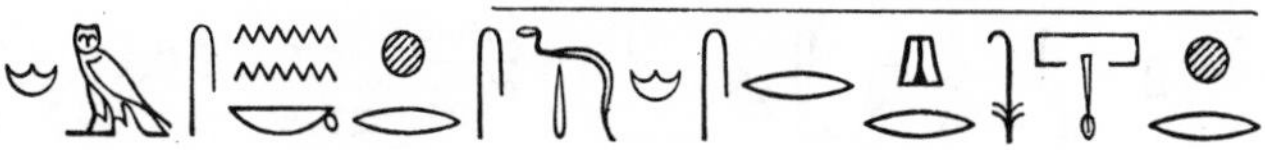

69. 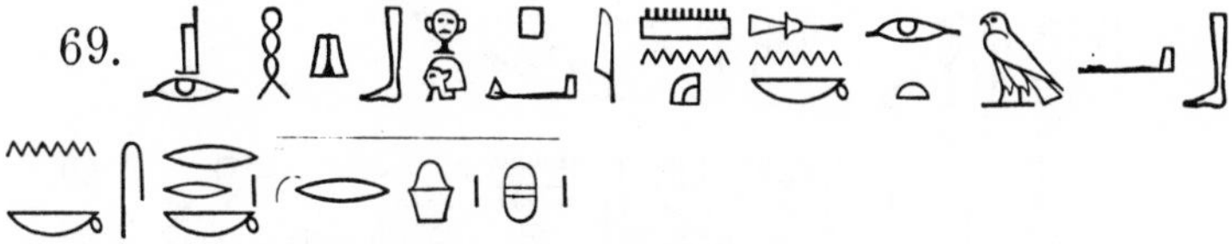

70. 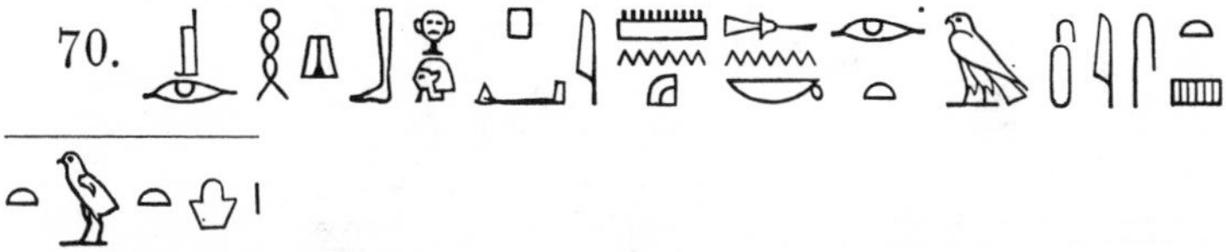

71. 

He who sitteth down by the offering shall say:—

"68. I have seated myself with it."

Here shall the priest present for the Ush a Ṭua cake and a Shens cake, and say:—

"69. O Osiris, the chief KHER ḤEB PEṬĀ-ÅMEN-ÅP, "the Eye of Horus hath been presented unto thee, and "it hath been offered to thee for thy mouth."

Here shall the priest present a Tut cake, and say:—

"70. O Osiris, the chief KHER ḤEB PEṬĀ-ÅMEN-ÅP, "the Eye of Horus hath been presented unto thee for "the smiting down of Set."

Here shall the priest offer a Reth̤u cake, and say:—

"71. O Osiris, the chief KHER ḤEB PEṬĀ-ÅMEN-ÅP, "the Eye of Horus hath been presented unto thee "which was chained up [by Set]."

72. 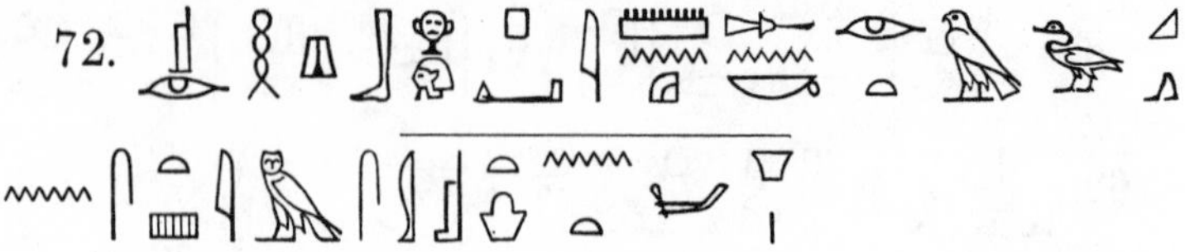

73. 

74. 

Here shall the priest offer a nemset vessel of Tcheser drink, and say:—

"72. O Osiris, the chief KHER ḤEB PEṬĀ-ÅMEN-ÅP, "the Eye of Horus hath been presented unto thee, "which entered into Set."

Here shall the priest offer a nemset vessel of Khenemes beer, and say:—

"73. O Osiris, the chief KHER ḤEB PEṬĀ-ÅMEN-ÅP, "the Eye of Horus hath been presented unto thee, "which hath been smitten, for thy mouth."

Here shall the priest lift up a cake and a vessel of beer, and say:—

"74. O Osiris, the chief KHER ḤEB PEṬĀ-ÅMEN-ÅP, "the Eye of Horus hath been presented unto thee, it

75. 

76. 

77. 

"hath been lifted for thee to thy face, Osiris, lifting "[it] to thy face, O PEṬĀ-ÅMEN-ÅP. May thy soul "advance from afar off. 75. Fix thy gaze intently on "that which cometh forth from it. That which is "corrupt in thee hath been washed away, O PEṬĀ-AMEN-"ÅP, and thy mouth hath been opened by the Eye of "Horus."

Here shall the priest offer as a shebu a Ṭua cake and a Shens cake, and say:—

"76. Let there be praise to thyself and to thy KA, "O Osiris, which hath been cut away from the hand of "him that doeth violence to the dead, O KHER ḤEB "PEṬĀ-ÅMEN-ÅP. Thou hast received 77. all these "cakes which have come forth from the Eye of Horus."

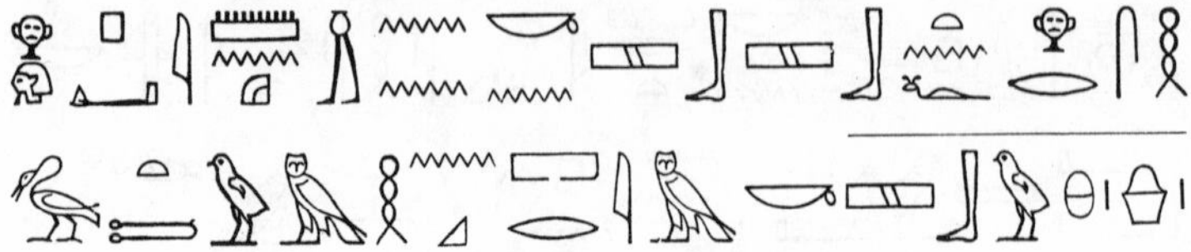

78.

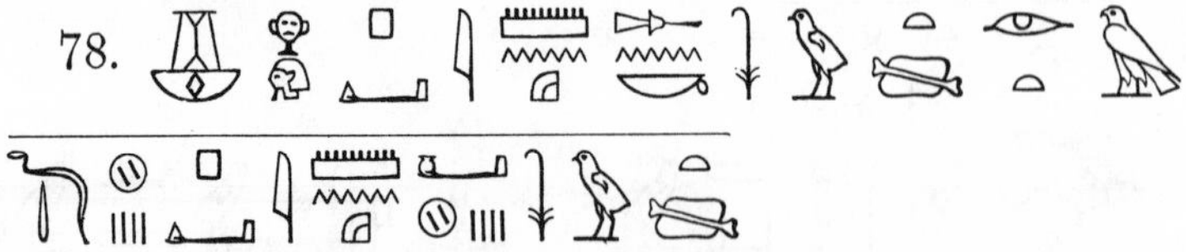

79.

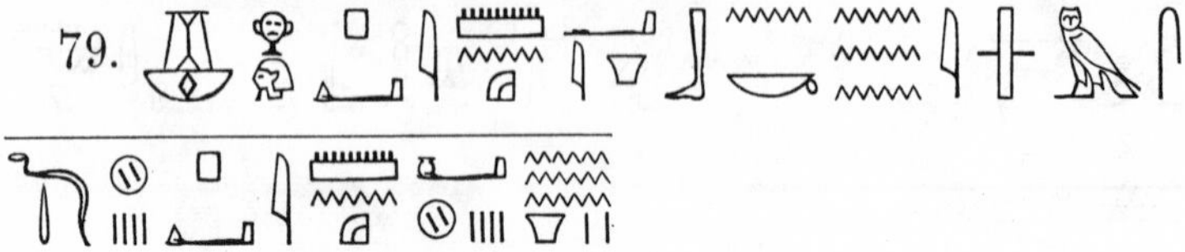

And he shall say :—

"O chief KHER ḤEB PETĀ-ȦMEN-ȦP, I have brought "unto thee that which was mixed for thee, so that "thou mayest be filled with that which hath been "pressed out and cometh forth from thee."

Here shall the priest offer the Sut joint of meat, and as he presenteth it four times to Peṭā-Ȧmen-ȧp, he shall say four times :—

"78. O chief KHER ḤEB PEṬĀ-ȦMEN-ȦP, the *Sut* joint "of meat hath been presented unto thee [as] the Eye "of Horus."

Here shall the priest offer two vases of water, and as he presenteth them to Peṭā-Ȧmen-ȧp four times, he shall say four times :—

"79. O chief KHER ḤEB PEṬĀ-ȦMEN-ȦP, the water "which is herein is offered unto thee."

80. 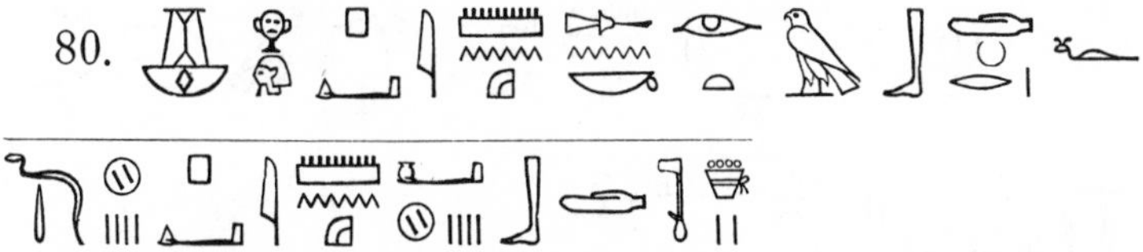

81. 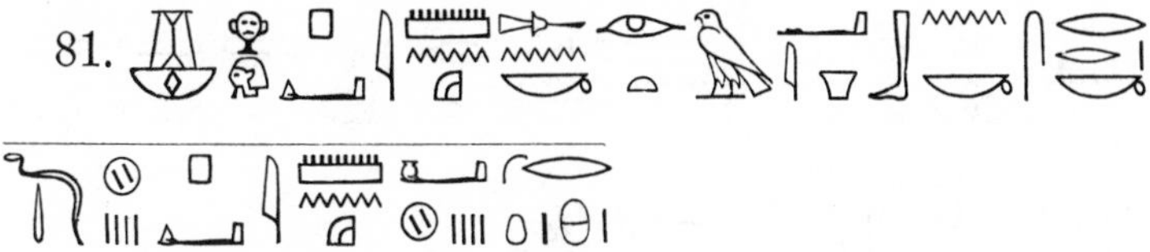

82. 

Here shall the priest offer two vessels of cakes of cleansing natron, and as he presenteth them four times to Peṭā-Åmen-åp, he shall say four times:—

"80. O chief KHER ḤEB PEṬĀ-ÅMEN-ÅP, the Eye of "Horus hath been presented unto thee that it may "purify thy mouth."

Here shall the priest offer for the Ush a Ṭua cake and a Shens cake, and as he presenteth them four times to Peṭā-Åmen-åp, he shall say four times:—

"81. O chief KHER ḤEB PEṬĀ-ÅMEN-ÅP, the Eye of "Horus hath been presented unto thee, and it hath "been offered unto thee for thy mouth."

Here shall the priest offer a Tut cake, and as he presenteth it to Peṭā-Åmen-åp four times, he shall say four times:—

"82. O chief KHER ḤEB PEṬĀ-ÅMEN-ÅP, the Eye of

83. 

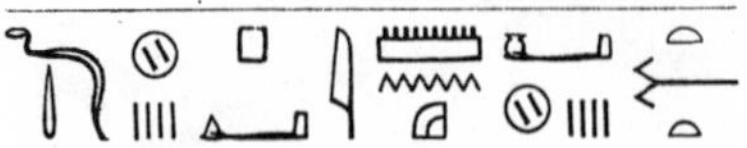

84. 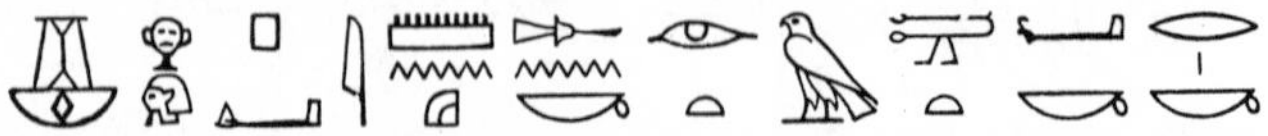

85. 

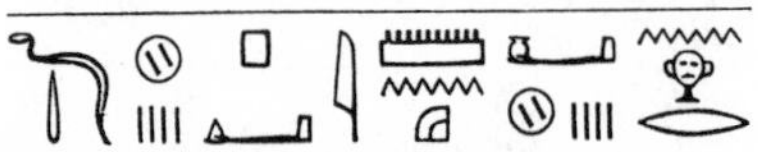

"Horus hath been presented unto thee, which struck "down Set."

Here shall the priest offer a Reṭhu cake, and as he presenteth it to Peṭā-Åmen-àp four times, he shall say four times:—

"83. O chief KHER ḤEB PEṬĀ-ÅMEN-ÀP, the Eye of "Horus hath been presented unto thee, which was put "under restraint [by Set]."

Here shall the priest offer a Ḥutcha cake, and as he presenteth it to Peṭā-Åmen-àp four times, he shall say four times:—

"84. O chief KHER ḤEB PEṬĀ-ÅMEN-ÀP, the Eye of "Horus hath been presented unto thee, that thou "mayest seize it for thy mouth."

86. 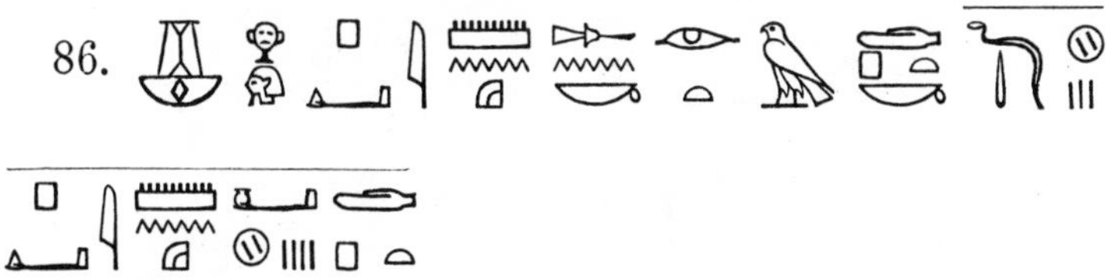

87. 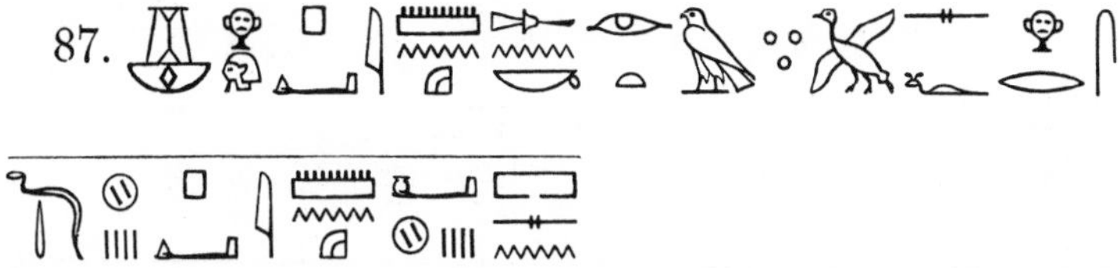

Here shall the priest offer a Neḥer cake, and as he presenteth it to Peṭā-Åmen-åp four times, he shall say four times:—

"85. O chief KHER ḤEB PEṬĀ-ÅMEN-ÅP, there hath "been brought unto thee that which is intended for thy "mouth."

Here shall the priest offer a Ṭept cake, and as he presenteth it to Peṭā-Åmen-åp four times, he shall say four times:—

"86. O chief KHER ḤEB PEṬĀ-ÅMEN-ÅP, the Eye of "Horus hath been presented unto thee, that thou "mayest taste [it]."

Here shall the priest offer a Pasen cake, and as he presenteth it to Peṭā-Åmen-åp four times, he shall say four times:—

"87. O chief KHER ḤEB PEṬĀ-ÅMEN-ÅP, the Eye of "Horus, the glorious one, hath been presented unto "thee; it hath been baked thereby."

88. 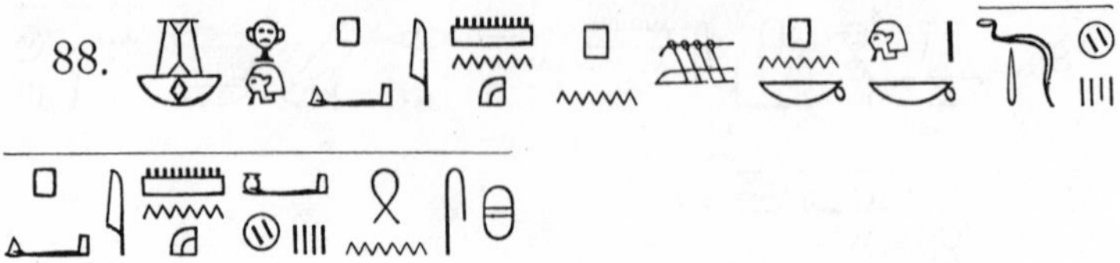

89. 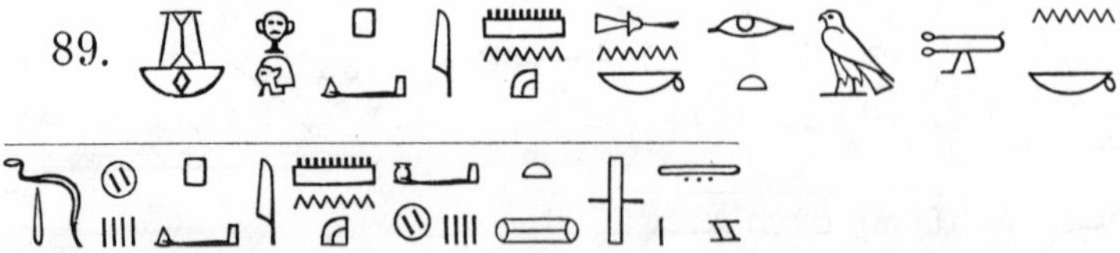

90. 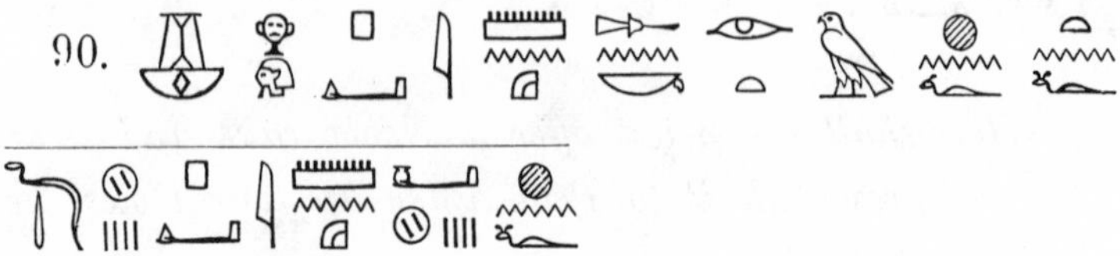

Here shall the priest offer a Shens cake, and as he presenteth it to Peṭā-Ȧmen-ȧp four times, he shall say four times:—

"88. O chief KHER ḤEB PEṬĀ-ȦMEN-ȦP, thou hast "received thy head."

Here shall the priest offer an Ȧm-ta cake, and as he presenteth it to Peṭā-Ȧmen-ȧp four times, he shall say four times:—

"89. O chief KHER ḤEB PEṬĀ-ȦMEN-ȦP, the Eye of "Horus hath been presented unto thee [that] thou "mayest seize it."

Here shall the priest offer a Khenf cake, and as he presenteth it to Peṭā-Ȧmen-ȧp four times, he shall say four times:—

"90. O chief KHER ḤEB PEṬĀ-ȦMEN-ȦP, the Eye of

91.

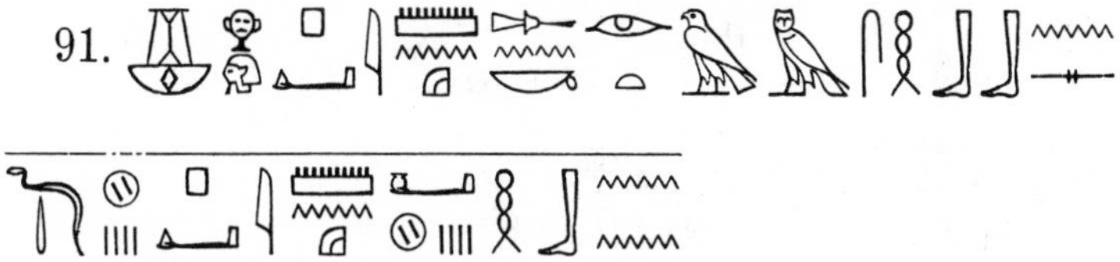

92.

93.

"Horus hath been presented unto thee, which hath "been made in the form of a fish scale for thee."

Here shall the priest offer a cake of Ḥebnen paste, and as he presenteth it four times, he shall say four times:—

"91. O chief KHER ḤEB PEṬĀ-ÅMEN-ÅP, the Eye of "Horus hath been presented unto thee, so that it may "well up before thee."

Here shall the priest offer a cake made of fine white flour, and as he presenteth it to Peṭā-Åmen-åp four times, he shall say four times:—

"92. O chief KHER ḤEB PEṬĀ-ÅMEN-ÅP, the Eye of "Horus hath been presented unto thee, which was "fettered [by Set]."

94. 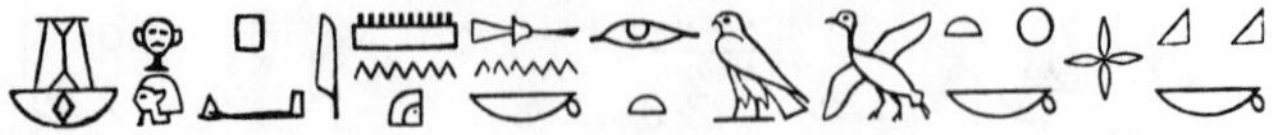

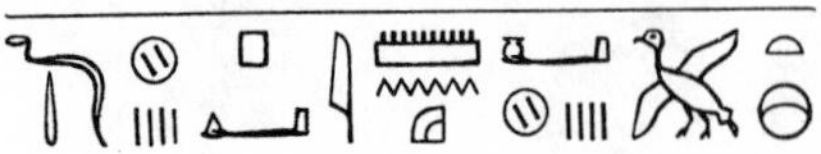

95. 

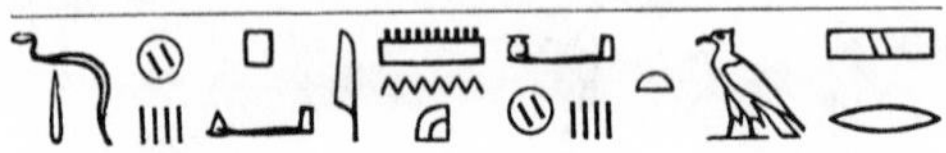

Here shall the priest offer an Ȧṭen cake, and as he presenteth it to Peṭā-Ȧmen-ȧp four times, he shall say four times :—

"93. O chief KHER ḤEB PEṬĀ-ȦMEN-ȦP, the Eye of "Horus hath been presented unto thee, and placed for "thee in thy mouth."

Here shall the priest offer a cake (Paut), and as he presenteth it to Peṭā-Ȧmen-ȧp four times, he shall say four times :—

"94. O chief KHER ḤEB PEṬĀ-ȦMEN-ȦP, the Eye of "Horus hath been presented unto thee, thy cake which "thou eatest."

Here shall the priest offer a baked cake (Ta asher), and as he presenteth it to Peṭā-Ȧmen-ȧp four times, he shall say four times :—

"95. O chief KHER ḤEB PEṬĀ-ȦMEN-ȦP, there hath "been presented unto thee that which is destined for "thee."

96. 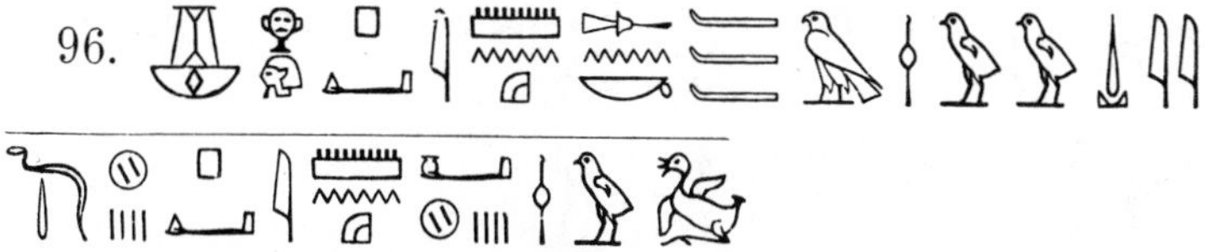

97. 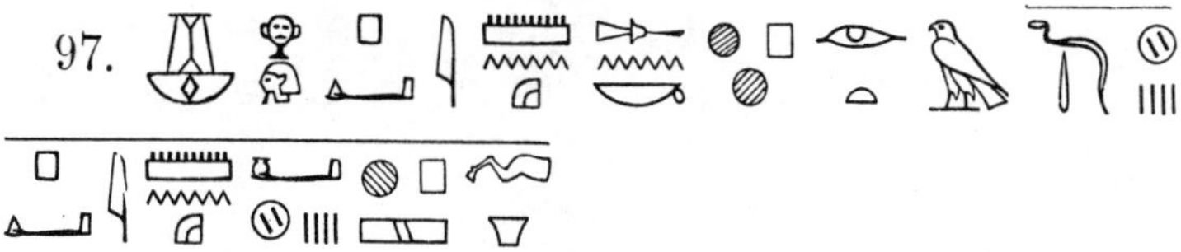

98. 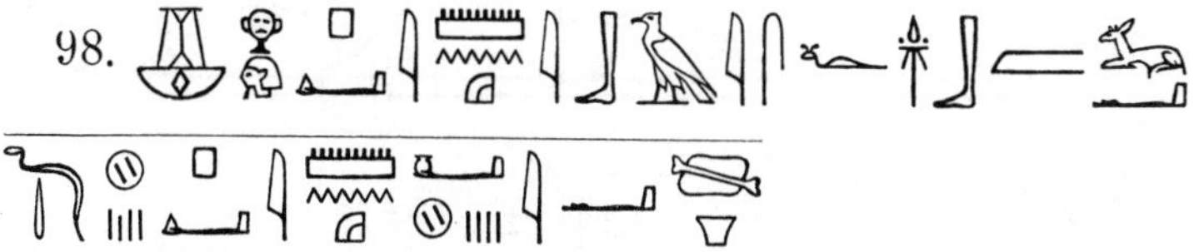

Here shall the priest offer a bunch of onions, and as he presenteth them to Peṭā-Ȧmen-ȧp four times, he shall say four times :—

"96. O chief KHER ḤEB PETĀ-ȦMEN-ȦP, the white "teeth of Horus have been presented unto thee, which "are strength[-giving]."

Here shall the priest offer a haunch of beef, and as he presenteth it to Peṭā-Ȧmen-ȧp four times, he shall say four times :—

"97. O chief KHER ḤEB PEṬĀ-ȦMEN-ȦP, the thigh "hath been presented unto thee [as] the Eye of "Horus."

Here shall the priest offer an Ȧā joint, and as he presenteth it to Peṭā-Ȧmen-ȧp four times, he shall say four times :—

"98. O chief KHER ḤEB PEṬĀ-ȦMEN-ȦP, the mark of "that which is abominable is burnt into the *Ȧā* joint."

99. 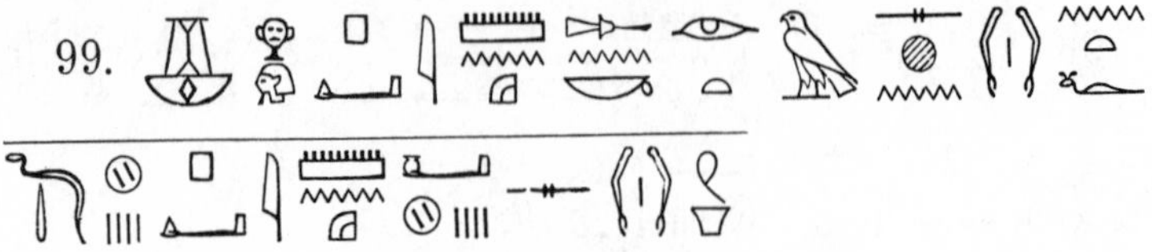

100. 

101. 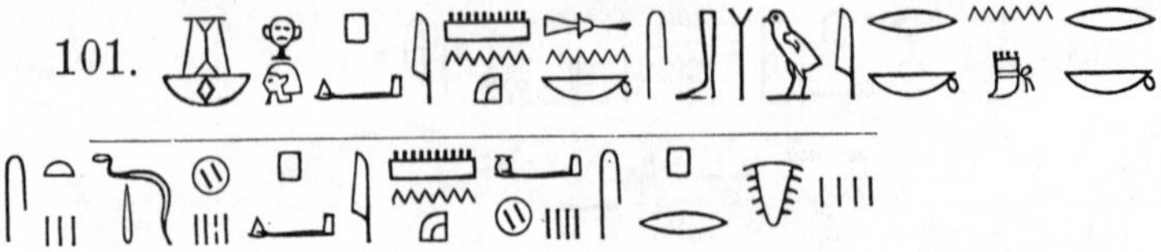

Here shall the priest offer a joint from the breast of the animal, and as he presenteth it to Peṭā-Ȧmen-ȧp four times, he shall say four times:—

"99. O chief KHER ḤEB PEṬĀ-ȦMEN-ȦP, the Eye of "Horus hath been presented unto thee so that it may "embrace thee."

Here shall the priest offer the Sut joint, and as he presenteth it to Peṭā-Ȧmen-ȧp four times, he shall say four times:—

"100. O chief KHER ḤEB PEṬĀ-ȦMEN-ȦP, the *Sut* joint "hath been presented unto thee as the Eye of Horus."

Here shall the priest offer four ribs of the animal, and as he presenteth them to Peṭā-Ȧmen-ȧp four times, he shall say four times:—

"101. O chief KHER HEB PEṬĀ-ȦMEN-ȦP, the enemies "have been presented unto thee, for they are thine, "and thou hast smitten them."

102. 

103. 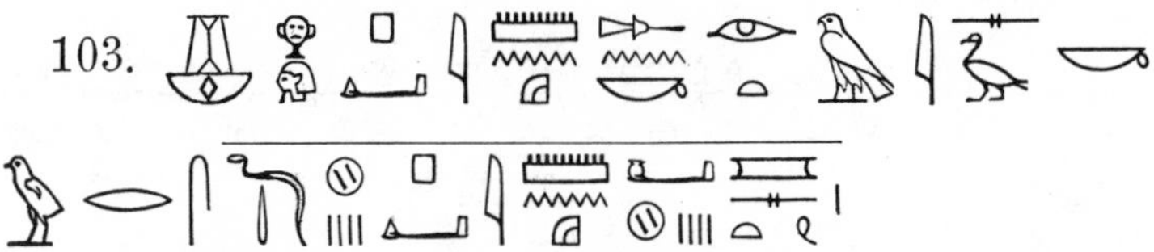

104. 

Here shall the priest offer four pieces of roasted flesh, and as he presenteth them to Peṭā-Ȧmen-ȧp four times, he shall say four times :—

"102. O chief KHER ḤEB PEṬĀ-ȦMEN-ȦP, there have "been presented unto thee the things which are ordained "for thee."

Here shall the priest offer a liver, and as he presenteth it to Peṭā-Ȧmen-ȧp four times, he shall say four times :—

"103. O chief KHER ḤEB PEṬĀ-ȦMEN-ȦP, the Eye of "Horus hath been presented unto thee, that thou "mayest go about with it."

Here shall the priest offer three pieces of the joint Ne[n]shem, and as he presenteth them to Peṭā-Ȧmen-ȧp four times, he shall say four times :—

"104. O chief KHER ḤEB PETȦ-ȦMEN-ȦP, the Eye of

105. 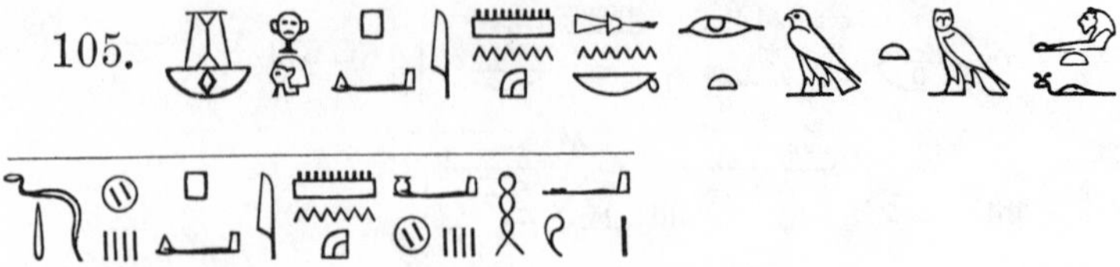

106. 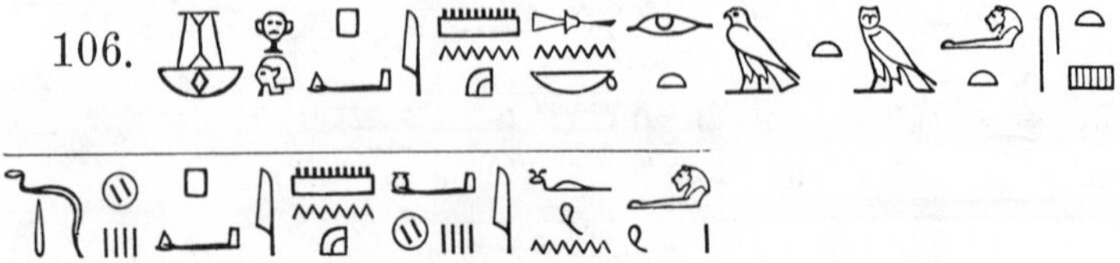

107. 

"Horus hath been presented unto thee, and one cometh "unto thee with it."

Here shall the priest offer the Ḥā joint (shoulder), and as he presenteth it to Peṭā-Åmen-åp four times, he shall say four times:—

"105. O chief KHER ḤEB PEṬĀ-ÅMEN-ÅP, the Eye of "Horus hath been presented unto thee in the form of "his forepart (i.e., shoulder of Set)."

Here shall the priest offer the flesh of the shoulder, and as he presenteth it to Peṭā-Åmen-åp four times, he shall say four times:—

"106. O chief KHER ḤEB PEṬĀ-ÅMEN-ÅP, the Eye "of Horus there hath been presented unto thee as the "shoulder of Set."

108. 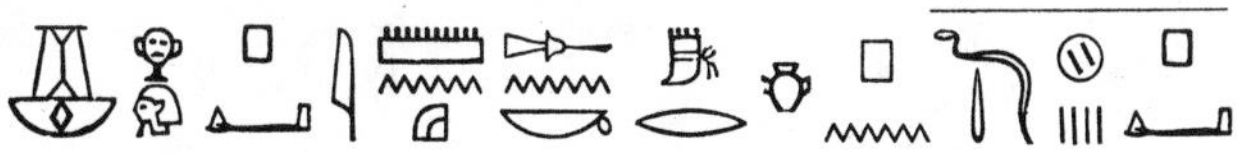

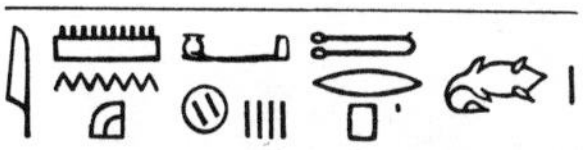

109. 

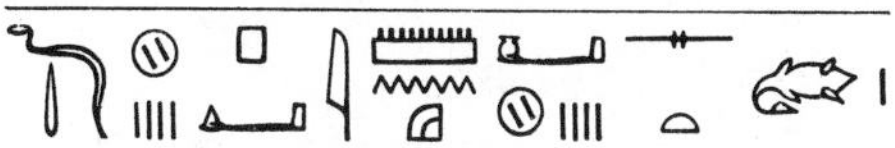

Here shall the priest offer a goose, and as he presenteth it unto Peṭă-Ȧmen-ȧp four times, he shall say four times:—

"107. O chief Kher ḥeb Peṭā-Ȧmen-ȧp, a *Serȧ* goose "hath been presented unto thee instead of the heads of "the followers of Set."

Here shall the priest offer a Therp goose, and as he presenteth it to Peṭă-Ȧmen-ȧp four times, he shall say four times:—

"108. O chief Kher ḥeb Peṭā-Ȧmen-ȧp, this [goose] "according to the desire of [thy] heart hath been pre- "sented unto thee."

Here shall the priest offer a Set goose, and as he presenteth it to Peṭă-Ȧmen-ȧp four times, he shall say four times:—

"109. O chief Kher ḥeb Peṭā-Ȧmen-ȧp, the Eye of "Horus hath been presented unto thee, and one beareth "it unto thee."

110. 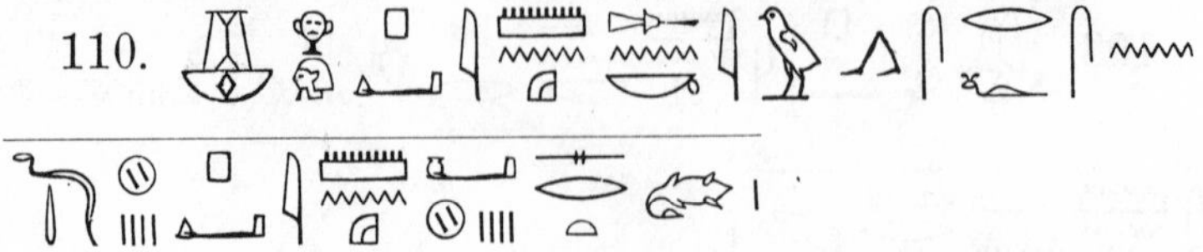

111. 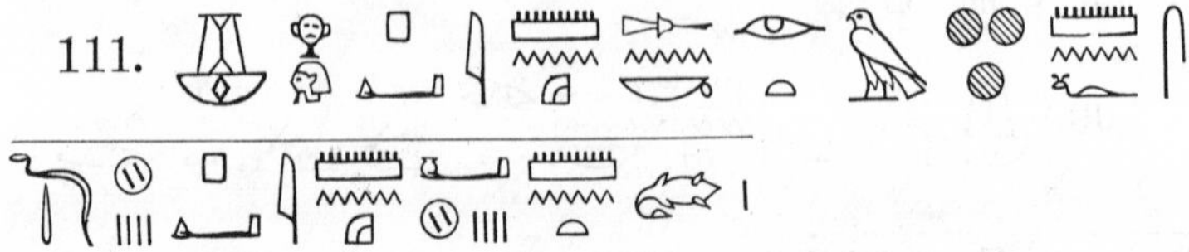

112. 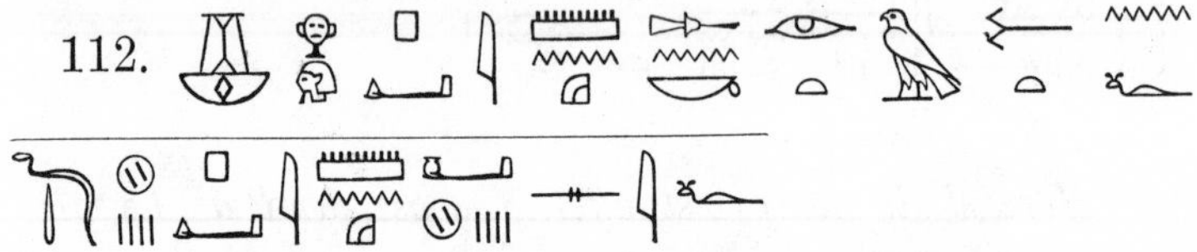

Here shall the priest offer a Sert goose, and as he presenteth it unto Peṭā-Āmen-āp four times, he shall say four times :—

"110. O chief KHER ḤEB PEṬĀ-ĀMEN-ĀP, have been "presented unto thee the things which come for thee."

Here shall the priest offer a dove, and as he presenteth it to Peṭā-Āmen-āp four times, he shall say four times :—

"111. O chief KHER ḤEB PEṬĀ-ĀMEN-ĀP, the Eye of "Horus hath been presented unto thee, the glorious "one, the dove which is ordained (?) for thee"

Here shall the priest offer some Sāf meal, and as he presenteth it to Peṭā-Āmen-āp four times, he shall say four times :—

"112. O chief KHER ḤEB PEṬĀ-ĀMEN-ĀP, the Eye of "Horus, which was fettered by him [i.e., Set], hath been "presented unto thee."

113. 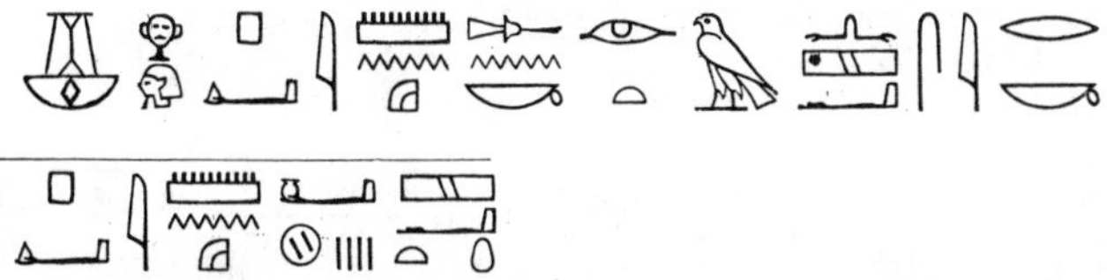

114. 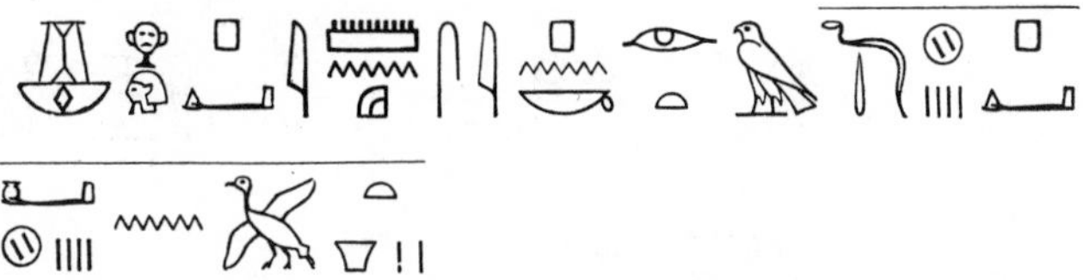

115. 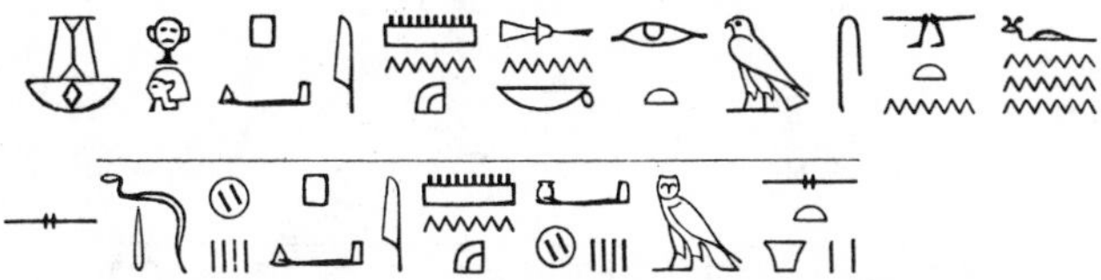

Here shall the priest offer some Shāt dough, and as he presenteth it to Peṭā-Ȧmen-ȧp four times, he shall say four times:—

"113. O chief KHER ḤEB PEṬĀ-ȦMEN-ȦP, the Eye of "Horus hath been presented unto thee, and thou shalt "not participate in its cutting off."

Here shall the priest offer two vessels of Nepat grain, and as he presenteth them to Peṭā-Ȧmen-ȧp four times, he shall say four times:—

"114. O chief KHER ḤEB PEṬĀ-ȦMEN-ȦP, the Eye of "Horus, which hath been reckoned up, [hath been pre-"sented unto thee]."

Here shall the priest offer two vessels of Mest grain, and as he presenteth them to Peṭā-Ȧmen-ȧp four times, he shall say four times:—

"115. O chief KHER ḤEB PEṬĀ-ȦMEN-ȦP, the Eye of

116. 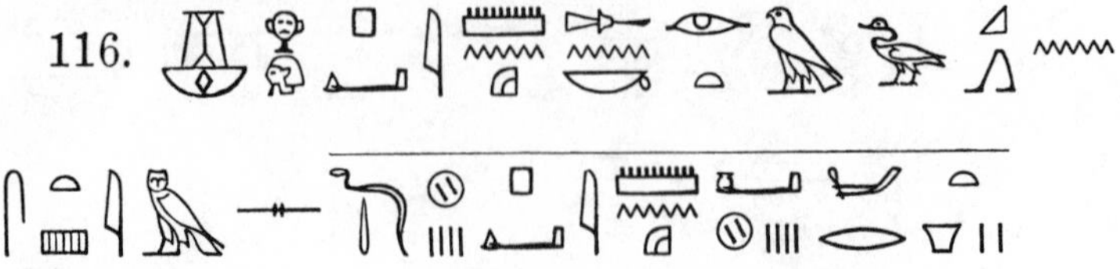

117. 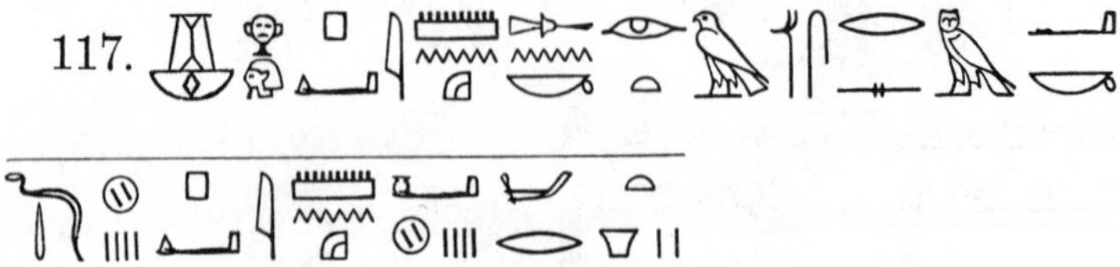

118. 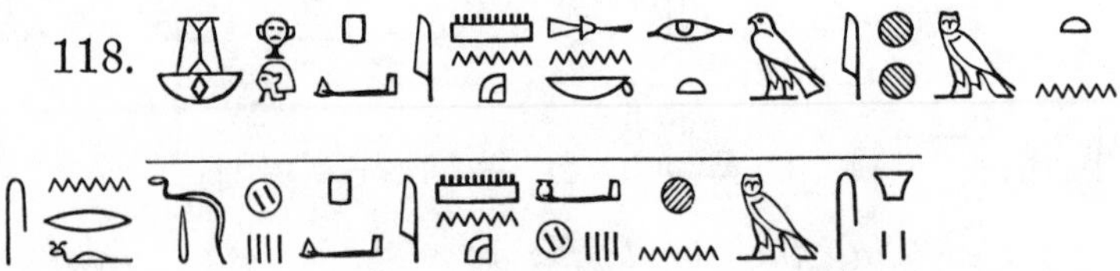

"Horus hath been presented unto thee, and that which "floweth from it [hath been brought to thee]."

Here shall the priest offer two vessels of Tchesert beer, and as he presenteth them to Peṭā-Ȧmen-ȧp four times, he shall say four times:—

"116. O chief Kher ḥeb Peṭā-Ȧmen-ȧp, the Eye of "Horus hath been presented unto thee, [which] entered "into Set."

Here shall the priest offer two vessels of Tchesert beer, and as he presenteth them to Peṭā-Ȧmen-ȧp four times, he shall say four times:—

"117. O chief Kher ḥeb Peṭā-Ȧmen-ȧp, the Eye of "Horus hath been presented unto thee, and there is "power to it in thine hand."

119. 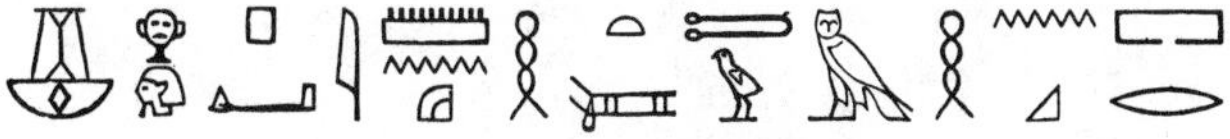

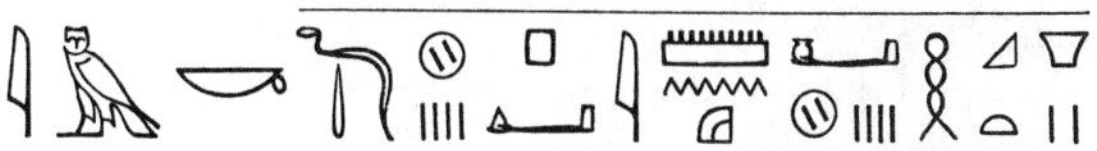

120. 

Here shall the priest offer two vessels of Khenemes beer, and as he presenteth them to Peṭā-Ȧmen-ȧp four times, he shall say four times:—

"118. O chief KHER ḤEB PEṬĀ-ȦMEN-ȦP, the Eye of "Horus hath been presented unto thee, and the fire of "wrath rageth in him against thee."

Here shall the priest offer two vessels of Ḥeqt beer, and as he presenteth them to Peṭā-Ȧmen-ȧp four times, he shall say four times:—

"119. O chief KHER ḤEB PEṬĀ-ȦMEN-ȦP, [thou art] "filled with that which hath been pressed out and hath "come forth from thee."

Here shall the priest offer two vessels of Sekh-pet grain, and as he presenteth them to Peṭā-Ȧmen-ȧp four times, he shall say four times:—

"120. O chief KHER ḤEB PEṬĀ-ȦMEN-ȦP, [thou art] "filled with that which hath been pressed out and hath "come forth from thee."

121.

122.
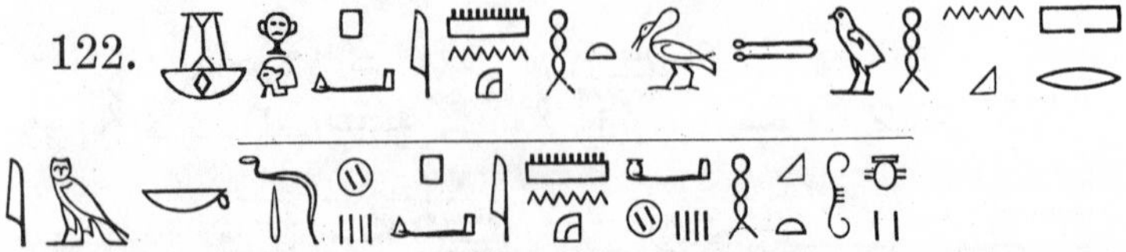

123.

Here shall the priest offer two vessels of Pekh grain, and as he presenteth them to Peṭā-Ȧmen-āp four times, he shall say four times:—

"121. O chief KHER ḤEB PEṬĀ-ȦMEN-ȦP, thou art "filled with that which hath been pressed out and hath "come forth from thee."

Here shall the priest offer two vessels of Ḥeqt and Nubian beer, and as he presenteth them to Peṭā-Ȧmen-āp four times, he shall say four times:—

"122. O chief KHER ḤEB PEṬĀ-ȦMEN-ȦP, thou art "filled with that which hath been pressed out and hath "come forth from thee."

Here shall the priest offer two baskets of figs, and as he presenteth them to Peṭā-Ȧmen-āp four times, he shall say four times:—

"123. O chief KHER ḤEB PEṬĀ-ȦMEN-ȦP, the breast

124.

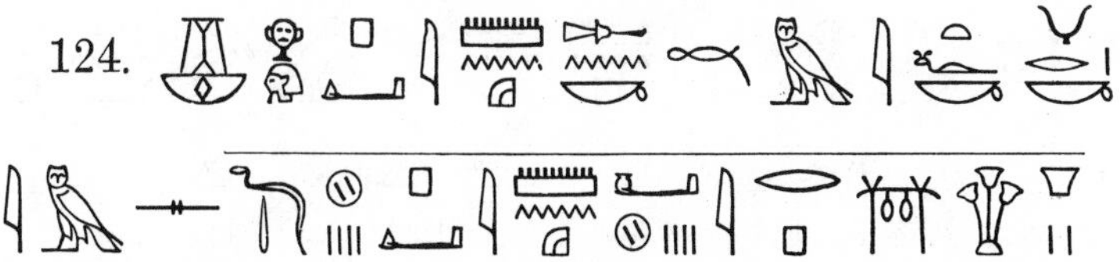

125.

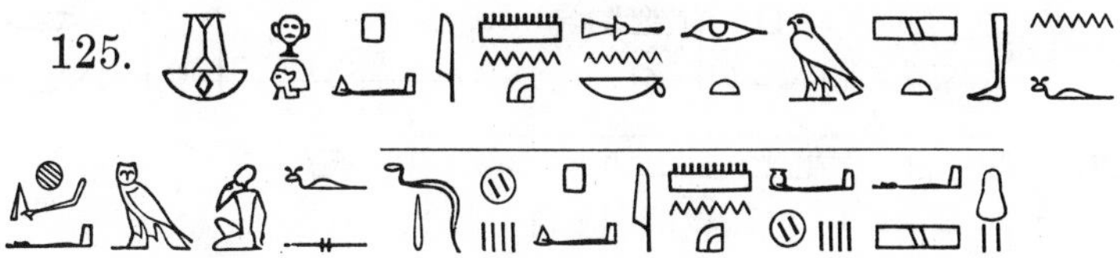

126.

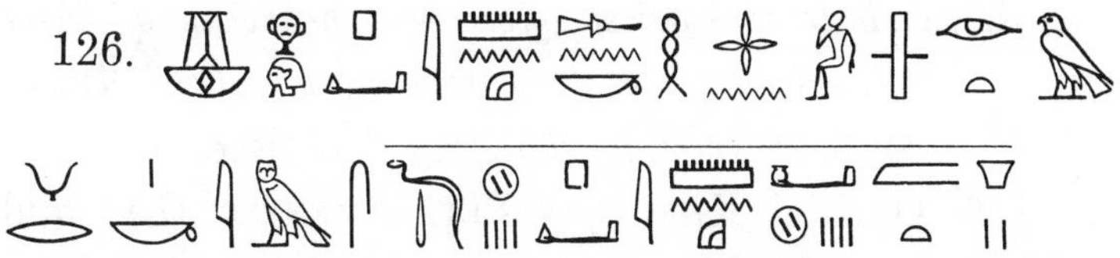

" of Horus hath been presented unto thee, and the gods " eat it together with thee."

Here shall the priest offer two vessels of wine of the North, and as he presenteth them to Peṭā-Åmen-åp four times, he shall say four times :—

" 124. O chief KHER ḤEB PEṬĀ-ÅMEN-ÅP, there hath " been presented unto thee that which filled thy father, " and thy mouth hath been opened thereby."

Here shall the priest offer two measures of white wine, and as he presenteth them to Peṭā-Åmen-åp four times, he shall say four times :—

" 125. O chief KHER ḤEB PEṬĀ-ÅMEN-ÅP, the Eye of " Horus hath been presented unto thee, which was " vomited by him [i.e., Set], the glorious one which he " devoured."

127. 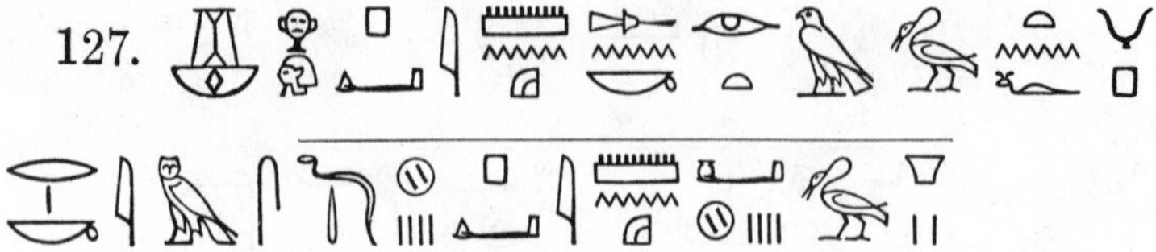

128. 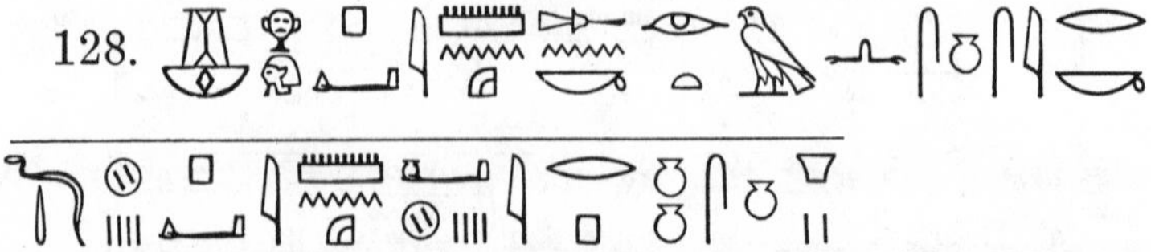

Here shall the priest offer two measures of Ȧmt wine, and as he presenteth them to Peṭā-Ȧmen-ȧp four times, he shall say four times:—

"126. O chief KHER ḤEB PEṬĀ-ȦMEN-ȦP, the child "(i.e., pupil) which is in the Eye of Horus hath been "presented unto thee, and thou hast opened thy mouth "by means of it."

Here shall the priest offer two measures of Ḥetem wine, and as he presenteth them to Peṭā-Ȧmen-ȧp four times, he shall say four times:—

"127. O chief KHER ḤEB PEṬĀ-ȦMEN-ȦP, the Eye of "Horus which was snared in a net hath been presented "unto thee, and thou hast opened thy mouth by means "of it."

Here shall the priest offer two measures of Senu wine, and as he presenteth them to Peṭā-Ȧmen-ȧp four times, he shall say four times:—

"128. O chief KHER ḤEB PEṬĀ-ȦMEN-ȦP, the Eye of "Horus hath been presented unto thee, there is nothing "like unto it, and it belongeth unto thee."

129. 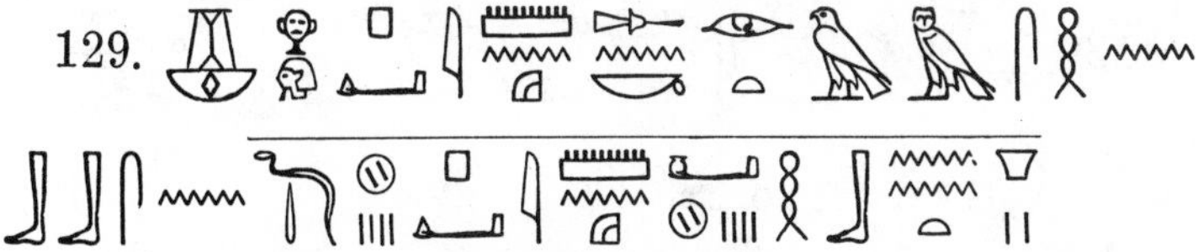

130. 

131. 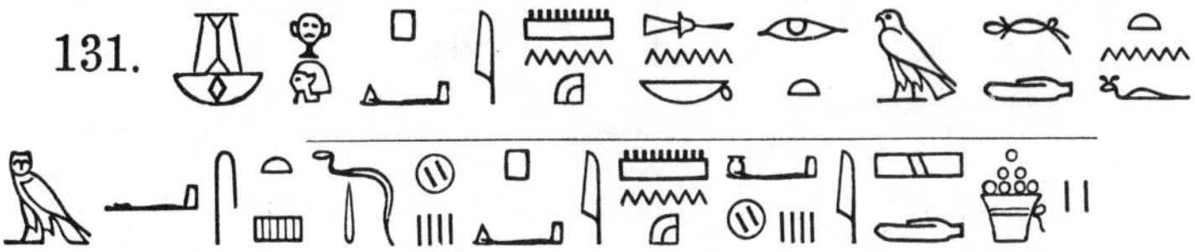

Here shall the priest offer two measures of Ḥebnent wine, and as he presenteth them to Peṭā-Åmen-åp four times, he shall say four times:—

"129. O chief KHER ḤEB PEṬĀ-ÅMEN-ÅP, the Eye of "Horus hath been presented unto thee, and it hath "brought about their overthrow (i.e., of the companions "of Set)."

Here shall the priest offer two measures of Khenfu cakes, and as he presenteth them to Peṭā-Åmen-åp four times, he shall say four times:—

"130. O chief KHER ḤEB PEṬĀ-ÅMEN-ÅP, the Eye of "Horus hath been presented unto thee, which is made "in the form of scale-shaped [cakes] for thee."

Here shall the priest offer two measures of Åsheṭ fruit, and as he presenteth them to Peṭā-Åmen-åp four times, he shall say four times:—

"131. O chief KHER ḤEB PEṬĀ-ÅMEN-ÅP, the Eye of

132. 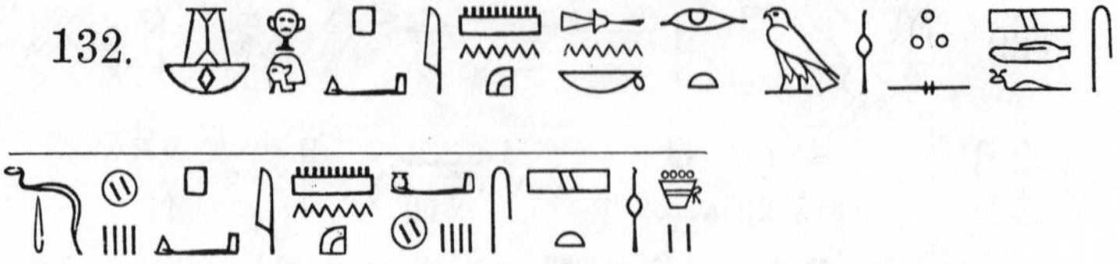

133. 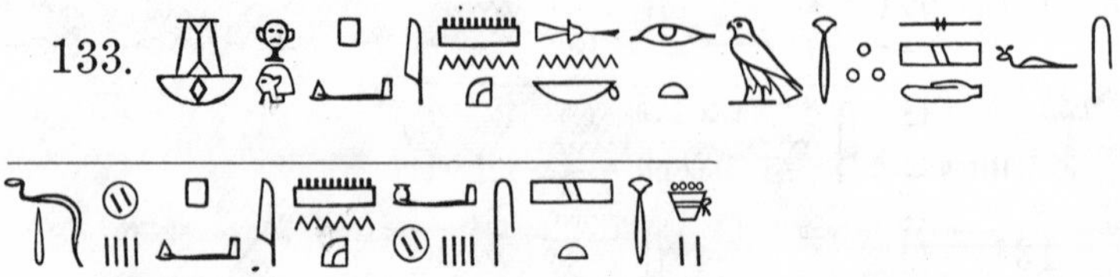

134. 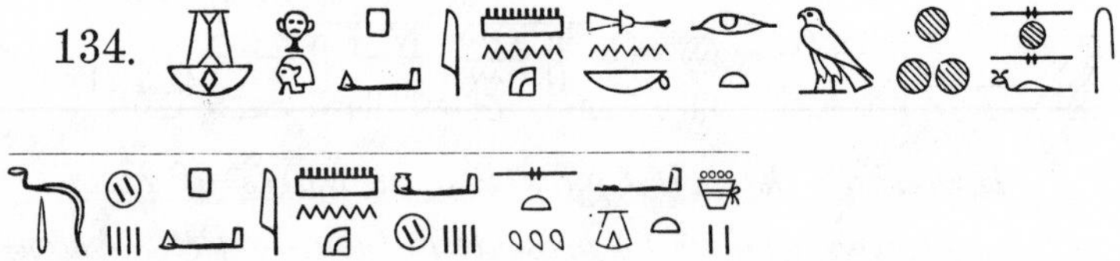

"Horus hath been presented unto thee, which was "snatched out of the hand of Set."

Here shall the priest offer two measures of White Seshet grain, and as he presenteth them to Peṭā-Ȧmen-ȧp four times, he shall say four times:—

"132. O chief KHER ḤEB PEṬĀ-ȦMEN-ȦP, the Eye of "Horus hath been presented unto thee, the White one, "and it shall serve for thy food."

Here shall the priest offer two measures of Green Seshet grain, and as he presenteth them to Peṭā-Ȧmen-ȧp four times, he shall say four times:—

"133. O chief KHER ḤEB PEṬĀ-ȦMEN-ȦP, the Eye of "Horus hath been presented unto thee, the Green one, "and it shall serve for thy food."

135. 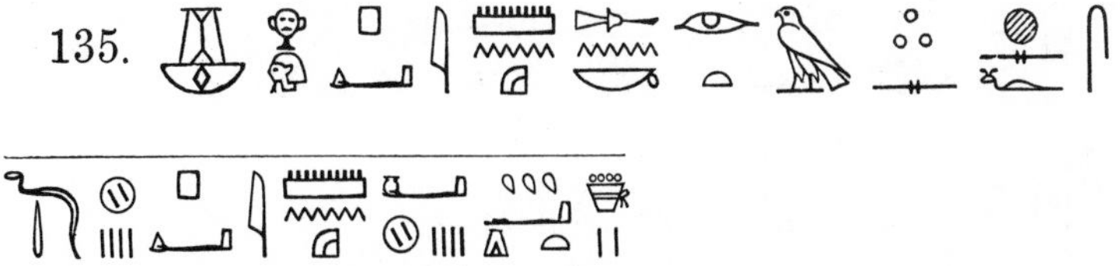

136. 

Here shall the priest offer two measures of roasted Set grain, and as he presenteth them to Peṭā-Ȧmen-ȧp four times, he shall say four times:—

"134. O chief KHER ḤEB PEṬĀ-ȦMEN-ȦP, the Eye of "Horus, the glorious one, hath been presented unto "thee, and it shall repulse attack on thee."

Here shall the priest offer two measures of roasted Set grain, and as he presenteth them to Peṭā-Ȧmen-ȧp four times, he shall say four times:—

"135. O chief KHER ḤEB PEṬĀ-ȦMEN-ȦP, the Eye of "Horus, the protected one, hath been presented unto "thee, and it shall repulse attack on thee."

Here shall the priest offer two measures of Babat grain, and as he presenteth them to Peṭā-Ȧmen-ȧp four times, he shall say four times:—

"136. O chief KHER ḤEB PEṬĀ-ȦMEN-ȦP, the Eye of "Horus hath been presented unto thee, and it is from "the hand of Baba."

137. 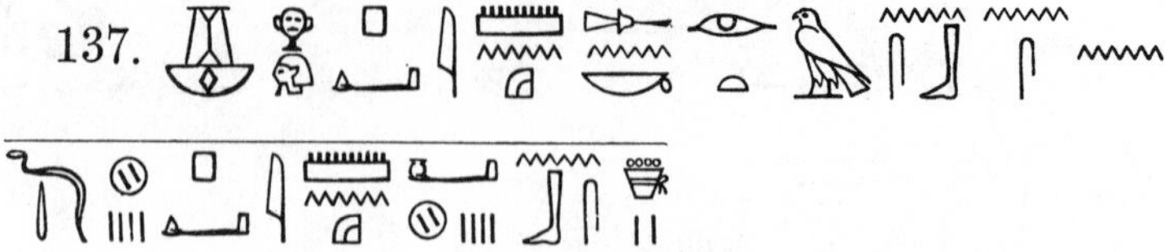

138. 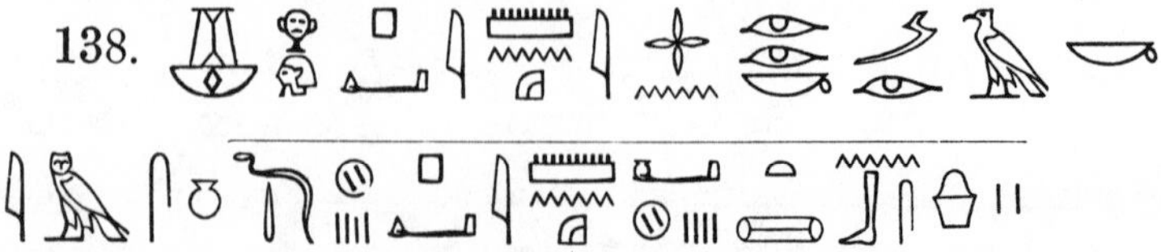

139. 

Here shall the priest offer two measures of Nebes fruit (mulberries?), and as he presenteth them to Peṭā-Ȧmen-ȧp four times, he shall say four times:—

"137. O chief KHER ḤEB PEṬĀ-ȦMEN-ȦP, the Eye of "Horus hath been presented unto thee, which burned "with fire against them (i.e., the fiends of Set)."

Here shall the priest offer two measures of Nebes cakes, and as he presenteth them to Peṭā-Ȧmen-ȧp four times, he shall say four times:—

"138. O chief KHER ḤEB PEṬĀ-ȦMEN-ȦP, thine eyes "have been opened, and thou seest with them."

Here shall the priest offer two measures of Ḥuā grain, and as he presenteth them to Peṭā-Ȧmen-ȧp four times, he shall say four times:—

"139. O chief KHER ḤEB PEṬĀ-ȦMEN-ȦP, the Eye of

140. 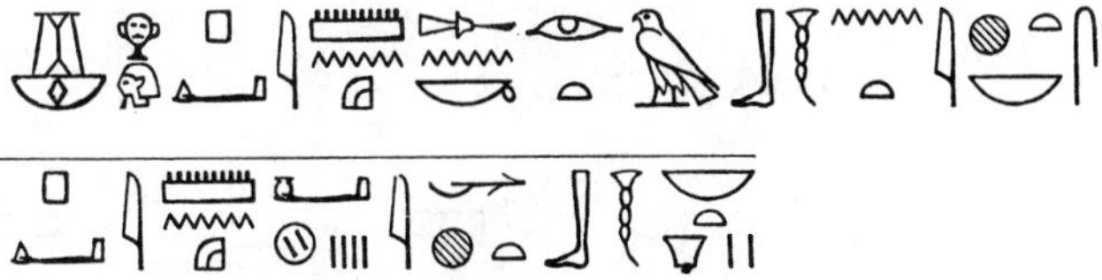

141. 

142. 

"Horus hath been presented unto thee, the glorious "one who was in his (i.e., Set's) throat."

Here shall the priest offer two measures of all kinds of sweet things, and as he presenteth them to Peṭā-Åmen-åp four times, he shall say four times:—

"140. O chief KHER ḤEB PEṬĀ-ÅMEN-ÅP, the Eye of "Horus hath been presented unto thee, which is sweet "in everything that belongeth to it."

Here shall the priest offer a basket of all kinds of spring products, and as he presenteth it to Peṭā-Åmen-åp four times, he shall say four times:—

"141. O chief KHER ḤEB PEṬĀ-ÅMEN-ÅP, the Eye of "Horus hath been presented unto thee, and thou hast "had experience of it."

143.

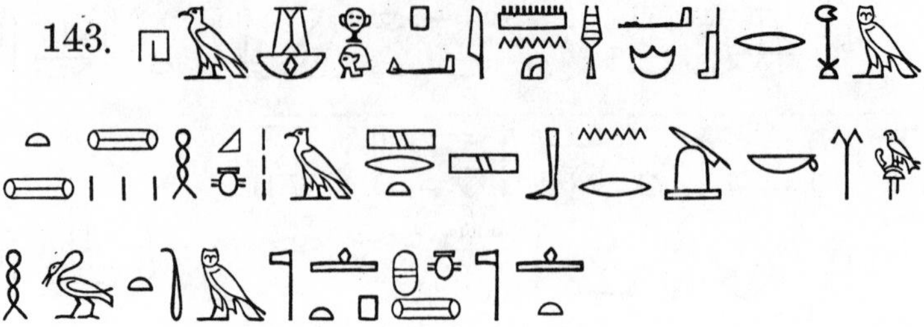

Here shall the priest offer a measure of gifts of all kinds, and as he presenteth it to Peṭā-Åmen-åp four times, he shall say four times:—

"142. O chief KHER ḤEB PEṬĀ-ÅMEN-ÅP, the Eye of "Horus hath been presented unto thee, and there hath "gone down into the throat for thee that which be-"longeth to thee.

"143. Hail, chief KHER ḤEB PEṬĀ-ÅMEN-ÅP, one "standeth and sitteth down by the thousands of cakes, "and [vessels of] beer, and roasted meat, by thine altar "in Åmentet, which is filled with holy offerings for the "meals of the dead."

INDEX

Åāt offering, 148, 181, 239
Abt, grain offering, 147
Aḥ cake, or offering, 81, 162, 218
Aḥā, 147
Åḥā . . . . ., Festival of, 11
Aḥu, a god, 14.
Almonds, offering, 92
Åmenemḥāt, of Beni Hasan, 10
Åmentet, the Other World, 256
Åmset (read Ḳeset, see Ḳesthå), 5
Amt (Pelusium), wine of, 135, 188, 250
Åm-ta cakes, an offering, 116, 178, 236
Ānep, Festival of, 18
Angle amulets, 66, 210
Ani, Papyrus of, 35
Ānkh-mā-ka, tomb of, 8
Ånnu (On, Heliopolis), 13
Ånpu (Anubis), 28, 29, 150
Ånpu, a man, 43, 83
Ånpu-khenti - Åmenti, 92, 168, 225
Āntchet, 150
Anubis, 21, 22, 23, 24, 31, 35; Festival of, 11
Āpep (Apophis), spell-bound, 17
Apple of the eye, 136
Aru Islanders, 55
Ashert cakes, 119
Åsheṭ, fruit offering, 139, 189
Åsht cakes, 180, 251
Ạswân, wine of, 137
Åten cake, an offering, 238
Åtet cakes, an offering, 118, 179
Aura, 46
Axe-heads, 66

BABA, first-born son of Osiris, 142, 191, 253

Babat fruit, 141, 191, 253
Backbone (Ṭeṭ), 49, 95
Baluba, death of chief of, 55
Bandlets, various kinds of, 92, 93
Baptism of the Dead, 44
Bat grain, an offering, 146
Bata, brother of Ȧnpu, 44, 52, 83
Beer offering, 85
Beer of everlastingness, 6
Beer, Nubian, 133, 248
Beni Hasan, 10
Bes grain, an offering, 146
Besen grain, an offering, 146
Beṭ, Beṭȧ, Beṭu, kind of incense, 111, 176
Bitumen, 165
Blacksmiths, 58
Boat of Rā, 61
Book of traversing Eternity, 18.
Bread for the journey, 74
Bread of everlastingness, 6, 80
Bread offering, 146
Breast offering, 83, 84, 121, 163, 181, 218, 240
Breast of Horus, 68, 158, 212
Breast of Isis, 158, 212
Butehai-Ȧmen, coffin of, 37, 38, 40
Buto (Pe-Ṭep), 93
Butter offering, 67

Cairo, 50
Calf of Kherȧ, 61
Cedar oil, 166
Censer, 48
Censing, 47
Ceremonies, 2, 3
Cheese cakes, 211
Cheese offerings, 67; of the North and South, 158
Chiefs, the, a class of gods, 4
Child in the Eye, 136
Coffin, wicker work, 56
Communication with the dead, 54
Copper, eye-paint, 91

Dâr Fûr, 18
Day, offerings of, 24, 72, 73, 160
Days, the Five Epagomenal, 11
Dead, baptism of, 44

Dead raised by means of water, 44
Dead, souls of, 101
Death, the second, 4
Delta, 70
Doubles (Kau) of gods and the dead, 19, 20
Doves, offerings of, 127, 184, 244

Eclipse, 77, 100
Effluxes of the dead, 53, 54
Eileithyiapolis (Nekhebet), 50
Emerald Trees, 61
Emission of Hawk-gods, 57
Emission of Horus, 57
Emission of Set, 57
Epagomenal Days, the Five, 11
Erṭu, 53
Eye of Horus, 13, 48, 50, 52, 63, 77, 78, 96, 101, 200
Eye of Horus, the Black, 72, 213
Eye of Horus, the Green, 148
Eye of Horus, the Little, 130
Eye of Horus, the White, 147
Eye-paint, 92; see also under Mesṭem and Uatch

Festival, the daily, 10
Festivals, List of, 9–11
Field of Åaru, 15
Field of Rā, 15
Field of Salt, 50
Figs, offerings of, 133, 187, 248
Fire-altar, 9
Fish scales, cakes in form of, 116, 237
Flesh roasted, 123, 181, 241
Flour, fine, for offerings, 117, 179, 237
Fluid of life, 46, 152
Fluids of the dead, 55
Followers of Horus, 2, 58, 59, 155
Fore-quarter, offering of, 124
Formulae, importance of, 2, 27
Four quarters of the World, 45
Four sons of Horus, 2, 5; see Ḥāpi, Qebḥsennuf, Ṭuamutef

Geese, offerings of, 126 ff., 183, 243

General offerings, 192
Gifts to the dead, 3
Girdle, ceremonial, 150
Gnostics, their beliefs, 44
Gods, Great and Little Companies, 30
Grain, roasted, offering of, 190
Great Festival, 9, 11, 12
Great Heat, Festival of, 11
Great List of Offerings, 10

Ḥā joint, an offering, 182, 242
Haematite, 66
Half-month, Festivals of, 9, 11
Ḥāp, Ḥāpi, guardian of the dead, 5, 45
Haroeris, 58
Ḥātet āsh unguent, 58
Ḥātet Theḥennu unguent, 58
Hathes measure, 72, 76
Hathor, goddess, 13
Haunch of beef, 120, 180, 239
Hawk-gods, Horus and Set, 57
Heart of Rā, 101
Heat Festival, 9
Hebnen, Hebennet cakes, 117, 179
Hebnent wine, 138, 189, 251
Ḥeken, Ḥekenu, unguent, 88, 164, 221
Ḥem cake, an offering, 72
Ḥent beer, 79
Ḥent measure, 85, 86
Ḥeqt (beer), 131; and see under Beer.
Ḥesmen, natron, or salt, 57, 155
Ḥesi, tomb of, 7
Ḥetem, Ḥetemet, a kind of vessel, 86, 164, 219
Ḥetem, kind of wine, 188, 250
Ḥetep, offering and city of offerings, 20, 217
Ḥetep-ḥer-s, 7
Ḥeteptiu-ṭuau-Rā, 17
Ḥeth cakes, an offering, 113, 177
Ḥet-menkh, 94
Hippopotamus of Set, stamped on cakes, 72, 73, 106
Holy water, 44
Horus, 13, 47, 48, 49, 95, 152, 205, 224; ceremonies

performed by for Osiris, 2; son of Isis, 58
Horus, Eye of, 13, 48, 50, 52, 63, 77, 78, 96, 200
Horus, Followers of, 2, 58, 59, 155; see Ḥeru-khet
Horus, Four sons of, 2, 5
Horus of Pe-Ṭep (Buto), 93
Horus of Saïs, 93
Horus seeks for his Eye, 101; recovers his Eye, 101; Two Eyes of, 159; regions of, 149
Horus-Bes, 57, 59, 66
Horus the Great, 58, 59, 60
Ḥua grain, 143, 192, 254
Hu-nefer, Papyrus of, 36
Hunger of the dead, 4
Ḥutcha cake, 234

INCENSE, efficacy of, 50, 167, 209
Incense of the North, 50
Incense of the South, 51
Irenaeus, 44
Iron vessel for liquids, 86, 164, 219
Iron of North, 66, 157, 210
Iron of South, 66, 157, 210
Isis-Uatchit, 93

JAW-BONES, 65, 157
Judgment, the, 45
Jug, black, 161
Jug, white, 161

KA, food of the, 98 ff.
Ka-chamber, 20
Ka-priest, 20
Ka-statues, 19
Ka-ḥrȧ-ka, Festival of, 18
Ḳeb, 24
Kef-Pesesh instrument, 65, 210
Keḥa cakes, offering, 146
Ḳerḥ (night), 160
Khen, Festival of, 11
Khenem beer, an offering, 173
Khenemes, beer, or drink, 107, 131, 186, 230, 247
Khenf, Khenfu, cakes, 117, 138, 179, 189, 236, 251
Khenti-Ȧmenti, 22, 29
Khenti-Maati, 47, 48, 152, 205, 225
Kherȧ (?), a goddess, 61
Kheri-Khenfu, 147
Khet-ḳerḥ, Festival of, 11
Khufu, 8
Khufu-ānkh, 9

Kingsmills, 55
Koḥl, eye-paint, 92
Kurnai, 54

Lake of Heaven, 59
Lake of Ḥetep, 217
Lamp-black, 92
Lead, 92
Leopard's skin, 35
Letopolis (Sekhem), 47
Libation, 51, 56, 59, 70, 87, 96, 153, 220
Libation water, 56
Life, fluid of, 46, 152
Lifting up the face, 72, 216
Little Heat Festivals, 11, 12, 18
Little List of Offerings, 10
Liturgy of Funerary Offerings, 36 ff.
Loin-cloth, 150
Loin of beef, 120
Liver, offering of the, 123, 182, 241

Mace, 150
Manganese, oxide of, 92
Mareotis, 137
Maṣṭaba tombs, 7
Mekhir, month of, 9
Mendes, 49
Ment bird (dove), 184
Menu, Festival of appearance of, 9
Mesentiu, sculptors, or artizans, 58
Mest grain, an offering, 129, 185, 245
Mesṭem, Mesṭemet, Mesṭemut, eye-paint, 91, 167, 223, 224
Mesthȧ (read Ḳesthȧ), 45; see also Horus, Four sons of
Metal workers, 58
Metchet oil, 89
Milk, offering of, 212
Month, Twelve Festivals of, 9, 11
Moon eaten by Set, 77, 106
Morning Star, 61
Mouth, ceremonies of opening of, described, 34
Mulberries, 7, 142
Mulberry tree, 23

Natron, incense and libation of, 155, 156, 157, 208, 209, 220, 226
Natron of North and South, 51

Natron Valley, 50, 59
Nebes cakes and fruit, 142, 143, 191, 254
Neb-ḥetepet, 204
Nebseni, Papyrus of, 13
Needle for eye-paint, 92
Neḥrȧ cakes, an offering, 114, 177, 235
Neith, goddess of Saïs, 93, 224
Nekheb, 50, 56, 154, 206
Nem oil, 222
Nemset vessel, 230
Nenshem joint, an offering, 182, 241
Nepȧt grain, 129, 148, 184, 245
Neshnem unguent, 88, 165
Net (Neith), 92
Net of Horus, 167, 224
Net, Eye of Horus snared in, 250
Neter-khert, 35
Neter-ṭuai (Venus), 61
New Year Festival, 9, 10
Nif-urt, 18
Night, 160; offering of, 73, 214; power of, 72
Nile (Ḥāpi), 14
Nile Flood, Festival of, 11
Nipples of Isis, 68
North, incense of, 50
North, iron of, 66, 157
North, water of, 70, 159
North, wine of, 134, 147, 187
Nu, god, 5
Nu, Papyrus of, 18
Nubia, beer of, 133, 248

Offerings, doctrine of, 1 ff.
Offerings, List of, 7, 8, 16
Offerings, transmutation of, 99
Oil, cedar, 166
Oil and water, 44
Oils, address to, 90, 165, 222
Onions, offering of, 74, 119, 160, 180, 214, 239
Opening the Mouth, 34 ff.
Osiris, 22, 47
Osiris, first-born son of, 142
Osiris, resurrection of, 2
Other World, 3, 4, 16, 19, 33, 47, 58

Paḥeri, inscription of, 26
Palm-tree, 23
Panther (leopard) skin, 150
Pasen cake, 235
Pashons, the month, 9
Passes, the making of, 46

Pat, or Patu, cakes, 118, 179
Pati, Twelve Festivals of, 10
Paut cakes, 238
Pekh grain, 132, 187, 248
Pelusium, wine of, 135, 188
Pepi I., 6
Pepi II., 8, 24, 30
Pert-er-kheru, 26, 27
Pert kheru, 24, 25, 26, 100
Pert Menu, Festival of, 10
Pert Sem, Festival of, 11
Pert Sepṭ, Festival of, 11
Pesesh-kef instrument, 157
Peṭā-Åmen-åp, Liturgy in his tomb, 15 ff.
Pe-Ṭep, 92
Peten cakes, 115, 178
Pitch, 115
Plutarch, 72
Polenta, 81
Ptaḥ, god of Memphis, 35
Ptaḥ-khā-mert, 8
Ptaḥ-shepses, tomb of, 8
Puls, 81
Pupil of the Eye, 136
Purifications of the Ka statue, 42

QEBḤSENNUF, a son of Horus, 5, 45; and see Ḥāpi, Ṭuamutef

Qem wine, 137
Qemḥ (fine flour), 117

RĀ, the Sun-god, 17, 80, 214, 217
Rā = Day, 160
Rā feeds the dead, 5
Rā, heart of, 101
Rā-Harmachis, 61
Raisins, 7
Re goose, offering of, 125, 183
Re-birth, 2; effected by water, 44
Re-born man, the, 2
Reḥiu, 14
Rekhmårā, tomb of, 40
Rethu cake, an offering, 106, 113, 172, 177, 234
Ribs of beef, an offering, 122, 181, 240
"Royal offering," 21 ff., 26, 27, 75, 100, 104, 172, 215

SA, fluid of life, 43, 46, 47
Såf cake, 128, 184, 245
Saïs, 93, 94, 244
Sais, a priestess, 37
Ṣaḳḳârah, 76
Salt, 50
Salt in libations, 42
Sandals, 71, 153

Saṭ, Twelve Festivals of, 11
Satch, Festival of, 9
Seb, the Earth-god, 1, 16, 17, 24, 29, 30, 73, 102, 106, 107, 143, 149, 203, 228
Seft, Sefth, oil or unguent, 88, 221
Seker-khā-baiu, tomb of, 7
Sekhem (Letopolis), 47, 149
Sekhet-ḥemam, 50
Sekhpet grain, 132, 186, 247
Sem, Festival of, 11
Sem priest, 32, 36
Semȧn, Semmȧn, incense, or incense water, 56, 57, 155, 156, 207
Senu (Syene) wine, 137, 188
Sep, the god of the East, 45, 47, 48, 60, 62, 95, 153, 156, 208, 209, 225
Serȧ goose, 243
Sert goose, 127, 183, 244
Seshet grain, green, 140, 148, 190, 252
Seshet grain, white, 139, 147, 190, 252
Set, 14, 47, 77, 95, 101, 106, 107, 142, 152, 154, 168, 205, 208, 209, 217, 218, 224
Set, cake of, 72
Set devours the Moon, 101
Set, fore-quarter of, 125, 182
Set goose, 126, 183, 243
Set grain, 140, 141, 253
Set, harpooned by Rā, 135
Set, regions of, 149
Setep sa, ceremony of, 46
Seth ḥeb unguent, 88, 164, 221
Seti I., 16, 38, 39, 40
Seven loaves of Horus and Thoth, 13
Shȧku cakes, or offerings, 68, 158, &c.
Shāt cakes, 128, 184
Shāt dough, 245
Sheba offering, 149
Shebu offerings, 109, 175, 231
Sheku cakes, 211
Shemsu Ḥeru (Followers of Horus), 58, 155
Shens cake, 104, 112, 115, 176, 229
Sheshu(*sic*)-Ḥeru, 155
Shetchet-shā, Festival of, 11
Sheṭ-pet incense, 50, 155, 206
Shoulder joint, 242

Shu, god, 5, 14
Shu finds the Eye of Horus, 101
Sixth-day Festivals, the twelve, 11
Smer priest, 215
Soda, 42
Sothis, Festival of, 11
Souls, the, in heaven, 19
Souls of the East, 61
South, incense of, 51
South, iron of, 66, 157
Spearer of the enemy, 148
Speech, efficacy of, 53
Spells, casting of, 17
Spirits, the, 149, 225
Spirits of inanimate beings, 4
Spirits of offerings, 4
Spleen offering, 124
Spring, offerings of the, 255
Stand for offerings, 79
Sucking calf, 61, 156
Sunrise, Mountain of, 61; see also Bakha
Sut joint, an offering, 110, 122, 175, 181, 232, 240
Suten-ḥetep cakes, 102, 171
Suten-ṭā-ḥetep, the Royal Offering, 21 ff., 26, 75, 104, 172, 215
Swathings, 167, 224
Syene, 137
Syene wine, 188, 250

TA-ASHER cake, 238
Taȧt, goddess, 92, 167
Taȧtet, goddess, 224
Table of offerings, 162, 171, 217
Takhart-p-seru-ȧbtiu, Papyrus of, 18
Tatet, 167
Ṭaṭṭu, 13
Tchesert drink, 106, 130 173, 185, 230, 247
Tchesert standard, 79, 81
Tcheṭ = Ṭeṭ, 49
Teben grain, 148
Teeth of Horus, 75, 119, 160, 215
Tefnut, goddess, 5
Tenbes cake, 191
Ṭep-pe (Buto), 167, 224
Ṭept cakes, 81, 114, 162, 177, 217, 235
Ṭeṭ, setting up the, 18, 48
Tetȧ, 5, 6
Theḥennu oil, 166, 222
Thenem drink, 147
Therp goose, 126, 163, 243

Thigh offering, 239
Thirst of the dead, 4
Thoth, 13, 14, 59, 62, 78, 95, 101, 152, 155, 205, 206, 209, 225, 227; as advocate, 45; remover of evil, 43
Thoth, Festival of, 9, 10
Thoth, month of, 9
Thoth and Horus, 43
Timorlaut, 55
Transmutation of offerings, 99
Trees of Emerald, 61
Tree trunk of Mendes, 49
Ṭua cake, 104, 112, 176, 229
Tua, or Ṭuat, oil, 221
Ṭuamutef, 5, 45
Ṭuat, Other World, 17
Ṭuat chamber, 41, 204
Tuatu unguent, 88, 165
Turt cakes, 141
Tut cake, 105, 172
Typhon, cake of, 72

UATCH eye-paint, 91, 167, 223
Uatch wine, 147
Uatch-ān, 150
Unȧs, 5, 6, 15, 38, 40, 49
Ur-ā, 92, 167, 224
Urerit Crown, 30
Ur-ḥekau, Ur-ḥekaut, Ur-ḥekat, instrument, 35, 36
Usekh, or Usekht, hall, 23, 103, 146
User-en-Rā, 8
Ush offering, 112, 227, 233
Uten cake, 75, 161, 215
Uaḥ, Festival of, 9, 11
Uaḥ-ākh, Festival of, 9

VENUS, 61
Vessel, black, 213
Vessel, white, 213
Voice, 53

WÂDÎ an-Naṭrûn, 50
Water, ceremonial use of, 43
Water offering, 111, 212
Water and oil, 44
Water of the North and South, 70, 159, 212
Wave offering, 84
Weighing words, 45
Whey offering, 69, 158
Wine, 76; black wine, 71 white, 71, 134, 188, 249

Wine of Åmt, 188, 250
Wine of eternity, 80
Wine of Ḥebnent, 189, 251
Wine of Ḥetem, 188, 250
Wine of Mareotis, 137
Wine of the North, 249
Wine of the South, 249
Wine of Syene, 188, 250

YEAR, Festival of beginning of, 9

A CATALOG OF SELECTED

DOVER BOOKS

IN ALL FIELDS OF INTEREST

A CATALOG OF SELECTED DOVER BOOKS IN ALL FIELDS OF INTEREST

CONCERNING THE SPIRITUAL IN ART, Wassily Kandinsky. Pioneering work by father of abstract art. Thoughts on color theory, nature of art. Analysis of earlier masters. 12 illustrations. 80pp. of text. 5⅜ × 8½. 23411-8 Pa. $3.95

ANIMALS: 1,419 Copyright-Free Illustrations of Mammals, Birds, Fish, Insects, etc., Jim Harter (ed.). Clear wood engravings present, in extremely lifelike poses, over 1,000 species of animals. One of the most extensive pictorial sourcebooks of its kind. Captions. Index. 284pp. 9 × 12. 23766-4 Pa. $10.95

CELTIC ART: The Methods of Construction, George Bain. Simple geometric techniques for making Celtic interlacements, spirals, Kells-type initials, animals, humans, etc. Over 500 illustrations. 160pp. 9 × 12. (USO) 22923-8 Pa. $8.95

AN ATLAS OF ANATOMY FOR ARTISTS, Fritz Schider. Most thorough reference work on art anatomy in the world. Hundreds of illustrations, including selections from works by Vesalius, Leonardo, Goya, Ingres, Michelangelo, others. 593 illustrations. 192pp. 7⅛ × 10¼. 20241-0 Pa. $8.95

CELTIC HAND STROKE-BY-STROKE (Irish Half-Uncial from "The Book of Kells"): An Arthur Baker Calligraphy Manual, Arthur Baker. Complete guide to creating each letter of the alphabet in distinctive Celtic manner. Covers hand position, strokes, pens, inks, paper, more. Illustrated. 48pp. 8¼ × 11. 24336-2 Pa. $3.95

EASY ORIGAMI, John Montroll. Charming collection of 32 projects (hat, cup, pelican, piano, swan, many more) specially designed for the novice origami hobbyist. Clearly illustrated easy-to-follow instructions insure that even beginning papercrafters will achieve successful results. 48pp. 8¼ × 11. 27298-2 Pa. $2.95

THE COMPLETE BOOK OF BIRDHOUSE CONSTRUCTION FOR WOODWORKERS, Scott D. Campbell. Detailed instructions, illustrations, tables. Also data on bird habitat and instinct patterns. Bibliography. 3 tables. 63 illustrations in 15 figures. 48pp. 5¼ × 8½. 24407-5 Pa. $1.95

BLOOMINGDALE'S ILLUSTRATED 1886 CATALOG: Fashions, Dry Goods and Housewares, Bloomingdale Brothers. Famed merchants' extremely rare catalog depicting about 1,700 products: clothing, housewares, firearms, dry goods, jewelry, more. Invaluable for dating, identifying vintage items. Also, copyright-free graphics for artists, designers. Co-published with Henry Ford Museum & Greenfield Village. 160pp. 8¼ × 11. 25780-0 Pa. $8.95

HISTORIC COSTUME IN PICTURES, Braun & Schneider. Over 1,450 costumed figures in clearly detailed engravings—from dawn of civilization to end of 19th century. Captions. Many folk costumes. 256pp. 8⅜ × 11¾. 23150-X Pa. $10.95

FRANK LLOYD WRIGHT'S HOLLYHOCK HOUSE, Donald Hoffmann. Lavishly illustrated, carefully documented study of one of Wright's most controversial residential designs. Over 120 photographs, floor plans, elevations, etc. Detailed perceptive text by noted Wright scholar. Index. 128pp. 9¼ × 10¾.
27133-1 Pa. $10.95

THE MALE AND FEMALE FIGURE IN MOTION: 60 Classic Photographic Sequences, Eadweard Muybridge. 60 true-action photographs of men and women walking, running, climbing, bending, turning, etc., reproduced from rare 19th-century masterpiece. vi + 121pp. 9 × 12. 24745-7 Pa. $10.95

1001 QUESTIONS ANSWERED ABOUT THE SEASHORE, N. J. Berrill and Jacquelyn Berrill. Queries answered about dolphins, sea snails, sponges, starfish, fishes, shore birds, many others. Covers appearance, breeding, growth, feeding, much more. 305pp. 5¼ × 8¼. 23366-9 Pa. $7.95

GUIDE TO OWL WATCHING IN NORTH AMERICA, Donald S. Heintzelman. Superb guide offers complete data and descriptions of 19 species: barn owl, screech owl, snowy owl, many more. Expert coverage of owl-watching equipment, conservation, migrations and invasions, etc. Guide to observing sites. 84 illustrations. xiii + 193pp. 5⅜ × 8½. 27344-X Pa. $7.95

MEDICINAL AND OTHER USES OF NORTH AMERICAN PLANTS: A Historical Survey with Special Reference to the Eastern Indian Tribes, Charlotte Erichsen-Brown. Chronological historical citations document 500 years of usage of plants, trees, shrubs native to eastern Canada, northeastern U.S. Also complete identifying information. 343 illustrations. 544pp. 6½ × 9¼. 25951-X Pa. $12.95

STORYBOOK MAZES, Dave Phillips. 23 stories and mazes on two-page spreads: Wizard of Oz, Treasure Island, Robin Hood, etc. Solutions. 64pp. 8¼ × 11.
23628-5 Pa. $2.95

NEGRO FOLK MUSIC, U.S.A., Harold Courlander. Noted folklorist's scholarly yet readable analysis of rich and varied musical tradition. Includes authentic versions of over 40 folk songs. Valuable bibliography and discography. xi + 324pp. 5⅜ × 8½. 27350-4 Pa. $7.95

MOVIE-STAR PORTRAITS OF THE FORTIES, John Kobal (ed.). 163 glamor, studio photos of 106 stars of the 1940s: Rita Hayworth, Ava Gardner, Marlon Brando, Clark Gable, many more. 176pp. 8⅜ × 11¼. 23546-7 Pa. $10.95

BENCHLEY LOST AND FOUND, Robert Benchley. Finest humor from early 30s, about pet peeves, child psychologists, post office and others. Mostly unavailable elsewhere. 73 illustrations by Peter Arno and others. 183pp. 5⅜ × 8½.
22410-4 Pa. $4.95

YEKL and THE IMPORTED BRIDEGROOM AND OTHER STORIES OF YIDDISH NEW YORK, Abraham Cahan. Film Hester Street based on Yekl (1896). Novel, other stories among first about Jewish immigrants on N.Y.'s East Side. 240pp. 5⅜ × 8½. 22427-9 Pa. $5.95

SELECTED POEMS, Walt Whitman. Generous sampling from *Leaves of Grass.* Twenty-four poems include "I Hear America Singing," "Song of the Open Road," "I Sing the Body Electric," "When Lilacs Last in the Dooryard Bloom'd," "O Captain! My Captain!"—all reprinted from an authoritative edition. Lists of titles and first lines. 128pp. 5³⁄₁₆ × 8¼. 26878-0 Pa. $1.00

MY BONDAGE AND MY FREEDOM, Frederick Douglass. Born a slave, Douglass became outspoken force in antislavery movement. The best of Douglass' autobiographies. Graphic description of slave life. 464pp. 5⅜ × 8½. 22457-0 Pa. $7.95

FOLLOWING THE EQUATOR: A Journey Around the World, Mark Twain. Fascinating humorous account of 1897 voyage to Hawaii, Australia, India, New Zealand, etc. Ironic, bemused reports on peoples, customs, climate, flora and fauna, politics, much more. 197 illustrations. 720pp. 5⅜ × 8½. 26113-1 Pa. $15.95

THE PEOPLE CALLED SHAKERS, Edward D. Andrews. Definitive study of Shakers: origins, beliefs, practices, dances, social organization, furniture and crafts, etc. 33 illustrations. 351pp. 5⅜ × 8½. 21081-2 Pa. $7.95

THE MYTHS OF GREECE AND ROME, H. A. Guerber. A classic of mythology, generously illustrated, long prized for its simple, graphic, accurate retelling of the principal myths of Greece and Rome, and for its commentary on their origins and significance. With 64 illustrations by Michelangelo, Raphael, Titian, Rubens, Canova, Bernini and others. 480pp. 5⅜ × 8½. 27584-1 Pa. $9.95

PSYCHOLOGY OF MUSIC, Carl E. Seashore. Classic work discusses music as a medium from psychological viewpoint. Clear treatment of physical acoustics, auditory apparatus, sound perception, development of musical skills, nature of musical feeling, host of other topics. 88 figures. 408pp. 5⅜ × 8½. 21851-1 Pa. $8.95

THE PHILOSOPHY OF HISTORY, Georg W. Hegel. Great classic of Western thought develops concept that history is not chance but rational process, the evolution of freedom. 457pp. 5⅜ × 8½. 20112-0 Pa. $8.95

THE BOOK OF TEA, Kakuzo Okakura. Minor classic of the Orient: entertaining, charming explanation, interpretation of traditional Japanese culture in terms of tea ceremony. 94pp. 5⅜ × 8½. 20070-1 Pa. $2.95

LIFE IN ANCIENT EGYPT, Adolf Erman. Fullest, most thorough, detailed older account with much not in more recent books, domestic life, religion, magic, medicine, commerce, much more. Many illustrations reproduce tomb paintings, carvings, hieroglyphs, etc. 597pp. 5⅜ × 8½. 22632-8 Pa. $9.95

SUNDIALS, Their Theory and Construction, Albert Waugh. Far and away the best, most thorough coverage of ideas, mathematics concerned, types, construction, adjusting anywhere. Simple, nontechnical treatment allows even children to build several of these dials. Over 100 illustrations. 230pp. 5⅜ × 8½. 22947-5 Pa. $5.95

DYNAMICS OF FLUIDS IN POROUS MEDIA, Jacob Bear. For advanced students of ground water hydrology, soil mechanics and physics, drainage and irrigation engineering, and more. 335 illustrations. Exercises, with answers. 784pp. 6⅛ × 9¼. 65675-6 Pa. $19.95

SONGS OF EXPERIENCE: Facsimile Reproduction with 26 Plates in Full Color, William Blake. 26 full-color plates from a rare 1826 edition. Includes "The Tyger," "London," "Holy Thursday," and other poems. Printed text of poems. 48pp. 5¼ × 7. 24636-1 Pa. $3.95

OLD-TIME VIGNETTES IN FULL COLOR, Carol Belanger Grafton (ed.). Over 390 charming, often sentimental illustrations, selected from archives of Victorian graphics—pretty women posing, children playing, food, flowers, kittens and puppies, smiling cherubs, birds and butterflies, much more. All copyright-free. 48pp. 9¼ × 12¼. 27269-9 Pa. $5.95

EARLY NINETEENTH-CENTURY CRAFTS AND TRADES, Peter Stockham (ed.). Extremely rare 1807 volume describes to youngsters the crafts and trades of the day: brickmaker, weaver, dressmaker, bookbinder, ropemaker, saddler, many more. Quaint prose, charming illustrations for each craft. 20 black-and-white line illustrations. 192pp. 4⅝ × 6. 27293-1 Pa. $4.95

VICTORIAN FASHIONS AND COSTUMES FROM HARPER'S BAZAR, 1867-1898, Stella Blum (ed.). Day costumes, evening wear, sports clothes, shoes, hats, other accessories in over 1,000 detailed engravings. 320pp. 9⅜ × 12¼. 22990-4 Pa. $12.95

GUSTAV STICKLEY, THE CRAFTSMAN, Mary Ann Smith. Superb study surveys broad scope of Stickley's achievement, especially in architecture. Design philosophy, rise and fall of the Craftsman empire, descriptions and floor plans for many Craftsman houses, more. 86 black-and-white halftones. 31 line illustrations. Introduction. 208pp. 6½ × 9¼. 27210-9 Pa. $9.95

THE LONG ISLAND RAIL ROAD IN EARLY PHOTOGRAPHS, Ron Ziel. Over 220 rare photos, informative text document origin (1844) and development of rail service on Long Island. Vintage views of early trains, locomotives, stations, passengers, crews, much more. Captions. 8⅞ × 11¾. 26301-0 Pa. $13.95

THE BOOK OF OLD SHIPS: From Egyptian Galleys to Clipper Ships, Henry B. Culver. Superb, authoritative history of sailing vessels, with 80 magnificent line illustrations. Galley, bark, caravel, longship, whaler, many more. Detailed, informative text on each vessel by noted naval historian. Introduction. 256pp. 5⅜ × 8½. 27332-6 Pa. $6.95

TEN BOOKS ON ARCHITECTURE, Vitruvius. The most important book ever written on architecture. Early Roman aesthetics, technology, classical orders, site selection, all other aspects. Morgan translation. 331pp. 5⅜ × 8½. 20645-9 Pa. $8.95

THE HUMAN FIGURE IN MOTION, Eadweard Muybridge. More than 4,500 stopped-action photos, in action series, showing undraped men, women, children jumping, lying down, throwing, sitting, wrestling, carrying, etc. 390pp. 7⅞ × 10⅝. 20204-6 Clothbd. $24.95

TREES OF THE EASTERN AND CENTRAL UNITED STATES AND CANADA, William M. Harlow. Best one-volume guide to 140 trees. Full descriptions, woodlore, range, etc. Over 600 illustrations. Handy size. 288pp. 4½ × 6⅜. 20395-6 Pa. $4.95

SONGS OF WESTERN BIRDS, Dr. Donald J. Borror. Complete song and call repertoire of 60 western species, including flycatchers, juncoes, cactus wrens, many more—includes fully illustrated booklet. Cassette and manual 99913-0 $8.95

GROWING AND USING HERBS AND SPICES, Milo Miloradovich. Versatile handbook provides all the information needed for cultivation and use of all the herbs and spices available in North America. 4 illustrations. Index. Glossary. 236pp. 5⅜ × 8½. 25058-X Pa. $5.95

BIG BOOK OF MAZES AND LABYRINTHS, Walter Shepherd. 50 mazes and labyrinths in all—classical, solid, ripple, and more—in one great volume. Perfect inexpensive puzzler for clever youngsters. Full solutions. 112pp. 8⅛ × 11. 22951-3 Pa. $3.95

PIANO TUNING, J. Cree Fischer. Clearest, best book for beginner, amateur. Simple repairs, raising dropped notes, tuning by easy method of flattened fifths. No previous skills needed. 4 illustrations. 201pp. 5⅜ × 8½. 23267-0 Pa. $4.95

A SOURCE BOOK IN THEATRICAL HISTORY, A. M. Nagler. Contemporary observers on acting, directing, make-up, costuming, stage props, machinery, scene design, from Ancient Greece to Chekhov. 611pp. 5⅜ × 8½. 20515-0 Pa. $10.95

THE COMPLETE NONSENSE OF EDWARD LEAR, Edward Lear. All nonsense limericks, zany alphabets, Owl and Pussycat, songs, nonsense botany, etc., illustrated by Lear. Total of 320pp. 5⅜ × 8½. (USO) 20167-8 Pa. $5.95

VICTORIAN PARLOUR POETRY: An Annotated Anthology, Michael R. Turner. 117 gems by Longfellow, Tennyson, Browning, many lesser-known poets. "The Village Blacksmith," "Curfew Must Not Ring Tonight," "Only a Baby Small," dozens more, often difficult to find elsewhere. Index of poets, titles, first lines. xxiii + 325pp. 5⅝ × 8¼. 27044-0 Pa. $7.95

DUBLINERS, James Joyce. Fifteen stories offer vivid, tightly focused observations of the lives of Dublin's poorer classes. At least one, "The Dead," is considered a masterpiece. Reprinted complete and unabridged from standard edition. 160pp. 5³⁄₁₆ × 8¼. 26870-5 Pa. $1.00

THE HAUNTED MONASTERY and THE CHINESE MAZE MURDERS, Robert van Gulik. Two full novels by van Gulik, set in 7th-century China, continue adventures of Judge Dee and his companions. An evil Taoist monastery, seemingly supernatural events; overgrown topiary maze hides strange crimes. 27 illustrations. 328pp. 5⅜ × 8½. 23502-5 Pa. $7.95

THE BOOK OF THE SACRED MAGIC OF ABRAMELIN THE MAGE, translated by S. MacGregor Mathers. Medieval manuscript of ceremonial magic. Basic document in Aleister Crowley, Golden Dawn groups. 268pp. 5⅜ × 8½. 23211-5 Pa. $7.95

NEW RUSSIAN-ENGLISH AND ENGLISH-RUSSIAN DICTIONARY, M. A. O'Brien. This is a remarkably handy Russian dictionary, containing a surprising amount of information, including over 70,000 entries. 366pp. 4½ × 6⅛. 20208-9 Pa. $8.95

HISTORIC HOMES OF THE AMERICAN PRESIDENTS, Second, Revised Edition, Irvin Haas. A traveler's guide to American Presidential homes, most open to the public, depicting and describing homes occupied by every American President from George Washington to George Bush. With visiting hours, admission charges, travel routes. 175 photographs. Index. 160pp. 8¼ × 11. 26751-2 Pa. $10.95

NEW YORK IN THE FORTIES, Andreas Feininger. 162 brilliant photographs by the well-known photographer, formerly with *Life* magazine. Commuters, shoppers, Times Square at night, much else from city at its peak. Captions by John von Hartz. 181pp. 9¼ × 10¾. 23585-8 Pa. $12.95

INDIAN SIGN LANGUAGE, William Tomkins. Over 525 signs developed by Sioux and other tribes. Written instructions and diagrams. Also 290 pictographs. 111pp. 6⅛ × 9¼. 22029-X Pa. $3.50

THE WIT AND HUMOR OF OSCAR WILDE, Alvin Redman (ed.). More than 1,000 ripostes, paradoxes, wisecracks: Work is the curse of the drinking classes; I can resist everything except temptation; etc. 258pp. 5⅜ × 8½. 20602-5 Pa. $4.95

SHAKESPEARE LEXICON AND QUOTATION DICTIONARY, Alexander Schmidt. Full definitions, locations, shades of meaning in every word in plays and poems. More than 50,000 exact quotations. 1,485pp. 6½ × 9¼. 2-vol. set.
Vol. 1: 22726-X Pa. $15.95
Vol. 2: 22727-8 Pa. $15.95

SELECTED POEMS, Emily Dickinson. Over 100 best-known, best-loved poems by one of America's foremost poets, reprinted from authoritative early editions. No comparable edition at this price. Index of first lines. 64pp. 5³⁄₁₆ × 8¼.
26466-1 Pa. $1.00

CELEBRATED CASES OF JUDGE DEE (DEE GOONG AN), translated by Robert van Gulik. Authentic 18th-century Chinese detective novel; Dee and associates solve three interlocked cases. Led to van Gulik's own stories with same characters. Extensive introduction. 9 illustrations. 237pp. 5⅜ × 8½.
23337-5 Pa. $5.95

THE MALLEUS MALEFICARUM OF KRAMER AND SPRENGER, translated by Montague Summers. Full text of most important witchhunter's "bible," used by both Catholics and Protestants. 278pp. 6⅝ × 10. 22802-9 Pa. $10.95

SPANISH STORIES/CUENTOS ESPAÑOLES: A Dual-Language Book, Angel Flores (ed.). Unique format offers 13 great stories in Spanish by Cervantes, Borges, others. Faithful English translations on facing pages. 352pp. 5⅜ × 8½.
25399-6 Pa. $7.95

THE CHICAGO WORLD'S FAIR OF 1893: A Photographic Record, Stanley Appelbaum (ed.). 128 rare photos show 200 buildings, Beaux-Arts architecture, Midway, original Ferris Wheel, Edison's kinetoscope, more. Architectural emphasis; full text. 116pp. 8¼ × 11. 23990-X Pa. $9.95

OLD QUEENS, N.Y., IN EARLY PHOTOGRAPHS, Vincent F. Seyfried and William Asadorian. Over 160 rare photographs of Maspeth, Jamaica, Jackson Heights, and other areas. Vintage views of DeWitt Clinton mansion, 1939 World's Fair and more. Captions. 192pp. 8⅞ × 11. 26358-4 Pa. $12.95

CAPTURED BY THE INDIANS: 15 Firsthand Accounts, 1750–1870, Frederick Drimmer. Astounding true historical accounts of grisly torture, bloody conflicts, relentless pursuits, miraculous escapes and more, by people who lived to tell the tale. 384pp. 5⅜ × 8½. 24901-8 Pa. $7.95

THE WORLD'S GREAT SPEECHES, Lewis Copeland and Lawrence W. Lamm (eds.). Vast collection of 278 speeches of Greeks to 1970. Powerful and effective models; unique look at history. 842pp. 5⅜ × 8½. 20468-5 Pa. $12.95

THE BOOK OF THE SWORD, Sir Richard F. Burton. Great Victorian scholar/adventurer's eloquent, erudite history of the "queen of weapons"—from prehistory to early Roman Empire. Evolution and development of early swords, variations (sabre, broadsword, cutlass, scimitar, etc.), much more. 336pp. 6⅛ × 9¼. 25434-8 Pa. $8.95